FACTS ABOUT CHAMPAGNE
AND OTHER SPARKLING WINES

FACTS ABOUT CHAMPAGNE
AND OTHER SPARKLING WINES

HENRY VIZETELLY

ISBN: 978-93-89560-72-5

Published: 1879

© 2020
LECTOR HOUSE LLP

LECTOR HOUSE LLP
E-MAIL: lectorpublishing@gmail.com

**THE DISGORGING, LIQUEURING, CORKING, STRINGING, AND WIR-
ING OF CHAMPAGNE**

(Frontispiece)

FACTS ABOUT CHAMPAGNE AND OTHER SPARKLING WINES,

COLLECTED DURING NUMEROUS VISITS TO THE CHAMPAGNE AND OTHER VITICULTURAL DISTRICTS OF FRANCE, AND THE PRINCIPAL REMAINING WINE-PRODUCING COUNTRIES OF EUROPE.

BY

HENRY VIZETELLY,

Chevalier of the Order of Franz Josef.
Wine Juror for Great Britain at the Vienna and Paris Exhibitions of 1873 and 1878.
Author of "The Wines of the World Characterized and Classed," &c.

WITH ONE HUNDRED AND TWELVE ILLUSTRATIONS,
DRAWN BY JULES PELCOQ, W. PRATER, BERTALL, ETC.,
FROM ORIGINAL SKETCHES.

1879.

THIS little book scarcely needs a preface, as it speaks sufficiently for itself. It is for the most part the result of studies on the spot of everything of interest connected with the various sparkling wines which it professes to describe. Neither pains nor expense have been spared to render it both accurate and complete, and the large number of authentic engravings with which it is illustrated will conduce, it is hoped, to its value.

Uniform with the present work and the Author's "Facts About Sherry,"

FACTS ABOUT PORT

AND MADEIRA,

Including Chapters on the Wines Vintaged Around Lisbon
and the Wines of Teneriffe.

Illustrated with 80 Engravings from Original Sketches.

CONTENTS

CHAPTER III.

THE VINEYARDS OF THE MOUNTAIN.

CHAPTER IV.

THE VINES OF THE CHAMPAGNE AND THE SYSTEM OF CULTIVATION.

CHAPTER V.

PREPARATION OF CHAMPAGNE.

CHAPTER VI.

THE REIMS CHAMPAGNE ESTABLISHMENTS.

CHAPTER VII.

THE REIMS ESTABLISHMENTS (CONTINUED).

CHAPTER VIII.

THE REIMS ESTABLISHMENTS (CONTINUED).

CHAPTER IX.

THE REIMS ESTABLISHMENTS (CONCLUDED).

CHAPTER X.

EPERNAY CHAMPAGNE ESTABLISHMENTS.

CHAPTER XI.

CHAMPAGNE ESTABLISHMENTS AT AY AND MAREUIL.

CHAPTER XII.

CHAMPAGNE ESTABLISHMENTS AT AVIZE AND RILLY.

CHAPTER XIII.

SPARKLING SAUMUR AND SPARKLING SAUTERNES.

CHAPTER XIV.

THE SPARKLING WINES OF BURGUNDY AND THE JURA.

CHAPTER XV.

THE SPARKLING WINES OF THE SOUTH OF FRANCE.

CHAPTER XVIII.

THE SPARKLING WINES OF AUSTRO-HUNGARY, SWITZER-LAND, ITALY, SPAIN, RUSSIA, &C.

CHAPTER XIX.

THE SPARKLING WINES OF THE UNITED STATES.

CHAPTER XX.

CONCLUDING FACTS AND HINTS.

CONTENTS xvii

FACTS ABOUT CHAMPAGNE
AND OTHER SPARKLING WINES.

CHAPTER I.

THE ORIGIN OF CHAMPAGNE.

The Early Vineyards of the Champagne—Their Produce esteemed by
Popes and Kings, Courtiers and Prelates—Controversy regarding
the rival Merits of the Wines of Burgundy and the Champagne—
Dom Perignon's happy Discovery of Sparkling Wine—Its Patrons
under Louis Quatorze and the Regency—The Ancient Church
and Abbey of Hautvillers—Farre and Co.'s Champagne Cellars—
The Abbey of St. Peter now a Farm—Existing Remains of the
Monastic Buildings—The Tombs and Decorations of the Ancient
Church—The Last Resting-Place of Dom Perignon—The Legend
of the Holy Dove—Good Champagne the Result of Labour, Skill,
Minute Precaution, and Careful Observation.

Strong men, we know, lived before Agamemnon; and strong wine was made
in the fair province of Champagne long before the days of the sagacious Dom Perignon, to whom we are indebted for the sparkling vintage known under the now
familiar name. The chalky slopes that border the Marne were early recognised
as offering special advantages for the culture of the vine. The priests and monks,
whose vows of sobriety certainly did not lessen their appreciation of the good
things of this life, and the produce of whose vineyards usually enjoyed a higher
reputation than that of their lay neighbours, were clever enough to seize upon the
most eligible sites, and quick to spread abroad the fame of their wines. St. Remi,
baptiser of Clovis, the first Christian king in France, at the end of the fifth century left by will, to various churches, the vineyards which he owned at Reims and
Laon, together with the "vilains" employed in their cultivation. Some three and a
half centuries later we find worthy Bishop Pardulus of Laon imitating Paul's ad-

vice to Timothy, and urging Archbishop Hincmar to drink of the wines of Epernay and Reims for his stomach's sake. The crusade-preaching Pope, UrbanII., who was born among the vineyards of the Champagne, dearly loved the wine of Ay; and his energetic appeals to the princes of Europe to take up arms for the deliverance of the Holy Sepulchre may have owed some of their eloquence to his favourite beverage.

The red wine of the Champagne sparkled on the boards of monarchs in the Middle Ages when they sat at meat amidst their mailclad chivalry, and quaffed mighty beakers to the confusion of the Paynim. Henry of Andely has sung in his *fabliau* of the "Bataille des Vins," how, when stout Philip Augustus and his chaplain constituted themselves the earliest known wine-jury, the *crûs* of Espernai, Auviler, Chaalons, and Reims were amongst those which found most favour in their eyes, though nearly a couple of centuries elapsed before Eustace Deschamps recorded in verse the rival merits of those of Cumières and Ay. King Wenceslaus of Bohemia, amighty toper, got so royally drunk day after day upon the vintages of the Champagne, that he forgot all about the treaty with Charles VI., that had formed the pretext of his visit to France, and would probably have lingered, goblet in hand, in the old cathedral city till the day of his death, but for the presentation of a little account for wine consumed, which sobered him to repentance and led to his abrupt departure. Dunois, Lahire, Xaintrailles, and their fellows, when they rode with Joan of Arc to the coronation of Charles VII., drank the same generous fluid, through helmets barred, to the speedy expulsion of the detested English from the soil of France.

The vin d'Ay—*vinum Dei* as Dominicus Baudoin punningly styled it—was, according to old Paulmier, the ordinary drink of the kings and princes of his day. It fostered bluff King Hal's fits of passion and the tenth Leo's artistic extravagance; consoled FrancisI. for the field of Pavia, and solaced his great rival in his retirement at St. Just. All of them had their commissioners at Ay to secure the best wine for their own consumption. Henri Quatre, whose *vendangeoir* is still shown in the village, held the wine in such honour that he was wont to style himself the Seigneur d'Ay, just as James of Scotland was known as the Gudeman of Ballangeich. When his son, Louis XIII., was crowned, the wines of the Champagne were the only growths allowed to grace the board at the royal banquet. Freely too did they flow at the coronation feast of the Grand Monarque, when the crowd of assembled courtiers, who quaffed them in his honour, hailed them as the finest wines of the day.

But the wines which drew forth all these encomiums were far from resembling the champagne of modern times. They were not, as has been asserted, all as red as burgundy and as flat as port; for at the close of the sixteenth, century some of them were of a *fauve* or yellowish hue, and of the intermediate tint between red and white which the French call *clairet*, and which our old writers translate as the "complexion of a cherry" or the "colour of a partridge's eye." But, as a rule, the wines of the Champagne up to this period closely resembled those produced in the adjacent province, where Charles the Bold had once held sway; aresemblance, no doubt, having much to do with the great medical controversy regarding their respective merits which arose in 1652. In that year a young medical student, hard pressed for the subject of his inaugural thesis, and in the firm faith that

> "None but a clever dialectician
> Can hope to become a good physician,
> And that logic plays an important part
> In the mystery of the healing art,"

propounded the theory that the wines of Burgundy were preferable to those of the Champagne, and that the latter were irritating to the nerves and conducive to gout. The faculty of medicine at Reims naturally rose in arms at this insolent assertion. They seized their pens and poured forth a deluge of French and Latin in defence of the wines of their province, eulogising alike their purity, their brilliancy of colour, their exquisite flavour and perfume, their great keeping powers, and, in a word, their general superiority to the Burgundy growths. The partisans of the latter were equally prompt in rallying in their defence, and the faculty of medicine of Beaune, having put their learned periwigs together, enunciated their views and handled their opponents without mercy. The dispute spread to the entire medical profession, and the champions went on pelting each other with pamphlets in prose and tractates in verse, until in 1778—long after the bones of the original disputants were dust and their lancets rust—the faculty of Paris, to whom the matter was referred, gave a final and formal decision in favour of the wines of the Champagne.

Meanwhile an entirely new kind of wine, which was to carry the name of the province producing it to the uttermost corners of the earth, had been introduced. On the picturesque slopes of the Marne, about fifteen miles from Reims, and some four or five miles from Epernay, stands the little hamlet of Hautvillers, which, in pre-revolutionary days, was a mere dependency upon a spacious abbey dedicated to St. Peter. Here the worthy monks of the order of St. Benedict had lived in peace and prosperity for several hundred years, carefully cultivating the acres of vineland extending around the abbey, and religiously exacting a tithe of all the other wine pressed in their district. The revenue of the community thus depending in no small degree upon the vintage, it was natural that the post of "celerer" should be one of importance. It happened that about the year 1688 this office was conferred upon a worthy monk named Perignon. Poets and roasters, we know, are born, and not made; and the monk in question seems to have been a heaven-born cellarman, with a strong head and a discriminating palate. The wine exacted from the neighbouring cultivators was of all qualities—good, bad, and indifferent; and with the spirit of a true Benedictine, Dom Perignon hit upon the idea of "marrying" the produce of one vineyard with that of another. He had noted that one kind of soil imparted fragrance and another generosity, and discovered that a white wine could be made from the blackest grapes, which would keep good, instead of turning yellow and degenerating like the wine obtained from white ones. Moreover, the happy thought occurred to him that a piece of cork was a much more suitable stopper for a bottle than the flax dipped in oil which had heretofore served that purpose.

The white, or, as it was sometimes styled, the grey wine of the Champagne grew famous, and the manufacture spread throughout the province, but that of

Hautvillers held the predominance. To Dom Perignon the abbey's well-stocked cellar was a far cheerfuller place than the cell. Nothing delighted him more than

> "To come down among this brotherhood
> Dwelling for ever underground,
> Silent, contemplative, round and sound,
> Each one old and brown with mould,
> But filled to the lips with the ardour of youth,
> With the latent power and love of truth,
> And with virtues fervent and manifold."

Ever busy among his vats and presses, barrels and bottles, Perignon alighted upon a discovery destined to be most important in its results. He found out the way of making an effervescent wine—awine that burst out of the bottle and over-flowed the glass, that was twice as dainty to the taste, and twice as exhilarating in its effects. It was at the close of the seventeenth century that this discovery was made—when the glory of the Roi Soleil was on the wane, and with it the splendour of the Court of Versailles. Louis XIV., for whose especial benefit liqueurs had been invented, recovered a gleam of his youthful energy as he sipped the creamy foaming vintage that enlivened his dreary *têtes-à-têtes* with the widow of Scarron. It found its chief patrons however, amongst the bands of gay young roysterers, the future *roues* of the Regency, whom the Duc d'Orléans and the Duc de Vendôme had gathered round them, at the Palais Royal and at Anet. It was at one of the famous *soupers* d'Anet that the Marquis de Sillery—who had turned his sword into a pruning-knife, and applied himself to the cultivation of his paternal vineyards on the principles inculcated by the celerer of St. Peter's—first introduced the sparkling wine bearing his name. The flower-wreathed bottles, which, at a given signal, adozen of blooming young damsels scantily draped in the guise of Bacchanals placed upon the table, were hailed with rapture, and thenceforth sparkling wine was an indispensable adjunct at all the *petits soupers* of the period. In the highest circles the popping of champagne-corks seemed to ring the knell of sadness, and the victories of Marlborough were in a measure compensated for by this happy discovery.

Why the wine foamed and sparkled was a mystery even to the very makers themselves; for as yet Baume's aerometer was unknown, and the connection between sugar and carbonic acid undreamt of. The general belief was that the degree of effervescence depended upon the time of year at which the wine was bottled, and that the rising of the sap in the vine had everything to do with it. Certain wiseacres held that it was influenced by the age of the moon at the time of bottling; whilst others thought the effervescence could be best secured by the addition of spirit, alum, and various nastinesses. It was this belief in the use and efficacy of drugs that led to a temporary reaction against the wine about 1715, in which year Dom Perignon departed this life. In his latter days he had grown blind, but his discriminating taste enabled him to discharge his duties with unabated efficiency to the end. Many of the tall tapering glasses invented by him have been emptied to the memory of the old Benedictine, whose remains repose beneath a black marble slab in the chancel of the archaic abbey church of Hautvillers.

THE VINEYARDS AND ABBEY OF HAUTVILLERS.

Time and the iconoclasts of the great Revolution have spared but little of the royal abbey of St. Peter where Dom Perignon lighted upon his happy discovery of the effervescent quality of champagne. The quaint old church, scraps of which date back to the 12th century, the remnants of the cloisters, and a couple of ancient gateways, marking the limits of the abbey precincts, are all that remain to testify to the grandeur of its past. It was the proud boast of the brotherhood that it had given nine archbishops to the see of Reims, and two-and-twenty abbots to various celebrated monasteries, but this pales beside the enduring fame it has acquired from having been the cradle of the sparkling vintage of the Champagne.

THE ESTABLISHMENT OF MESSRS. CHARLES FARRE & CO., AT HAUT-VILLERS.

It was in the budding springtime when we made our pilgrimage to Hautvillers across the swollen waters of the Marne at Epernay. Our way lay for a time along a straight level poplar-bordered road, with verdant meadows on either hand, then diverged sharply to the left and we commenced ascending the vine-clad hills, on a narrow plateau of which the church and abbey remains are picturesquely perched. Vines climb the undulating slopes to the summit of the plateau, and wooded heights rise up beyond, affording shelter from the bleak winds sweeping over from the north. As we near the village of Hautvillers we notice on our left hand a couple of isolated buildings overlooking a small ravine with their bright tiled roofs flashing in the sunlight. These prove to be a branch establishment of Messrs. Charles Farre and Co., awell-known champagne firm having its head-quarters at Reims. The grassy space beyond, dotted over with low stone shafts giving light and ventilation to the cellars beneath, is alive with workmen unloading waggons densely packed with new champagne bottles, while under a neighbouring shed is a crowd of women actively engaged in washing the bottles as they are brought to them. The large apartment aboveground, known as the *cellier*, contains wine in cask already blended, and to bottle which preparations are now being made. On descending into the cellars, which, excavated in the chalk and of regular construction, comprise a series of long, lofty, and well-ventilated galleries, we find them stocked with bottles of fine wine reposing in huge compact piles ready for transport to the head establishment, where they will undergo their final manipulation. The cellars consist of two stories, the lowermost of which has an iron gate communicating with the ravine already mentioned. On passing out here and looking up behind we see the buildings perched some hundred feet above us, hemmed in on every side with budding vines.

THE PORTE DES PRESSOIRS, HAUTVILLERS.

The church of Hautvillers and the remains of the neighbouring abbey are situated at the farther extremity of the village, at the end of its one long street, named, pertinently enough, the Rue de Bacchus. Passing through an unpretentious gateway we find ourselves in a spacious courtyard, bounded by buildings somewhat complex in character. On our right rises the tower of the church with the remains of the old cloisters, now walled-in and lighted by small square windows, and propped up by heavy buttresses. To the left stands the residence of the bailiff, and beyond it an 18th-century château on the site of the abbot's house, the abbey precincts being bounded on this side by a picturesque gateway tower leading to the vineyards, and known as the "porte des pressoirs," from its contiguity to the existing wine-presses. Huge barn-like buildings, stables, and cart-sheds inclose the court on its remaining sides, and roaming about are numerous live stock, indicating that what remains of the once-famous royal abbey of St. Peter has degenerated into an ordinary farm. To-day the abbey buildings and certain of its lands are the property of Messrs. Moët and Chandon, the great champagne manufacturers of Epernay, who maintain them as a farm, keeping some six-and-thirty cows there with the object of securing the necessary manure for the numerous vineyards which they own hereabouts.

The dilapidated cloisters, littered with old casks, farm implements, and the like, preserve ample traces of their former architectural character, and the Louis Quatorze gateway on the northern side of the inclosure still displays above its arch a grandiose carved shield, with surrounding palm-branches and half-obliterated bearings. Vine-leaves and bunches of grapes decorate some of the more ancient columns inside the church, and grotesque mediæval monsters, such as monkish architects habitually delighted in, entwine themselves around the capitals of others. The stalls of the choir are elaborately carved with cherubs' heads, medallions and figures of saints, cupids supporting shields, and free and graceful arabesques of the epoch of the Renaissance. In the chancel, close by the altar steps, are a couple of black marble slabs, with Latin inscriptions of dubious orthography, the one to Johannes Royer, who died in 1527, and the other setting forth the virtues and merits of Dom Petrus Perignon, the discoverer of champagne. In the central aisle a similar slab marks the resting-place of Dom Thedoricus Ruynart—obit 1709— an ancestor of the Reims Ruinarts, and little square stones interspersed among the tiles with which the side aisles of the church are paved record the deaths of other members of the Benedictine brotherhood during the 17th and 18th centuries. Several large pictures grace the walls of the church, the most interesting one representing St. Nivard, Bishop of Reims, and his friend, St. Berchier, designating to some mediæval architect the site the contemplated abbey of St. Peter was to occupy. There was a monkish legend that about the middle of the 7th century this pair of saints set out in search of a suitable site for the future monastery. The way was long, the day was warm, and St. Nivard and St. Berchier as yet were simply mortal. Weary and faint, they sat them down to rest at a spot identified by tradition with a vineyard at Dizy, belonging to-day to the Messrs. Bollinger, but at that period forming part of the forest of the Marne. St. Nivard fell asleep with his head on his companion's lap, and the one in a dream, and the other with waking eyes, saw a snow-white dove—the same, firm believers in miracles suggested, which had brought down the holy oil for the anointment of Clovis at his coronation at Reims—flutter through the wood, and finally alight on the stump of a tree.

In those superstitious times such a significant omen was not to be disregarded, the site thus miraculously indicated was at once decided upon, the high altar of the abbey church being erected upon the precise spot where the tree stood on which the snow-white dove had alighted.

The celerer of St. Peter's found worthy successors, and thenceforward the manufacture and the popularity of champagne went on steadily increasing, until to-day its production is carried on upon a scale and with an amount of painstaking care that would astonish its originator. For good champagne does not rain down from the clouds, or gush out from the rocks, but is the result of incessant labour, patient skill, minute precaution, and careful observation. In the first place, the soil imparts to the natural wine a special quality which it has been found impossible to imitate in any other quarter of the globe. To the wine of Ay it lends a flavour of peaches, and to that of Avenay the savour of strawberries; the vintage of Hautvillers, though fallen from its former high estate, is yet marked by an unmistakably nutty taste; while that of Pierry smacks of the locally-abounding flint, the well-known *pierre à fusil* flavour. So on the principle that a little leaven leavens the whole lump, the produce of grapes grown in the more favoured vineyards is added in certain proportions to secure certain special characteristics, as well as to maintain a fixed standard of excellence.

CHAPTER II.

THE VINTAGE IN THE CHAMPAGNE. THE VINE-YARDS OF THE RIVER.

Ay, the Vineyard of Golden Plants—Summoning the Vintagers by Beat of Drum—Excitement in the Surrounding Villages—The Pickers at Work—Sorting the Grapes—Grapes Gathered at Sunrise the Best—Varieties of Vines in the Ay Vineyards—Few of the Growers in the Champagne Crush their own Grapes—Squeezing the Grapes in the "Pressoir" and Drawing off the Must—Cheerful Glasses Round—The Vintage at Mareuil—Bringing in the Grapes on Mules and Donkeys—The Vineyards of Avenay, Mutigny, and Cumières—Damery and Adrienne Lecouvreur, Maréchal de Saxe, and the obese Anna Iwanowna—The Vineyards of the Côte d'Epernay—Boursault and its Château—Pierry and its Vineyard Cellars—The Clos St. Pierre—Moussy and Vinay—A Hermit's Cave and a Miraculous Fountain—Ablois St. Martin—The Côte d'Avize—The Grand Premier Crû of Cramant—Avize and its Wines—The Vineyards of Oger and Le Mesnil—The Old Town of Vertus and its Vine-clad Slopes—Their Red Wine formerly celebrated.

With the exception of certain famous vineyards of the Rhône, the vinelands of the Champagne may, perhaps, be classed among the most picturesque of the more notable vine districts of France. Between Paris and Epernay even, the banks of the Marne present a series of scenes of quiet beauty. The undulating ground is everywhere cultivated like a garden. Handsome châteaux and charming country houses peep out from amid luxuriant foliage. Picturesque antiquated villages line the river's bank or climb the hill sides, and after leaving La Ferté-sous-Jouarre, the cradle of the Condés, all the more favoured situations commence to be covered with vines.

This is especially the case in the vicinity of Château-Thierry—the birthplace of La Fontaine—where the view is shut in on all sides by vine-clad slopes, which the spring frosts seldom spare. Hence merely one good vintage out of four gladdens the hearts of the peasant proprietors, who find eager purchasers for their produce among the lower-class manufacturers of champagne. In the same way the *petit vin de Chierry*, dexterously prepared and judiciously mingled with other growths, often figures as "Fleur de Sillery" or "Ay Mousseux." In reality it is not until we have passed the ornate modern Gothic château of Boursault, erected in her declining years by the wealthy Veuve Clicquot, by far the shrewdest manipulator of the sparkling products of Ay and Bouzy of her day, and the many towers and turrets of which, rising above umbrageous trees, crown the loftiest height within eyeshot of Epernay, that we find ourselves within that charmed circle of vineyards whence champagne—the wine, not merely of princes, as it has been somewhat obsequiously termed, but essentially the *vin de société*—is derived.

The vinelands in the vicinity of Epernay, and consequently near the Marne, are commonly known as the "Vineyards of the River," whilst those covering the slopes in the neighbourhood of Reims are termed the "Vineyards of the Mountain." The Vineyards of the River comprise three distinct divisions—first, those lining the right bank of the Marne and enjoying a southern and south-eastern aspect, among which are Ay, Hautvillers, Cumières, Dizy, and Mareuil; secondly, the Côte d'Epernay on the left bank of the river, of which Pierry, Moussy, and Vinay form part; and thirdly, the Côte d'Avize (the region *par excellence* of white grapes), which stretches towards the south-east, and includes the vinelands of Cramant, Avize, Oger, Le Mesnil, and Vertus. The entire vineyard area is upwards of 40,000 acres.

The Champagne vineyards most widely celebrated abroad are those of Ay and Sillery, although the last-named are really the smallest in the Champagne district. Ay, distant only a few minutes by rail from Epernay, is in the immediate centre of the vinelands of the river, having Mareuil and Avenay on the east, and Dizy, Hautvillers, and Cumières on the west. Sillery, on the other hand, lies at the foot of the so-called Mountain of Reims, and within an hour's drive of the old cathedral city.

The pleasantest season of the year to visit the Champagne is certainly during the vintage. When this is about to commence, the vintagers—some of whom come from Sainte Menehould, forty miles distant, while others hail from as far as Lorraine—are summoned at daybreak by beat of drum in the market-places of the villages adjacent to the vineyards, and then and there a price is made for the day's labour. This is generally either a franc and a half, with food consisting of three meals, or two francs and a half without food, children being paid a franc and a half. The rate of wage satisfactorily arranged, the gangs start off to the vineyards, headed by their overseers.

It was on one of those occasional sunshiny days in the early part of October (1871) when I first visited Ay, the vineyard of golden plants, the unique *premier crû* of the Wines of the River. The road lay between two rows of closely-planted poplar-trees reaching almost to the village of Dizy, whose quaint grey church tower, with its gabled roof, is dominated by the neighbouring vine-clad slopes, which extend from Avenay to Venteuil, some few miles beyond Hautvillers, the cradle, so to speak, of the *vin mousseux* of the Champagne.

Everywhere was bustle and excitement; every one was big with the business in hand. In these ordinarily quiet little villages the majority of the inhabitants were afoot, the feeble feminine half with the juveniles threading their way through the rows of vines half-way up the mountain, basket on arm, while the sturdy masculine portion were mostly passing to and fro between the press-houses and the wine-shops. Carts piled up with baskets, or crowded with peasants from a distance on their way to the vineyards, jostled the low railway trucks laden with brannew casks, and the somewhat rickety cabriolets of the agents of the big champagne houses, reduced to clinch their final bargain for a hundred or more *pièces* of the peerless wine of Ay, beside the reeking wine-press.

There was a pleasant air of jollity over all, for in the wine-producing districts every one participates in the interest excited by the vintage, which influences the takings of all the artificers and all the tradespeople, bringing grist to the mill of the baker and the bootmaker, as well as to the café and the cabaret. The various contending interests were singularly satisfied, the vintagers getting their two francs and a half a day, and the men at the pressoirs their three francs and their food. The plethoric *commissionaires-en-vins* wiped their perspiring foreheads with satisfaction at having at last secured the full number of hogsheads they had been instructed to buy—at a high figure it was true, still this was no disadvantage to them, as their commission mounted up all the higher. And, as regarded the small vine proprietors, even the thickest-skulled among them, who make all their calculations on their fingers, could see at a glance that they were gainers, for, although the crop was no more than half an average one, yet, thanks to the ill-disguised anxiety of the agents to secure all the wine they required, prices had gradually crept up until they doubled those of ordinary years, and this with only half the work in the vineyard and at the wine-press to be done.

On leaving Dizy the road runs immediately at the base of the vine-clad slopes, broken up by an occasional conical peak detaching itself from the mass, and tinted from base to summit with richly-variegated hues, in which deep purple, yellow, green, grey, and crimson by turns predominate. Dotting these slopes like a swarm of huge ants are a crowd of men, women, and children, intent on stripping the vines of their luscious-looking fruit. The men are mostly in blue blouses, and the women in closely-fitting neat white caps, or wearing old-fashioned unbleached straw-bonnets of the contemned coal-scuttle type. They detach the grapes with scissors or hooked knives, technically termed "serpettes," and in some vineyards proceed to remove all damaged, decayed, or unripe fruit from the bunches before placing them in the baskets hanging on their arms, the contents of which are from time to time emptied into a larger basket resembling a deep clothes-basket in shape, numbers of these being dispersed about the vineyard for the purpose, and invariably in the shade. When filled they are carried by a couple of men to the roadside, along which dwarf stones carved with initials, and indicating the boundaries of the respective properties, are encountered every eight or ten yards, into such narrow strips are the vineyards divided. Large carts with railed open sides are continually passing backwards and forwards to pick these baskets up, and when one of them has secured its load it is driven slowly—in order that the grapes may not be shaken—to the neighbouring pressoir, so extreme is the care observed throughout every stage of the process of champagne manufacture.

In many of the vineyards the grapes are inspected in bulk instead of in detail before being sent to the wine-press. The hand-baskets, when filled, are all brought to a particular spot, where their contents are minutely examined by some half-dozen men and women, who pluck off all the bruised, rotten, and unripe berries, and fling them aside into a separate basket. In one vineyard we came upon a party of girls, congregated round a wicker sieve perched on the top of a large tub by the roadside, who were busy sorting the grapes, pruning away the diseased stalks, and picking off all the doubtful berries, and letting the latter fall through the interstices of the sieve, the sound fruit being deposited in large baskets standing by their side, which, as soon as filled, were conveyed to the pressoir.

A VINTAGE SCENE IN THE CHAMPAGNE.

The picking ordinarily commences with daylight, and the vintagers assert that the grapes gathered at sunrise always produce the lightest and most limpid wine. Moreover by plucking the grapes when the early morning sun is upon them they are believed to yield a fourth more juice. Later on in the day, too, spite of all precautions, it is impossible to prevent some of the detached grapes from partially fermenting, which frequently suffices to give a slight excess of colour to the must, athing especially to be avoided—no matter how rich and ripe the fruit may be—in a high-class champagne. When the grapes have to be transported in open baskets for some distance to the press-house, jolting along the road either in carts or on the backs of mules, and exposed to the torrid rays of a bright autumnal sun, the juice expressed from the fruit, however gently the latter may be squeezed, is occasionally of a positive purple tinge, and consequently useless for conversion into champagne.

On the right of the road leading from Dizy to Ay we pass a vineyard called Le Léon, which tradition asserts to be the one whence Pope Leo the Magnificent, the patron of Michael Angelo, Raffaelle, and Da Vinci, drew his supply of Ay wine. The village of Ay lies right before us at the foot of the vine-clad slopes, with the tapering spire of its ancient church rising above the neighbouring hills and cutting sharply against the bright blue sky. The vineyards, which spread themselves over a calcareous declivity, have mostly a full southern aspect, and the predominating vines are those known as golden plants, the fruit of which is of a deep purple colour. After these comes the *plant vert doré*, and then a moderate proportion of the *plant gris*, the latter a white variety, as its name implies. Alimited quantity of wine from white grapes is likewise made in the neighbouring vineyards of Dizy.

We visited the pressoir of the principal producer of *vin brut* at Ay, who, although the owner of merely five hectares, or about twelve and a half acres of vines, expected to make as many as 1,500 pièces of wine that year, mainly of course from grapes purchased from other growers. One peculiarity of the Champagne district is that, contrary to the prevailing practice in the other wine-producing regions of France, where the owner of even a single acre of vines will crush his grapes himself, only a limited number of vine-proprietors press their own grapes. The large champagne houses, possessing vineyards, always have their pressoirs in the neighbourhood, and other large vine-proprietors will press the grapes they grow, but the multitude of small cultivators invariably sell the produce of their vineyards to one or other of the former at a certain rate, either by weight or else per caque, ameasure estimated to hold sixty kilogrammes (equal to 132lbs.) of grapes. The price which the fruit fetches varies of course according to the quality of the vintage and the requirements of the manufacturers. In 1873, in all the higher-class vineyards, as much as two francs and a quarter per kilogramme (10d. per lb.) were paid, or between treble and quadruple the average price. And yet the vintage was a most unsatisfactory one owing to the deficiency of sun and abundance of wet throughout the summer. The market, however, was in great need of wine, and the fruit while still ungathered was bought up at most exorbitant prices by the *spéculateurs* who supply the *vin brut* to the champagne manufacturers.

Carts laden with grapes were continually arriving at the pressoir, and after discharging their loads, and having them weighed, kept driving off for fresh ones. Four powerful presses of recent invention, each worked by a large fly-wheel requiring four sturdy men to turn it, were in operation. The grapes were spread over the floor of the press in a compact mass, and on being subjected to pressure—again and again repeated, the first squeeze only giving a high-class wine—the must filtered through a wicker basket into the reservoir beneath, whence, after remaining a certain time to allow of its ridding itself of the grosser lees, it is pumped through a gutta-percha tube into the casks. The wooden stoppers of the bungholes, instead of being fixed tightly in the apertures, are simply laid over them, and after the lapse of ten or twelve days fermentation usually commences, and during its progress the must, which is originally of a pale pink tint, fades to a light straw colour. The wine usually remains undisturbed until Christmas, when it is drawn off into fresh casks, and delivered to the purchaser.

On our way from Ay to Mareuil, along the lengthy Rue de Châlons, we looked in at the little auberge at the corner of the Boulevard du Sud, where we found a crowd of coopers and others connected in some way with the vintage taking their cheerful glasses round. The walls of the room were appropriately enough decorated with capering bacchanals squeezing bunches of purple grapes and flourishing their thyrsi about in a very tipsy fashion. All the talk—and there was an abundance of it—had reference to the yield of this particular vintage and the high rate the Ay wine had realised. Eight hundred francs the pièce of two hundred litres, equal to forty-four gallons, appeared to be the price fixed by the agents of the great champagne houses, and at this figure the bulk of the vintage was disposed of before a single grape passed through the wine-press.

At Mareuil, which is scarcely more than a mile from Ay, owing to the steepness of the slopes and to the roads through the vineyards being impracticable for carts, the grapes were being conveyed to the press-houses in baskets slung across the backs of mules and donkeys, who, on account of their known partiality for the ripe fruit, were most of them muzzled while thus employed. The *vin brut* here, inferior of course to that of Ay, found a ready market at from five to six hundred francs the pièce.

From Mareuil we proceeded to Avenay, a tumbledown little village in the direction of Reims, and the vineyards of which were of greater repute in the 13th century than they are to-day. Its best wine, extolled by Saint Evremond, the epicurean Frenchman, who emigrated to the gay court of CharlesII. at Whitehall to escape a gloomy cell in the Bastille, is vintaged up the slopes of Mont Hurlé. At Avenay we found the yield had been little more than the third of an average one, and that the wine from the first pressure of the grapes had been sold for five hundred francs the pièce. Here we tasted some very fair still red wine, made from the same grapes as champagne, remarkably deep in colour, full of body, and with that slight sweet bitterish flavour characteristic of certain of the better-class growths of the south of France. On leaving Avenay we ascended the hills to Mutigny, and wound round thence to Cumières, on the banks of the Marne, finding the vintage in full operation all throughout the route. The vineyards of Cumières—classed as a second crû—join those of Hautvillers on the one side and Damery on the other—the latter a cosy little river-side village, where the *"bon Roi Henri"* sought relaxation from the turmoils of war in the society of the fair Anne du Puy—*"sa belle hôtesse,"* as the gallant Béarnais was wont to style her. Damery too claims to be the birthplace of Adrienne Lecouvreur, the celebrated actress of the Regency, and mistress of the Maréchal de Saxe who coaxed her out of her £30,000 of savings to enable him to prosecute his suit with the obese Anna Iwanowna, niece of Peter the Great, which, had he only been successful in, would have secured the future hero of Fontenoy the coveted dukedom of Courland.

The vineyards of the Côte d'Epernay, south of the Marne, extend eastward from beyond Boursault, on whose wooded height Madame Clicquot built her fine château, in which her granddaughter, the Comtesse de Mortemart, to-day resides. They then follow the course of the river, and after winding round behind Epernay diverge towards the south-west. The vines produce only black grapes, and many of the vineyards are of great antiquity, one at Epernay, known as the Closet, having been bequeathed under that name six and a half centuries ago to a neighbouring Abbey of St. Martin. Ashort drive along the high road leading from Epernay to Troyes brings us to the village of Pierry cosily nestling amongst groves of poplars in the valley of the Cubry, with some half-score of châteaux of the last century belonging to well-to-do wine-growers of the neighbourhood, screened from the road by umbrageous gardens. Vines mount the slopes that rise around, the higher summits being crowned with forest, while here and there some pleasant village shelters itself under the brow of a lofty hill. Near Pierry many cellars have been excavated in the chalky soil, to the flints prevalent in which the village is said to owe its name.

The entrances to these cellars are closed by iron gateways, and on the skirts of the vineyards we come upon whole rows of them picturesquely overgrown with ivy. Early in the last century the wine vintaged in the Clos St. Pierre, belonging to an abbey of this name at Châlons, acquired a high reputation through the care bestowed upon it by Brother Jean Oudart, whose renown almost rivalled that of Dom Perignon himself, and to-day the Pierry vineyards, producing exclusively black grapes, hold a high rank among the second-class crûs of the Marne.

Crossing the Sourdon, a little stream which, bubbling up in the midst of huge rocks in the forest of Epernay, rushes down the hills and mingles its waters with that of the Cubry, we soon reach Moussy, where the vineyards, spite of their long pedigree and southern aspect, also rank as a second crû. Still skirting the vine-clad slopes we come to Vinay, noted for an ancient grotto—the comfortless abode of some rheumatic anchorite—and a pretended miraculous spring to which fever-stricken pilgrims to-day credulously resort. The water may possibly merit its renown, but the wine here produced is very inferior, due no doubt to the class of vines, the meunier being the leading variety cultivated. At Ablois St. Martin, picturesquely perched partway up a slope in the midst of hills covered with vines and crowned with forest trees, the Côte d'Epernay ends, and the produce becomes of a choicer character.

The Côte d'Avize lies to the south-east, so that we have to retrace our steps to Pierry and follow the road which there branches off, leaving the vineyards of Chavot, Monthelon, and Grauves, of no particular note, on our right hand. We pass through Cuis, where the slopes, planted with both black and white varieties of vines, are extremely abrupt, and eventually reach Cramant, one of the grand *premiers crûs* of the Champagne. From the vineyards around this picturesque little village, and extending along the somewhat precipitous Côte de Saran—aprominent object on which is M.Moët's handsome château—there is vintaged a wine from white grapes especially remarkable for lightness and delicacy and the richness of its bouquet, and an admixture of which is essential to every first-class champagne *cuvée*.

From Cramant the road runs direct to Avize, a large thriving village, lying at the foot of vineyard slopes, where numerous champagne firms have established themselves. Its prosperity dates from the commencement of the last century, when the Count de Lhery cleared away the remains of its ancient ramparts, filled up the moat, and planted the ground with vines, the produce of which was found admirably suited for the sparkling wines then coming into vogue. To-day the light delicate wine of Avize is classed, like that of Cramant, as a *premier crû*. It is the same with the wine of Oger, lying a little to the south, while the neighbouring growths of Le Mesnil hold a slightly inferior rank. The latter village and its grey Gothic church lie under the hill in the midst of vines that almost climb the forest-crowned summit. The stony soil hereabouts is said to be better adapted to the cultivation of white than of black grapes, besides which the wines of Le Mesnil are remarkable for their effervescent properties.

Vertus forms the southern limit of the Côte d'Avize, and the vineyard slopes subsiding at their base into a broad expanse of fertile fields, and crested as usual with dense forest, rise up behind the picturesque old town which the English assailed and partly burnt five centuries ago, spite of its fortifications, of which to-day a dilapidated gateway alone remains. The church is ancient and curious, and a few quaint old houses are here and there met with, notably one with a florid Gothic window enriched with a moulding of grapes and vine-leaves. The vineyards of Vertus were originally planted with vines from Burgundy, and in the 14th century yielded a red wine held in high repute, while later on the Vertus growths formed the favourite beverage of William III. of England. To-day the growers find it more profitable to make white instead of red wine from their crops of black grapes, the former commanding a good price for conversion into *vin mousseux*, it being in the opinion of some manufacturers especially valuable for binding a *cuvée* together. The wine of Vertus ranks among the second-class champagne crûs.

CHATEAU OF SILLERY.

CHAPTER III.

THE VINEYARDS OF THE MOUNTAIN.

The Wine of Sillery—Origin of its Renown—The Marechale d'Estrées a successful Marchande de Vin—From Reims to Sillery—Failure of the Jacquesson Vineyards—Château of Sillery—Wine Making at M.Fortel's—Sillery sec—The Vintage and Vendangeoirs at Verzenay—The Verzy Vineyards—Edward III. at the Abbey of St. Basle—From Reims to Bouzy—The Herring Procession at St. Remi—Rilly, Chigny, and Ludes—The Knights Templars' "Pot" of Wine—Mailly and the View over the Plains of the Champagne—Wine Making at Mailly—The Village in the Wood—Village and Château of Louvois—Louis le Grand's War Minister—Bouzy, its Vineyards and Church Steeple, and the Lottery of the Great Gold Ingot—MM.Werlé's and Moët and Chandon's Vendangeoirs—Pressing the Grapes—Still Red Bouzy—Ambonnay—APeasant Proprietor—The Vineyards of Ville-Dommange and Sacy, Hermonville, and St. Thierry—The Still Red Wine of the latter.

The smallest of the Champagne vineyards are those of Sillery, and yet no wine of the Marne enjoys a greater renown, due originally to the intelligence and energy of the Maréchale d'Estrées, the clever daughter of a Jew financier, who brought the wine of Sillery prominently into notice during the latter half of the seventeenth century. She had vineyards at Mailly, Verzy, and Verzenay, as well as at Sillery, and concentrated their produce in the capacious cellars of her château, afterwards sending it forth with her own guarantee, under the general name of Sillery, which, like Aaron's serpent, thus swallowed up the others. The Maréchale's social position enabled her to secure for her wines the recognition they really merited, added to which she was a keen woman of business. She also possessed much taste, and whenever she gave one of her rare entertainments nothing could be more exquisite or more magnificent. At the same time, she was so sordid that when her daughter, who was covered with jewels, fell down at a ball, her first cry was, not like Shylock's, "my daughter," but "my diamonds," as rushing forward she strove to pick up, not the fallen dancer, but her scattered gems.

The drive from Reims to Sillery has nothing attractive about it. Along, straight, level road bordered by trees intersects a broad tract of open country, skirted on the right by the Petite Montagne of Reims, with antiquated villages nestled among the dense woodland. After crossing the Châlons line of railway—near where one of the new forts constructed for the defence of Reims rises up behind the villages and vineyards of Cernay and Nogent l'Abbesse—the country becomes more undulating. Poplars border the broad Marne canal, and a low fringe of foliage marks the course of the languid river Vesle, on the banks of which is Taissy, famous in the old days for its wines, great favourites with Sully, and which almost lured Henri Quatre from his allegiance to the vintages of Ay and Arbois that he loved so well.

To the left rises Mont de la Pompelle, where the first Christians of Reims suffered martyrdom, and where in 1658 the Spaniards under Montal, when attempting to ravage the vineyards of the district, were repulsed with terrible slaughter by the Remois militia, led on by Grandpré. Aquarter of a century ago the low ground on our right near Sillery was planted with vines by M.Jacquesson, the owner of the Sillery estate, and a large champagne manufacturer at Châlons, who was anxious to resuscitate the ancient reputation of the domain. Under the advice of Dr. Guyot, the well-known writer on viticulture, he planted the vines in deep trenches, which led to the vineyards being punningly termed Jacquesson's *celery* beds. To shield the vines from hailstorms prevalent in the district, and the more dangerous spring frosts, so fatal to vines planted in low-lying situations, long rolls of straw-matting were stored close at hand with which to roof them over when needful. These precautions were scarcely needed, however; the vines languished through moisture at the roots, and eventually were mostly rootedup.

After again crossing the railway, we pass the trim, restored turrets of the famous château of Sillery, with its gateways, moats, and drawbridges, flanked by trees and floral parterres. It was here that the Maréchale d'Estrées carried on her successful business as a *marchande de vins*, and the pragmatic and pedantic Comtesse de Genlis, governess of the Orleans princes, spent, as she tells us, the happiest days of her life. The few thriving vineyards of Sillery cover a gentle eminence which rises out of the plain, and present on the one side an eastern and on the other a western aspect. To-day the Vicomte de Brimont and M.Fortel of Reims, the latter of whom cultivates about forty acres of vines, yielding ordinarily about 300 hogsheads, are the only wine-growers at Sillery. Before pressing his grapes—of course for sparkling wine—M.Fortel has them thrown into a trough, at the bottom of which are a couple of grooved cylinders, each about eight inches in diameter, and revolving in contrary directions, the effect of which, when set in motion, is to disengage the grapes partially from their stalks. Grapes and stalks are then placed under the press, which is on the old cyder-press principle, and the must runs into a reservoir beneath, whence it is pumped into large vats, each holding from 250 to 500 gallons. Here it remains from six to eight hours, and is then run off into casks, the spigots of which are merely laid lightly over the holes, and in the course of twelve days the wine begins to ferment. It now rests until the end of the year, when it is drawn off into new casks and delivered to the buyer, invariably one or other of the great champagne houses, who willingly pay an exceptionally high price for it. The second and third pressures of the grapes yield an inferior wine, and from the husks and stalks *eau de vie*, worth about five shillings a gallon, is distilled.

The wine known as Sillery sec is a full, dry, pleasant-flavoured, and some-what spirituous amber-coloured wine. Very little of it is made now-a-days, and most that is comes from the adjacent vineyards of Verzenay and Mailly, and is principally reserved by the growers for their own consumption. One of these candidly admitted to me that the old reputation of the wine had exploded, and that better white Bordeaux and Burgundy wines were to be obtained for less money. In making dry Sillery, which locally is esteemed as a valuable tonic, it is essential that the grapes should be subjected to only slight pressure, while to have it in perfection it is equally essential that the wine should be kept for ten years in the wood according to some, and eight years in bottle according to others, to which circumstance its high price is in all probability to be attributed. In course of time it forms a deposit, and has the disadvantage common to all the finer still wines of the Champagne district of not travelling well.

Beyond Sillery the vineyards of Verzenay unfold themselves, spreading over the extensive slopes and stretching to the summit of the steep height to the right, where a windmill or two is perched. Everywhere the vintagers are busy detaching the grapes with their little hook-shaped *serpettes*, the women all wearing projecting, close-fitting bonnets, as though needlessly careful of their anything but blonde complexions. Long carts laden with baskets of grapes block the narrow roads, and donkeys, duly muzzled, with baskets slung across their backs, toil up and down the steeper slopes. Half way up the principal hill, backed by a dense wood and furrowed with deep trenches, whence soil has been removed for manuring the vineyards, is the village of Verzenay, overlooking a veritable sea of vines. Rising up in front of the old grey cottages, encompassed by orchards or gardens, are the white walls and long red roofs of the vendangeoirs belonging to the great champagne houses—Moët and Chandon, Clicquot, G.H. Mumm, Roederer, Deutz and Geldermann, and others—all teeming with bustle and excitement, and with the vines almost reaching to their very doors. Moët and Chandon have as many as eight presses in full work, and own no less than 120 acres of vines on the neighbouring slopes, besides the Clos de Romont—in the direction of Sillery, and yielding a wine of the Sillery type—belonging to M.Moët Romont. At Messrs. G.H. Mumm's the newly-delivered grapes are either being weighed and emptied into one of the pressoirs, or else receiving their first gentle squeeze. Verzenay ranks as a *premier crû*, and for three years in succession—1872, 3, and4—its wines fetched a higher price than either those of Ay or Bouzy. In 1873 the *vin brut* commanded the exceptionally large sum of 1,030 francs the hogshead of 44 gallons. All the inhabitants of Verzenay are vine proprietors, and several million francs are annually received by them for the produce of their vineyards from the manufacturers of champagne. The wine of Verzenay, remarkable for its body and vinosity, has always been held in high repute, which is more than can be said for the probity of the inhabitants, for according to an old Champagne saying—"Whenever at Verzenay 'Stop thief' is cried every one takes to his heels."

THE VINEYARDS OF VERZENAY.

Just over the mountain of Reims is the village of Verzy, the vineyards of which adjoin those of Verzenay, and are almost exclusively planted with white grapes, the only instance of the kind to be met with in the district. In the clos St. Basse, however—taking its name from the abbey of St. Basle, of which the village was a dependency, and where Edward III. of England had his head-quarters during the siege of Reims—black grapes alone are grown, and its produce is almost on a par with the wines of Verzenay. Southwards of Verzy are the third-class crûs of Villers-Marmery and Trépail.

On leaving Reims on our excursion to the vineyards of Bouzy we pass the quaint old church of St. Remi, one of the sights of the Champagne capital, and notable among other things for its magnificent ancient stained-glass windows, and the handsome modern tomb of the popular Remois saint. It was here in the middle ages that that piece of priestly mummery, the procession of the herrings, used to take place at dusk on the Wednesday before Easter. Preceded by a cross the canons of the church marched in double file up the aisles, each trailing a cord after him, with a herring attached. Every one's object was to tread on the herring in front of him, and prevent his own herring from being trodden upon by the canon who followed behind—adifficult enough proceeding which, if it did not edify, certainly afforded much amusement to the lookers-on.

Soon after crossing the canal and the river Vesle we leave the grey antiquated-looking village of Cormontreuil on our left, and traverse a wide stretch of cultivated country streaked with patches of woodland. Occasional windmills dot the distant heights, while villages nestle among the trees up the mountain sides and in the quiet hollows. Soon a few vineyards occupying the lower slopes, and thronged by bands of vintagers, come in sight, and the country too gets more picturesque. We pass successively on our right hand Rilly, producing a capital red wine, then Chigny, and afterwards Ludes, all three more or less up the mountain, with vines in all directions, relieved by a dark background of forest trees. In the old days the Knights Templars of the Commanderie of Reims had the right of *vinage* at Ludes, and exacted their modest "pot" (about half a gallon) per pièce on all the wine the village produced. On our left hand is Mailly, the vineyards of which join those of Verzenay, and yield a wine noted for *finesse* and bouquet. From the wooded knolls hereabouts a view is gained of the broad plains of the Champagne, dotted with white villages and scattered homesteads among the poplars and the limes, the winding Vesle glittering in the sunlight, and the dark towers of Notre Dame de Reims, with all their rich Gothic fretwork, rising majestically above the distant city.

At one vendangeoir we visited at Mailly between 350 and 400 pièces of wine were being made at the rate of some thirty pièces during the long day of twenty hours, five men being engaged in working the old-fashioned press, closely resembling a cyder press, and applying its pressure longitudinally. The must was emptied into large vats, holding about 450 gallons, and remained there for two or three days before being drawn off into casks. Of the above thirty pièces, twenty resulting from the first pressure were of the finest quality, four produced by the second pressure were partly reserved to replace what the first might lose during fermentation, the residue serving for second-class champagne. The six pièces which came from the final pressure, after being mixed with common wine of the district, were converted into champagne of inferior quality.

We now cross the mountain, sight Ville-en-Selve—the village in the wood—among the distant trees, and eventually reach Louvois, whence the Grand Monarque's domineering war minister derived his marquisate, and where his château, aplain but capacious edifice, may still be seen nestled in a picturesque and fertile valley, and surrounded by lordly pleasure grounds. Soon afterwards the vineyards of Bouzy appear in sight, with the prosperous-looking little village rising out of the plain at the foot of the vine-clad slopes stretching to Ambonnay, and the glittering Marne streaking the hazy distance. The commodious new church was indebted for its spire, we were told, to the lucky gainer — who chanced to be a native of Bouzy — of the great gold ingot lottery prize, value £16,000, drawn some years ago. The Bouzy vineyards occupy a series of gentle inclines, and have the advantage of a full southern aspect. The soil, which is of the customary calcareous formation, has a marked ruddy tinge, indicative of the presence of iron, to which the wine is in some degree indebted for its distinguishing characteristics — its delicacy, spirituousness, and pleasant bouquet. Vintagers are passing slowly in between the vines, and carts laden with grapes come rolling over the dusty roads. The mountain which rises behind is scored up its sides and fringed with foliage at its summit, and a small stone bridge crosses the deep ravine formed by the swift descending winter torrents.

THE VINEYARDS OF BOUZY.

The principal vineyard proprietors at Bouzy, which ranks, of course, as a *premier crû*, are M.Werlé, M.Irroy, and Messrs. Moët and Chandon, the first and last of whom have capacious vendangeoirs here, M.Irroy's pressing-house being in the neighbouring village of Ambonnay. M.Werlé possesses at Bouzy from forty to fifty acres of the finest vines, forming a considerable proportion of the entire vineyard area. At the Clicquot-Werlé vendangeoir, containing as many as eight presses, about 1,000 pièces of wine are made annually. At the time of our visit, grapes gathered that morning were in course of delivery, the big basketfuls being measured off in caques — wooden receptacles, holding two-and-twenty gallons — while the florid-faced foreman ticked them off with a piece of chalk on the head of an adjacent cask.

PRESSING GRAPES AT M. WERLÉ'S VENDANGEOIR AT BOUZY.

As soon as the contents of some half-hundred or so of these baskets had been emptied on to the floor of the press, the grapes undetached from their stalks were smoothed compactly down, and a moderate pressure was applied to them by turning a huge wheel, which caused the screw of the press to act—agradual squeeze rather than a powerful one, and given all at once, coaxing out, it was said, the finer qualities of the fruit. The operation was repeated as many as six times; the yield from the three first pressures being reserved for conversion into champagne, while the result of the fourth squeeze would be applied to replenishing the loss, averaging 7½ per cent., sustained by the must during fermentation. Whatever comes from the fifth pressure is sold to make an inferior champagne. The grapes are subsequently well raked about, and then subjected to a couple of final squeezes, known as the *rébêche*, and yielding a sort of *piquette*, given to the workmen employed at the pressoir to drink.

The small quantity of still red Bouzy wine made by M. Werlé at the same vendangeoir only claims to be regarded as a wine of especial mark in good years. The grapes before being placed beneath the press are allowed to remain in a vat for as many as eight days. The must undergoes a long fermentation, and after being drawn off into casks is left undisturbed for a couple of years. In bottle, where, by the way, it invariably deposits a sediment, which is indeed the case with all the wines of the Champagne, still or sparkling, it will outlive, we were told, any Burgundy.

Still red Bouzy has a marked and agreeable bouquet and a most delicate flavour, is deliciously smooth to the palate, and to all appearances as light as a wine of Bordeaux, while in reality it is quite as strong as Burgundy, to the finer crûs of which it bears a slight resemblance. It was, Ilearnt, most susceptible to travelling, amere journey to Paris being, it was said, sufficient to sicken it, and impart such a shock to its delicate constitution that it was unlikely to recover from it. To attain perfection, this wine, which is what the French term a *vin vif*, penetrating into the remotest corners of the organ of taste, requires to be kept a couple of years in wood and half-a-dozen or more years in bottle.

From Bouzy it was only a short distance along the base of the vine slopes to Ambonnay, where there are merely two or three hundred acres of vines, and where we found the vintage almost over. The village is girt with fir trees, and surrounded by rising ground fringed with solid belts or slender strips of foliage. An occasional windmill cuts against the horizon, which is bounded here and there by scattered trees. Inquiring for the largest vine proprietor we were directed to an open porte-cochère, and on entering the large court encountered half-a-dozen labouring men engaged in various farm occupations. Addressing one whom we took to be the foreman, he referred us to a wiry little old man, in shirt-sleeves and sabots, absorbed in the refreshing pursuit of turning over a big heap of rich manure with a fork. He proved to be M.Oury, the owner of I forget how many acres of vines, and a remarkably intelligent peasant, considering what dunderheads the French peasants as a rule are, who had raised himself to the position of a large vine proprietor. Doffing his sabots and donning a clean blouse, he conducted us into his little salon, afreshly-painted apartment about eight feet square, of which the huge fireplace occupied fully one-third, and submitted patiently to our catechizing.

At Ambonnay, as at Bouzy, they had that year, M. Oury said, only half an average crop; the caque of grapes had, moreover, sold for exactly the same price at both places, and the wine had realised about 800 francs the pièce. Each hectare (2½ acres) of vines had yielded 45 caques of grapes, weighing some 2¾ tons, which produced 6½ pièces, equal to 286 gallons of wine, or at the rate of 110 gallons per acre. Here the grapes were pressed four times, the yield from the second pressure being used principally to make good the loss which the first sustained during its fermentation. As the squeezes given were powerful ones, all the best qualities of the grapes were by this time extracted, and the yield from the third and fourth pressures would not command more than 80 francs the pièce. The vintagers who came from a distance received either a franc and a half per day and their food, consisting of three meals, or two francs and a half without food, the children being paid thirty sous. M.Oury further informed us that every year vineyards came into the market, and found ready purchasers at from fifteen to twenty thousand francs the hectare, equal to an average price of £300 the acre. Owing to the properties being divided into such infinitesimal portions, they were rarely bought up by the large champagne houses, who preferred not to be embarrassed with the cultivation of such tiny plots, but to buy the produce from their owners.

There are other vineyards of lesser note in the neighbourhood of Reims producing very fair wines which enter more or less into the composition of champagne. Noticeable among these are Ville-Dommange and Sacy, south-west of Reims, and Hermonville and St. Thierry—where the Black Prince took up his quarters during the siege of Reims—north-west of the city. The still red wine of St. Thierry, which recalls the growths of the Médoc by its tannin, and those of the Côte d'Or by its vinosity, is to-day almost a thing of the past, it being found here as elsewhere more profitable to press the grapes for sparkling in preference to still wine.

CHAPTER IV.

THE VINES OF THE CHAMPAGNE AND THE SYSTEM OF CULTIVATION.

The Vines chiefly of the Pineau Variety—The Plant doré of Ay, the Plant vert doré, the Plant gris, and the Epinette—The Soil of the Vineyards—Close Mode of Plantation—The Operation of Provinage—The Stems of the Vines never more than Three Years Old—Fixing the Stakes to the Vines—Manuring and General Cultivation—Spring Frosts in the Champagne—Various Modes of Protecting the Vines against them—Dr. Guyot's System—The Parasites that Prey upon the Vines.

In the Champagne the old rule holds good—poor soil, rich product; grand wine in moderate quantity. Four descriptions of vines are chiefly cultivated, three of them yielding black grapes, and all belonging to the Pineau variety, from which the grand Burgundy wines are produced, and so styled from the clusters taking the conical form of the pine. The first is the franc pineau, the plant doré of Ay, producing small round grapes, with thickish skins of a bluish black tint, and sweet and refined in flavour. The next is the plant vert doré, more robust and more productive than the former, but yielding a less generous wine, and the berries of which are dark and oval, very thin skinned and remarkably sweet and juicy. The third variety is the plant gris, or burot, as it is styled in the Côte d'Or, asomewhat delicate vine, whose fruit has a brownish tinge, and yields a light and perfumed wine. The remaining species is a white grape known as the épinette, avariety of the pineau blanc, and supposed by some to be identical with the chardonnet of Burgundy, which yields the famous wine of Montrachet. It is met with all along the Côte d'Avize, notably at Cramant, the delicate and elegant wine of which ranks immediately after that of Ay and Verzenay. The épinette is a prolific bearer, and its round transparent golden berries, which hang in no very compact clusters, are both juicy and sweet. It ripens, however, much later than either of the black varieties.

There are several other species of vines cultivated in the Champagne vineyards, notably the common meunier, or miller, bearing black grapes, and prevalent in the valley of Epernay, and which takes its name from the circumstance of the young leaves appearing to have been sprinkled with flour. There are also the black and white gouais, the meslier, aprolific white variety yielding a wine of fair quality, the black and white gamais, the leading grape in the Mâconnais, and chiefly found in the Vertus vineyards, together with the tourlon, the marmot, and half a score of others.

The soil of the Champagne vineyards is chalk, with a mixture of silica and light clay, combined with a varying proportion of oxide of iron. The vines are almost invariably planted on rising ground, the lower slopes which usually escape the spring frosts producing the best wines. The new vines are placed very close together, there often being as many as six within a square yard. When two or three years old they are ready for the operation of provinage universally practised in the Champagne, and which consists in burying in a trench, from 6 to 8 inches deep, dug on one side of the plant, the two lowest buds of the two principal shoots, left when the vine was pruned for this especial purpose. The shoots thus laid underground are dressed with a light manure, and in course of time take root and form new vines, which bear during their second year. This operation is performed in the spring, and is annually repeated until the vine is five years old, the plants thus being in a state of continual progression, asystem which accounts for the juvenescent aspect of the Champagne vineyards, where none of the wood of the vines showing aboveground is more than three years old. When the vine has attained its fifth year it is allowed to rest for a couple of years, and then the pruning is resumed, the shoots being dispersed in any direction throughout the vineyard. The plants remain in this condition henceforward, merely requiring to be renewed from time to time by judicious provining.

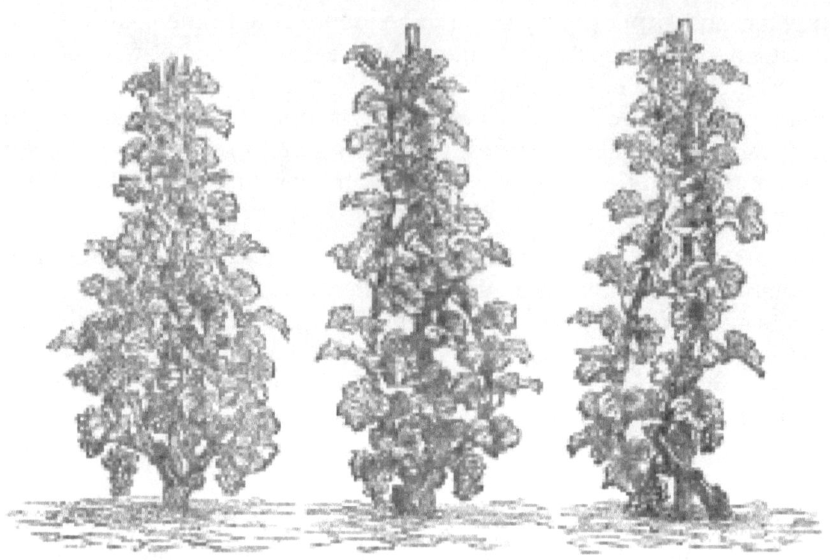

The vines are supported by stakes, when of oak costing sixty francs the thousand; and as in the Champagne a close system of plantation is followed, no less than 24,000 stakes are required on every acre of land, making the cost per acre of propping up the vines upwards of £57, or double what it is in the Médoc and quadruple what it is in Burgundy. These stakes are set up in the spring of the year by men or women, the former of whom force them into the ground by pressing against them with their chest, which is protected with a shield of stout leather. The women use a mallet, or have recourse to a special appliance, in working which the foot plays the principal part. The latter method is the least fatiguing, and in some localities is practised by the men. An expert labourer will set up as many as 5,000 of these stakes in the course of the day. After the vines have been hoed around their roots they are secured to the stakes, and the tops are broken off at a shoot to prevent them from growing above the regulation height, which is ordinarily from 30 to 33 inches. They are liberally manured with a kind of compost formed of the loose friable soil dug out from the sides of the mountain, and of supposed volcanic origin, mixed with animal and vegetable refuse. The vines are shortened back while in flower, and in the course of the summer the ground is hoed a second and a third time, the object being, first, to destroy the superficial roots of the vines and force the plants to live solely on their deep roots; and, secondly, to remove all pernicious weeds from round about them. After the third hoeing, which takes place in the middle of August, the vines are left to themselves until the period of the vintage. When this is over the stakes supporting the vines are pulled up and stacked in compact masses, with their ends out of the ground, the vine, which is left curled up in a heap, remaining undisturbed until the winter, when the earth around it is loosened. In the month of February it is pruned and sunk into the earth, as already described, so as to leave only the new wood aboveground. Owing to the vines being planted so closely together they starve one another, and numbers of them perish. When this is the case, or the stems get broken during the vintage, their places are filled up by provining.

The vignerons of the Champagne regard the numerous stakes which support the vines as affording some protection against the white frosts of the spring. To guard against the dreaded effects of these frosts, which invariably occur between early dawn and sunrise, and the loss arising from which is estimated to amount annually to 25 per cent. some of the cultivators place heaps of hay, faggots, dead leaves, &c., about twenty yards apart, taking care to keep them moderately damp. When a frost is feared the heaps on the side of the vineyard whence the wind blows are set light to, whereupon the dense smoke which rises spreads horizontally over the vines, producing the same result as an actual cloud, intercepting the rays of the sun, warming the atmosphere, and converting the frost into dew. Among other methods adopted to shield the vines from frosts is the joining of branches of broom together in the form of a fan, and afterwards fastening them to the end of a pole, which is placed obliquely in the ground, so that the fan may incline over the vine and protect it from the sun's rays. Asingle labourer can plant, it is said, as many as eight thousand of these fans in the ground in the course of a long day.

Dr. Guyot's system of roofing the vines with straw matting, to protect them alike against frost and hailstorms, is very generally followed in low situations in the Champagne, the value of the wine admitting of so considerable an expense being incurred. This matting, which is about a foot and a half in width, and in rolls of great length, is fastened either with twine or wire to the vine stakes, and it is estimated that half-a-dozen men can fix nearly 11,000 yards of it, or sufficient to roof over 2½acres of vines, during an ordinary day.

Owing to the system of cultivation by rejuvenescence, and the constant replenishing of the soil by well-compounded manures, the Champenois winegrowers entertain great hopes that their vineyards will escape the ravages of the phylloxera vastatrix. According to Dr. Plonquet of Ay they are already the prey of no less than fifteen varieties of insects, which feed upon the leaves, stalks, roots, or fruit of the vines. Between 1850 and 1860 the vineyards of Ay were devastated by the pyrale, aspecies of caterpillar, which feeds on the young leaves and shoots until the vine is left completely bare. The insect eventually becomes transformed into a small white butterfly, and deposits its eggs either in the crevices of the stakes or in the stalks of the vine. All the efforts made to rid the vineyards of this scourge proved ineffectual until the wet and cold weather of 1860 put a stop to the insect's ravages. More recently it has been discovered that its attacks can be checked by sulphurous acid.

CHAPTER V.

PREPARATION OF CHAMPAGNE.

Treatment of Champagne after it comes from the Wine-Press—Racking and Blending of the Wine—Deficiency and Excess of Effervescence—Strength and Form of Champagne Bottles—The "Tirage" or Bottling of the Wine—The Process of Gas-making commences—Inevitable Breakage follows—Wine Stacked in Piles—Formation of Sediment—Bottles placed "sur pointe" and Daily Shaken—Effect of this occupation on those incessantly engaged in it—"Claws" and "Masks"—Champagne Cellars—Their Construction and Aspect—Transforming the "vin brut" into Champagne—Disgorging and Liqueuring the Wine—The Corking, Stringing, Wiring, and Amalgamating—The Wine's Agitated Existence comes to an End—The Bottles have their Toilettes made—Champagne sets out on its beneficial Pilgrimage.

The special characteristic of champagne is that its manufacture only just commences where that of other wines ordinarily ends. The must flows direct from the press into capacious reservoirs, whence it is drawn off into large vats, and after being allowed to clear, is transferred to casks holding some forty-four gallons each.

Although the bulk of the new-made wine is left to repose at the vendangeoirs until the commencement of the following year, still when the vintage is over numbers of long narrow carts laden with casks of it are to be seen rolling along the dusty highways leading to those towns and villages in the Marne where the manufacture of champagne is carried on. Chief amongst these is the cathedral city of Reims, after which comes the rising town of Epernay, stretching to the very verge of the river, then Ay, nestled between the vine-clad slopes and the Marne canal, with the neighbouring village of Mareuil, and finally Avize, in the centre of the white grape district southwards of Epernay. Châlons, owing to its distance from the vineyards, would scarcely draw its supply of wine until the new year. The first fermentation lasts from a fortnight to a month, according as to whether the wine be *mou*—that is, rich in sugar—or the reverse. In the former case fermentation naturally lasts much longer than when the wine is *vert* or green. This active fermentation is converted into latent fermentation by transferring the wine to a cooler cellar, as it is essential it should retain a large proportion of its natural saccharine to ensure its future effervescence. The casks have previously been completely filled, and their bungholes tightly stopped, anecessary precaution to guard the wine from absorbing oxygen, the effect of which would be to turn it yellow and cause it to lose some of its lightness and perfume. After being racked and fined, the produce of the different vineyards is now ready for mixing together in accordance with the traditional theories of the various manufacturers, and should the vintage have been an indifferent one a certain proportion of old reserved wine of a good year enters into the blend.

The mixing is usually effected in gigantic vats holding at times as many as 12,000 gallons each, and having fan-shaped appliances inside, which, on being worked by handles, ensure a complete amalgamation of the wine. This process of marrying wine on a gigantic scale is technically known as making the *cuvée*. Usually four-fifths of wine from black grapes are tempered by one-fifth of the juice of white ones. It is necessary that the first should comprise a more or less powerful dash of the finer growths both of the Mountain of Reims and of the River, while, as regards the latter, one or other of the delicate vintages of the Côte d'Avize is essential to the perfect *cuvée*. The aim is to combine and develop the special qualities of the respective crûs, body and vinosity being secured by the red vintages of Bouzy and Verzenay, softness and roundness by those of Ay and Dizy, and lightness, delicacy, and effervescence by the white growths of Avize and Cramant. The proportions are never absolute, but vary according to the manufacturer's style of wine and the taste of the countries which form his principal markets. The wine at this period being imperfectly fermented and crude, the reader may imagine the delicacy and discrimination of palate requisite to judge of the flavour, finesse, and bouquet which the *cuvée* is likely eventually to develop.

These, however, are not the only matters to be considered. There is, above everything, the effervescence, which depends upon the quantity of carbonic acid gas the wine contains, and this, in turn, upon the amount of its natural saccharine. If the gas be present in excess, there will be a shattering of bottles and a flooding of cellars; and if there be a paucity the corks will refuse to pop, and the wine to sparkle aright in the glass. Therefore the amount of saccharine in the *cuvée* has to be accurately ascertained by means of a glucometer; and if it fails to reach the required standard, the deficiency is made up by the addition of the purest sugar-candy. If, on the other hand, there be an excess of saccharine, the only thing to be done is to defer the final blending and bottling until the superfluous saccharine matter has been absorbed by fermentation in the cask.

The *cuvée* completed, the blended wine, now resembling in taste and colour an ordinary acrid white wine, and giving to the uninitiated palate no promise of the exquisite delicacy and aroma it is destined to develop, is drawn off again into casks for further treatment. This comprises fining with some gelatinous substance, and, as a precaution against ropiness and other maladies, liquid tannin is at the same time frequently added to supply the place of the natural tannin which has departed from the wine with its reddish hue at the epoch of its first fermentation.

The operation of bottling the wine next ensues, when the Scriptural advice not to put new wine into old bottles is rigorously followed. For the tremendous pressure of the gas engendered during the subsequent fermentation of the wine is such that the bottle becomes weakened and can never be safely trusted again. It is because of this pressure that the champagne bottle is one of the strongest made, as indicated by its weight, which is almost a couple of pounds. To ensure this unusual strength it is necessary that its sides should be of equal thickness and the bottom of a uniform solidity throughout, in order that no particular expansion may ensue from sudden changes of temperature. The neck must, moreover, be perfectly round and widen gradually towards the shoulder. In addition—and this is of the utmost consequence—the inside ought to be perfectly smooth, as a rough interior causes the gas to make efforts to escape, and thus renders an explosion imminent. The composition of the glass, too, is not without its importance, as a manufactory established for the production of glass by a new process turned out champagne bottles charged with alkaline sulphurets, and the consequence was that an entire *cuvée* was ruined by their use, through the reciprocal action of the wine and these sulphurets. The acids of the former disengaged hydrosulphuric acid, and instead of champagne the result was a new species of mineral water.

Most of the bottles used for champagnes come from the factories of Loivre (which supplies the largest quantity), Folembray, Vauxrot, and Quiquengrogne, and cost on the average from 28 to 30 francs the hundred. They are generally tested by a practised hand, who, by knocking them sharply together, professes to be able to tell from the sound that they give the substance of the glass and its temper. The washing of the bottles is invariably performed by women, who at the larger establishments accomplish it with the aid of machines, sometimes provided with a revolving brush, although small glass beads are more generally used by preference. After being washed every bottle is minutely examined to make certain of its perfect purity.

With the different champagne houses the mode of bottling the wine, which may take place any time between April and August, varies in some measure, still the *tirage*, as this operation is called, is ordinarily effected as follows:—The wine is emptied from the casks into vats or tuns of varying capacity, whence it flows through pipes into oblong reservoirs, each provided with a row of syphon taps, on to which the bottles are slipped, and from which the wine ceases to flow directly the bottles become filled. Men or lads remove the full bottles, replacing them by empty ones, while other hands convey them to the corkers, whose guillotine machines are incessantly in motion; next the *agrafeurs* secure the corks by means of an iron staple, termed an agrafe; and then the bottles are conveyed either to a capacious apartment aboveground, known as a cellier, or to a cool cellar, according to the number of atmospheres the wine may indicate. It should be explained that air compressed to half its volume acquires twice its ordinary force, and to a quarter of its volume quadruple this force—hence the phrase of two, four, or more atmospheres. The exact degree of pressure is readily ascertained by means of a manometer, an instrument resembling a pressure gauge, with a hollow screw at the base which is driven through the cork of the bottle. A pressure of 5¾ atmospheres constitutes what is styled a "grand mousseux," and the wine exhibiting it may be safely conveyed to the coolest subterranean depths, for no doubt need be entertained as to its future effervescent properties. Should the pressure, however, scarcely exceed 4atmospheres, it is advisable to keep the wine in a cellier aboveground that it may more rapidly acquire the requisite sparkling qualities. If fewer than 4atmospheres are indicated it would be necessary to pour the wine back into the casks again, and add a certain amount of cane sugar to it, but such an eventuality very rarely happens, thanks to the scientific formulas and apparatus which enable the degree of pressure the wine will show to be determined beforehand to a nicety. Still mistakes are sometimes made, and there are instances where charcoal fires have had to be lighted in the cellars to encourage the effervescence to develop itself.

The bottles are placed in a horizontal position and stacked in rows of varying length and depth, one above the other, to about the height of a man, and with narrow laths between them. Thus they will spend the summer providing all goes well, but in about three weeks' time the process of gas-making inside the bottles is at its height, and may cause an undue number of them to burst. The glucometer notwithstanding, it is impossible to check a certain amount of breakage, especially when a hot season has caused the grapes, and consequently the raw wine, to be sweeter than usual. Moreover when once *casse* or breakage sets in on a large scale, the temperature of the cellar is raised by the volume of carbonic acid gas let loose, which is not without its effect on the remaining bottles. The only remedy is at once to remove the wine to a lower temperature when this is practicable. Amanufacturer of the pre-scientific days of the last century relates how one year, when the wine was rich and strong, he only preserved 120 out of 6,000 bottles; and it is not long since that 120,000 out of 200,000 were destroyed in the cellars of a well-known champagne firm. Over-knowing purchasers still affect to select a wine which has exploded in the largest proportion as being well up to the mark as regards its effervescence, and profess to make inquiries as to its performances in this direction.

It is evident that in spite of the teachings of science the bursting of champagne bottles has not yet been reduced to a minimum, for whereas in some cellars it averages 7 and 8 per cent., in others it rarely exceeds 2½ or3. In the month of October, the first and severest breakage being over, the newly-bottled wine is definitively stacked in the cellars in piles from two to half-a-dozen bottles deep, from six to seven feet high, and frequently a hundred feet or upwards in length. Usually the bottles remain in their horizontal position for about eighteen or twenty months, though some firms, who pride themselves upon shipping perfectly matured wines, leave them thus for double this space of time. All this while the temperature to which the wine is exposed is, as far as practicable, carefully regulated; for the risk of breakage, though greatly diminished, is never entirely at an end.

By this time the fermentation is over, but in the interval, commencing from a few days after the bottling of the wine, aloose dark-brown sediment has been forming which has now settled on the lower side of the bottle, and to get rid of which is a delicate and tedious task. The bottles are placed *sur pointe*, as it is termed—that is to say, slantingly in racks with their necks downwards, the inclination being increased from time to time to one more abrupt. The object of this change in their position is to cause the sediment to leave the side of the bottle where it has gathered; it afterwards becomes necessary to twist and turn it, and coagulate it, as it were, until it forms a kind of muddy ball, and eventually to get it well down into the neck of the bottle, so that it may be finally expelled with a bang when the temporary cork is removed and the proper one adjusted. To accomplish this the bottles are sharply turned in one direction every day for at least a month or six weeks, the time being indefinitely extended until the sediment shows a disposition to settle near the cork. The younger the wine the longer the period necessary for the bottles to be shaken, new wine often requiring as much as three months. Only a thoroughly practised hand can give the right amount of revolution and the requisite degree of slope; and in some of the cellars that we visited men were pointed out to us who had acquired such dexterity as to be able at a pinch to shake with their two hands as many as 50,000 bottles in a single day.

Some of these men have spent thirty or forty years of their lives engaged in this perpetual task. Fancy being entombed all alone day after day in vaults which are invariably dark and gloomy, and often cold and dank, and being obliged to twist sixty to seventy of these bottles every minute throughout the day of twelve hours. Why the treadmill and the crank with their periodical respites must be pastime compared to this maddeningly monotonous occupation, which combines hard labour, with the wrist at any rate, with next to solitary confinement. One can understand these men becoming gloomy and taciturn, and affirming that they sometimes see devils hovering over the bottle-racks and frantically shaking the bottles beside them, or else grinning at them as they pursue their humdrum task. Still it may be taken for granted that the men who reach this stage are accustomed to drink freely of raw spirits, and merely pay the penalty resulting from over-indulgence.

In former times the bottles used to be placed with their heads downwards on tables pierced with holes, from which they had to be removed and agitated. In 1818, however, aman named Muller, in the employment of Madame Clicquot, suggested that the bottles should remain in the tables whilst being shaken, and further that the holes should be cut obliquely so that the bottles might recline at varying angles. His suggestions were privately adopted by Madame Clicquot, but eventually the improved plan got wind, and the system now prevails throughout the Champagne. When the bottles have gone through their regular course of shaking they are examined before a lighted candle to ascertain whether the deposit has fallen and the wine become perfectly clear. Sometimes it happens that, twist these men never so wisely, the deposit refuses to stir, and takes the shape of a bunch of thread technically called a "claw," or an adherent mass styled a "mask." When this is the case an attempt is made to start it by tapping the part to which it adheres with a piece of iron, the result being frequently the sudden explosion of the bottle. As a precaution, therefore, the workman protects his face with a wire-mask or gigantic wire spectacles, which give to him a ghoul-like aspect.

The cellars of the champagne manufacturers are very varied in character. The wine that has been grown on the chalky hills undergoes development in vaults burrowed out of the calcareous strata underlying the entire district. In excavating these cellars the sides and roofs are frequently worked smooth and regular as finished masonry. The larger ones are composed of a number of spacious and lofty galleries, sometimes parallel with each other, but often ramifying in various directions, and evidently constructed on no definite plan. They are of one, two, and, in rare instances, of three stories, and now and then consist of a series of parallel galleries communicating with each other, lined with masonry, and with their stone walls and vaulted roofs resembling the crypt of some conventual building. Others of ancient date are less regular in their form, being merely so many narrow low winding corridors, varied, perhaps, by recesses hewn roughly out of the chalk, and resembling the brigands' cave of the melodrama, while a certain number of the larger cellars at Reims are simply abandoned quarries, the broad and lofty arches of which are suggestive of the nave and aisles of some Gothic church. In these varied vaults, lighted by solitary lamps in front of metal reflectors, or by the flickering tallow candles which we carry in our hands, we pass rows of casks filled with last year's vintage or reserved wine of former years, and piles after piles of bottles of *vin brut* in seemingly endless sequence—squares, so to speak, of raw champagne recruits awaiting their turn to be thoroughly drilled and disciplined. These are varied by bottles reposing necks downwards in racks at different degrees of inclination according to the progress their education has attained. Reports caused by exploding bottles now and then assail the ear, and as the echo dies away it becomes mingled with the rush of the escaping wine, cascading down the pile and finding its way across the sloping sides of the floor to the narrow gutter in the centre. The dampness of the floor and the shattered fragments of glass strewn about show the frequency of this kind of accident. The spilt wine, which flows along the gutter into reservoirs, is usually thrown away, though there is a story current to the effect that the head of one Epernay firm cooks nearly everything consumed in his house in the fluid thus let loose in his cellars.

In these subterranean galleries we frequently come upon parties of workmen engaged in transforming the perfected *vin brut* into champagne. Viewed at a distance while occupied in their monotonous task, they present in the semi-obscurity a series of picturesque Rembrandt-like studies. One of the end figures in each group is engaged in the important process of *dégorgement*, which is performed when the deposit, of which we have already spoken, has satisfactorily settled in the neck of the bottle. Baskets full of bottles with their necks downwards are placed beside the operator, who stands before an apparatus resembling a cask divided vertically down the middle. This nimble-figured manipulator seizes a bottle, holds it for a moment before the light to test the clearness of the wine and the subsidence of the deposit; brings it, still neck downwards, over a small tub at the bottom of the apparatus already mentioned; and with a jerk of the steel hook which he holds in his right hand loosens the *agrafe* securing the cork, Bang goes the latter, and with it flies out the sediment and a small glassful or so of wine, further flow being checked by the workman's finger, which also serves to remove any sediment yet remaining in the bottle's neck. Like many other clever tricks, this looks very easy when adroitly performed, though a novice would probably empty the bottle by the time he had discovered that the cork was out. Occasionally a bottle bursts in the *dégorgeur's* hand, and his face is sometimes scarred from such explosions. The sediment removed, he slips a temporary cork into the bottle, and the wine is ready for the important operation of the *dosage*, upon the nature and amount of which the character of the perfected wine, whether it be dry or sweet, light or strong, very much depends.

Different manufacturers have different recipes, more or less complex in character, and varying with the quality of the wine and the country for which it is intended; but the genuine liqueur consists of nothing but old wine of the best quality, to which a certain amount of sugar-candy and perhaps a dash of the finest cognac spirit has been added. The saccharine addition varies according to the market for which the wine is destined: thus the high-class English buyer demands a dry champagne, the Russian a wine sweet and strong as "ladies' grog," and the Frenchman and German a sweet light wine. To the extra-dry champagnes a modicum dose is added, while the so-called "*brut*" wines receive no more than from one to three per cent. of liqueur.

In some establishments the dose is administered with a tin can or ladle; but more generally an ingenious machine of pure silver and glass which regulates the percentage of liqueur to a nicety is employed. The *dosage* accomplished, the bottle passes to another workman known as the *égaliseur*, who fills it up with pure wine.

Should a pink champagne be required, the wine thus added will be red, although manufacturers of questionable reputation sometimes employ the solution known as *teinte de Fismes*. The *égaliseur* in turn hands the bottle to the corker, who places it under a machine furnished with a pair of claws, which compress the cork to a size sufficiently small to allow it to enter the neck of the bottle, and a suspended weight, which in falling drives it home. These corks, which are principally obtained from Catalonia and Andalucia, cost more than twopence each, and are delivered in huge sacks resembling hop-pockets. Before they are used they have been either boiled in wine, soaked in a solution of tartar, or else steamed by the cork merchants, both to prevent their imparting a bad flavour to the wine and to hinder any leakage. They are commonly handed warm to the corker, who dips them into a small vessel of wine before making use of them. Some firms, however, prepare their corks by subjecting them to cold water *douches* a day or two beforehand. The *ficeleur* receives the bottle from the corker, and with a twist of the fingers secures the cork with string, at the same time rounding its hitherto flat top. The *metteur de fil* next affixes the wire with like celerity; and then the final operation is performed by a workman seizing a couple of bottles by the neck and whirling them round his head, as though engaged in the Indian-club exercise, in order to secure a perfect amalgamation of the wine and the liqueur.

The final manipulation accomplished, the agitated course of existence through which the wine has been passing of late comes to an end, and the bottles are conveyed to another part of the establishment, where they repose for several days, or even weeks, in order that the mutual action of the wine and the liqueur upon each other may be complete. When the time arrives for despatching them they are confided to feminine hands to have their dainty toilettes made, and are tastefully labelled and either capsuled, or else have their corks and necks imbedded in sealing-wax, or swathed in gold or silver foil, whereby they are rendered presentable at the best-appointed tables.

Thus completed champagne sets out on its beneficial pilgrimage to promote the spread of mirth and lightheartedness, to drive away dull care and foment good-fellowship, to comfort the sick and cheer the sound. Wherever civilisation penetrates, champagne sooner or later is sure to follow; and if Queen Victoria's morning drum beats round the world, its beat is certain to be echoed before the day is over by the popping of champagne-corks. Now-a-days the exhilarating wine graces not merely princely but middle-class dinner-tables, and is the needful adjunct at every *petit souper* in all the gayer capitals of the world. It gives a flush to beauty at garden-parties and picnics, sustains the energies of the votaries of Terpsichore until the hour of dawn, and imparts to many a young gallant the necessary courage to declare his passion. It enlivens the dullest of *réunions*, brings smiles to the lips of the sternest cynics, softens the most irascible tempers, and loosens the most taciturn tongues. The grim Berliner and the gay Viennese both acknowledge its enlivening influence. It sparkles in crystal goblets in the great capital of the North, and the Moslem wipes its creamy foam from his beard beneath the very shadow of the mosque of St. Sophia; for the Prophet has only forbidden the use of wine, and of a surety—Allah be praised!—this strangely-sparkling delicious liquor, which gives to the true believer a foretaste of the joys of Paradise, cannot be wine.At the diamond-fields of South Africa and the diggings of Australia the brawny miner who has hit upon a big bit of crystallised carbon, or a nugget of virgin ore, strolls to the "saloon" and shouts for champagne. The mild Hindoo imbibes it quietly, but approvingly, as he watches the evolutions of the Nautch girls, and his partiality for it has already enriched the Anglo-Bengalee vocabulary and London slang with the word "simkin." It is transported on camel-backs across the deserts of Central Asia, and in frail canoes up the mighty Amazon. The two-sworded Daimio calls for it in the tea-gardens of Yokohama, and the New Yorker, when not rinsing his stomach by libations of iced-water, imbibes it freely at Delmonico's. Wherever civilised man has set his foot—at the base of the Pyramids and at the summit of the Cordilleras, in the mangrove swamps of Ashantee and the gulches of the Great Lone Land, in the wilds of the Amoor and on the desert isles of the Pacific—he has left traces of his presence in the shape of the empty bottles that were once full of the sparkling vintage of the Champagne.

DEVICES FROM THE COMMANDERIE AT REIMS.

CHAPTER VI.

THE REIMS CHAMPAGNE ESTABLISHMENTS.

Messrs. Werlé and Co., successors to the Veuve Clicquot-Ponsardin—
Their Offices and Cellars on the site of a Former Commanderie
of the Templars—Origin of the Celebrity of Madame Clicquot's
Wines—M.Werlé and his Son—The Forty-five Cellars of the Clic-
quot-Werlé Establishment—Our Tour of Inspection—Ingenious
Liqueuring Machine—An Explosion and its Consequences—M.
Werlé's Gallery of Paintings—Madame Clicquot's Renaissance
House and its Picturesque Bas-reliefs—The Werlé Vineyards and
Vendangeoirs—M.Louis Roederer's Establishment—Heidsieck
and Co. and their Famous "Monopole" Brand—The Firm Found-
ed in the Last Century—Their various Establishments Inside and
Outside Reims—The Matured Wines Shipped by them.

The cellars of the great champagne manufacturers of Reims are scattered in
all directions over the historical old city. They undermine its narrowest and most
insignificant streets, its broad and handsome boulevards, and on the eastern side
extend to its more distant outskirts. Messrs. Werlé and Co., the successors of the
famous Veuve Clicquot-Ponsardin, have their offices and cellars on the site of a

former Commanderie of the Templars in an ancient quarter of the city, and strangers passing by the spot would scarcely imagine that under their feet hundreds of busy hands are incessantly at work, disgorging, dosing, shaking, corking, storing, wiring, labelling, capsuling, waxing, tinfoiling, and packing hundreds of thousands of bottles of champagne destined for all parts of the civilised world.

The house of Clicquot, established in the year 1798 by the husband of La Veuve Clicquot-Ponsardin, who died in 1866, in her 89th year, was indebted for much of the celebrity of its wine to the lucky accident of the Russians occupying Reims in 1814 and 1815, and freely requisitioning the sweet champagne stored in the widow's capacious cellars. Madame Clicquot's wines were slightly known in Russia prior to this date, but the officers of the invading army, on their return home, proclaimed their merits throughout the length and breadth of the Muscovite Empire, and the fortune of the house was made. Madame Clicquot, as every one knows, amassed enormous wealth, and succeeded in marrying both her daughter and granddaughter to counts of the *ancien régime.*

MADAME VEUVE CLICQUOT AT EIGHTY YEARS OF AGE.
(From the Painting by Léon Coignet.)

The present head of the firm is M. Werlé, who comes of an old Lorraine family although born in the ancient free imperial town of Wetzlar on the Lahn, where Goethe lays the scene of his "Sorrows of Werther," the leading incidents of which really occurred here. M.Werlé entered the establishment, which he has done so much to raise to its existing position, so far back as the year 1821. His care and skill, exercised over more than half a century, have largely contributed to obtain for the Clicquot brand that high repute which it enjoys to-day all over the world. M.Werlé, who has long been naturalised in France, was for many years Mayor of

Reims and President of its Chamber of Commerce, as well as one of the deputies of the Marne to the Corps Législatif. He enjoys the reputation of being the richest man in Reims, and, like his late partner, Madame Clicquot, he has also succeeded in securing brilliant alliances for his children, his son, M.Alfred Werlé, having married the daughter of the Duc de Montebello, while his daughter espoused the son of M.Magne, Minister of Finance under the Second Empire.

THE CLICQUOT-WERLÉ ESTABLISHMENT AT REIMS.

Half-way down the narrow tortuous Rue du Temple is an ancient gateway, on which may be traced the half-effaced sculptured heads of Phœbus and Bacchus. Immediately in front is a green *porte-cochère* forming the entrance to the Clicquot-Werlé establishment, and conducting to a spacious trim-kept courtyard, set off with a few trees, with some extensive stabling and cart-sheds on the left, and on the right hand the entrance to the cellars. Facing us is an unpretending-looking edifice, where the firm has its counting-houses, with a little corner tower surmounted by a characteristic weathercock consisting of a figure of Bacchus seated astride a cask beneath a vine-branch, and holding up a bottle in one hand and a goblet in the other. The old Remish Commanderie of the Knights Templars existed until the epoch of the Great Revolution, and to-day a few fragments of the ancient buildings remain adjacent to the "celliers" of the establishment, which are reached through a pair of folding-doors and down a flight of stone steps, and whence, after being furnished with lighted candles, we set out on our tour of inspection, entering first of all the vast cellar of St. Paul, where the thousands of bottles requiring to be daily shaken are reposing necks downwards on the large perforated tables which crowd the apartment. It is a peculiarity of the Clicquot-Werlé establishment that each of the cellars—forty-five in number, and the smallest a vast apartment—has its special name. In the adjoining cellar of St. Matthew other bottles are similarly arranged, and here wine in cask is likewise stored. We pass rows of huge tuns, each holding its twelve or thirteen hundred gallons of fine reserved wine designed for blending with more youthful growths; next are threading our way between seemingly endless piles of hogsheads filled with later vintages, and anon are passing smaller casks containing the syrup with which the *vin préparé* is dosed. At intervals we come upon some square opening in the floor through which bottles of wine are being hauled up from the cellars beneath in readiness to receive their requisite adornment before being packed in baskets or cases according to the country to which they are destined to be despatched. To Russia the Clicquot champagne is sent in cases containing sixty bottles, while the cases for China contain as many as double that number.

REMAINS OF THE COMMANDERIE AT REIMS.

The ample cellarage which the house possesses has enabled M.Werlé to make many experiments which firms with less space at their command would find it difficult to carry out on the same satisfactory scale. Such, for instance, is the system of racks in which the bottles repose while the wine undergoes its diurnal shaking. Instead of these racks being, as they commonly are, at almost upright angles, they are perfectly horizontal, which, in M.Werlé's opinion, offers a material advantage, inasmuch as the bottles are all in readiness for disgorging at the same time instead of the lower ones being ready before those above, as is the case when the ancient system is followed, owing to the uppermost bottles getting less shaken than the others.

After performing the round of the celliers we descend into the *caves*, acomplete labyrinth of gloomy underground corridors excavated in the bed of chalk which underlies the city, and roofed and walled with solid masonry, more or less blackened by age. In one of these cellars we catch sight of rows of work-people engaged in the operation of dosing, corking, securing, and shaking the bottles of wine which have just left the hands of the *dégorgeur* by the dim light of half-a-dozen tallow candles. The latest invention for liqueuring the wine is being employed. Formerly, to prevent the carbonic acid gas escaping from the bottles while the process of liqueuring was going on, it was necessary to press a gutta-percha ball connected with the machine, in order to force the escaping gas back. The new machine, however, renders this unnecessary, the gas by its own power and composition forcing itself back into the wine.

In the adjoining cellar of St. Charles are stacks of bottles awaiting the manipulation of the *dégorgeur*, while in that of St. Ferdinand men are engaged in examining other bottles before lighted candles to make certain that the sediment is thoroughly dislodged and the wine perfectly clear before the disgorgement is effected. Here, too, the corking, wiring, and stringing of the newly-disgorged wine are going on. Another flight of steps leads to the second tier of cellars, where the moisture trickles down the dank dingy walls, and save the dim light thrown out by the candles we carried, and by some other far-off flickering taper stuck in a cleft stick to direct the workmen, who with dexterous turns of their wrists give a twist to the bottles, all is darkness. On every side bottles are reposing in various attitudes, the majority in huge square piles on their sides, others in racks slightly tilted, others, again, almost standing on their heads, while some, which through over-inflation have come to grief, litter the floor and crunch beneath our feet. Tablets are hung against each stack of wine indicating its age, and from time to time a bottle is held up before the light to show us how the sediment commences to form, or explain how it eventually works its way down the neck of the bottle, and finally settles on the cork. Suddenly we are startled by a loud report resembling a pistol-shot, which reverberates through the vaulted chamber, as a bottle close at hand explodes, dashing out its heavy bottom as neatly as though it had been cut by a diamond, and dislocating the necks and pounding in the sides of its immediate neighbours. The wine trickles down, and eventually finds its way along the sloping sides of the slippery floor to the narrow gutter in the centre.

Ventilating shafts pass from one tier of cellars to the other, enabling the temperature in a certain measure to be regulated, and thereby obviate an excess of breakage. M.Werlé estimates that the loss in this respect during the first eighteen months of a *cuvée* amounts to 7per cent., but subsequently is considerably less. In 1862 one champagne manufacturer lost as much as 45 per cent. of his wine by breakages. The Clicquot *cuvée* is made in the cave of St. William, where 120 hogsheads of wine are hauled up by means of a crane and discharged into the vat daily as long as the operation lasts. The *tirage* or bottling of the wine ordinarily commences in the middle of May, and occupies fully a month.

RENAISSANCE HOUSE AT REIMS, IN WHICH MADAME CLICQUOT RESIDED.

M. Werlé's private residence is close to the establishment in the Rue du Temple, and here he has collected a small gallery of high-class modern paintings by French and other artists, including Meissonnier's "Card-players," Delaroche's "Beatrice

Cenci on her way to Execution," Fleury's "CharlesV. picking up the brush of Titian," various works by the brothers Scheffer, Knaus's highly-characteristic *genre* picture, "His Highness on a Journey," and several fine portraits, among which is one of Madame Clicquot, painted by Léon Coignet, when she was eighty years of age, and another of M.Werlé by the same artist, regarded as a *chef-d'œuvre*. Before her father's death Madame Clicquot used to reside in the Rue de Marc, some short distance from the cellars in which her whole existence centered, in a handsome Renaissance house, said to have had some connection with the row of palaces that at one time lined the neighbouring and then fashionable Rue du Tambour. This, however, is extremely doubtful. Anumber of interesting and well-preserved bas-reliefs decorate one of the façades of the house looking on to the court. The figures are of the period of François Premier and his son HenriII., who inaugurated his reign with a comforting edict for the Protestants, ordaining that blasphemers were to have their tongues pierced with red-hot irons, and heretics to be burnt alive, and who had the ill-luck to lose his eye and life through a lance-thrust of the Comte de Montgomerie, captain of his Scotch guards, whilst jousting with him at a tournament held in honour of the marriage of his daughter Isabelle with the gloomy widower of Queen Mary of England, of sanguinary fame.

The first of these bas-reliefs represents two soldiers of the Swiss guard, the next a Turk and a Slav tilting at each other, and then comes a scroll entwined round a thistle, and inscribed with this enigmatical motto: "Giane le sur ou rien." In the third bas-relief a couple of passionate Italians are winding up a gambling dispute with a hand-to-hand combat, in the course of which table, cards, and dice have got cantered over; the fourth presenting us with two French knights, armed *cap-à-pie*, engaged in a tourney; while in the fifth and last a couple of German lansquenets essay their gladiatorial skill with their long and dangerous weapons. Several years back a tablet was discovered in one of the cellars of the house, inscribed "Ci-gist vénérable religieux maître Pierre Derclé, docteur en théologie, jadis prieur de céans. Priez Dieu pour luy. 1486," which would almost indicate that the house had originally a religious character, although the warlike spirit of the bas-reliefs decorating it renders any such supposition with regard to the existing building untenable.

The Messrs. Werlé own numerous acres of vineyards, comprising the very finest situations in the well-known districts of Verzenay, Bouzy, Le Mesnil, and

Oger, at all of which places they have vendangeoirs or pressing-houses of their own. Their establishment at Verzenay contains seven presses, that at Bouzy eight, at Le Mesnil six, and at Oger two, in addition to which grapes are pressed under their own supervision at Ay, Avize, and Cramant in vendangeoirs belonging to their friends.

Since the death of Madame Clicquot the legal style of the firm has been Werlé and Co., successors to Veuve Clicquot-Ponsardin, the mark, of which M.Werlé and his son are the sole proprietors, still remaining "Veuve Clicquot-Ponsardin," while the corks of the bottles are branded with the words "V.Clicquot-P.Werlé," encircling the figure of a comet. The style of the wine—light, delicate, elegant, and fragrant—is familiar to all connoisseurs of champagne. What, however, is not equally well known is that within the last few years the firm, in obedience to the prevailing taste, have introduced a perfectly dry wine of corresponding quality to the richer wine which made the fortune of the house.

The house of M. Louis Roederer, founded by a plodding German named Schreider, pursued the sleepy tenor of its way for years, until all at once it felt prompted to lay siege to the Muscovite connection of La Veuve Clicquot-Ponsardin and secure a market for its wine at Moscow and St. Petersburg. It next opened up the United States, and finally introduced its brand into England. The house possesses cellars in various parts of Reims, and has its offices in one of the oldest quarters of the city—namely, the Rue des Élus, or ancient Rue des Juifs, records of which date as far back as 1103. These offices are at the farther end of a courtyard beyond which is a second court, where carts being laden with cases of champagne seemed to indicate that some portion of the shipping business of the house is here carried on. M.Louis Roederer refused our request for permission to visit his establishments, so that it is only of their external appearance that we are able to speak. One of them—the façade of which is rather imposing, and which has a carved head of Bacchus surmounting the *porte-cochère*—is situated in the Boulevard du Temple, while the principal establishment, apicturesque range of buildings of considerable extent, is in the neighbouring Rue de la Justice.

The old-established firm of Heidsieck and Co., which has secured a reputation in both hemispheres for its famous Monopole and Dry Monopole brands, has its cellars scattered about Reims, the central ones, where the wine is prepared and packed, being situated in the narrow winding Rue Sedan, at no great distance from the Clicquot-Werlé establishment. The original firm dates back to 1785, when France was struggling with those financial difficulties that a few years later culminated in that great social upheaving which kept Europe in a state of turmoil for more than a quarter of a century. Among the archives of the firm is a patent, bearing the signature of the Minister of the Prussian Royal Household, appointing Heidsieck and Co. purveyors of champagne to Friedrich William III. The champagne-drinking Hohenzollern *par excellence*, however, was the son and successor of the preceding, who, from habitual over-indulgence in the exhilarating sparkling beverage during the last few years of his reign, acquired the *sobriquet* of King Clicquot.

On passing through the large *porte-cochère* giving entrance to Messrs.

Heidsieck's principal establishment, one finds oneself in a small courtyard with the surrounding buildings overgrown with ivy and venerable vines. On the left is a dwelling-house enriched with elaborate mouldings and cornices, and at the farther end of the court is the entrance to the cellars, surmounted by a sun-dial bearing the date 1829. The latter, however, is no criterion of the age of the buildings themselves, as these were occupied by the firm at its foundation, towards the close of the last century. We are first conducted into an antiquated-looking low cellier, the roof of which is sustained with rude timber supports, and here bottles of wine are being labelled and packed, although this is but a mere adjunct to the adjacent spacious packing-room provided with its loading platform and communicating directly with the public road. At the time of our visit this hall was gaily decorated with flags and inscriptions, the day before having been the fête of St. Jean, when the firm entertain the people in their employ with a banquet and a ball, at which the choicest wine of the house liberally flows. From the packing-room we descend into the cellars, which, like all the more ancient vaults in Reims, have been constructed on no regular plan. Here we thread our way between piles after piles of bottles, many of which having passed through the hands of the disgorger are awaiting their customary adornment. The lower tier of cellars is mostly stored with *vin sur pointe*, and bottles with their necks downwards are encountered in endless monotony along a score or more of long galleries. The only variation in our lengthened promenade is when we come upon some solitary workman engaged in his monotonous task of shaking his 30,000 or 40,000 bottles per diem.

The disgorging at Messrs. Heidsieck's takes place, in accordance with the good old rule, in the cellars underground, where we noticed large stocks of wine three and five years old, the former in the first stage of *sur-pointe*, and the latter awaiting shipment. It is a speciality of the house to ship only matured wine, which is necessarily of a higher character than the ordinary youthful growths, for a few years have a wonderful influence in developing the finer qualities of champagne. At the time of our visit, in the spring of 1877, when the English market was being glutted with the crude, full-bodied wine of 1874, Messrs. Heidsieck were continuing to ship wines of 1870 and 1872, beautifully rounded by keeping and of fine flavour and great delicacy of perfume, and of which the firm estimated they had fully a year's consumption still on hand.

Messrs. Heidsieck and Co. have a handsome modern establishment in the Rue Coquebert—acomparatively new quarter of the city where champagne establishments are the rule—the courtyard of which, alive with workmen at the time of our visit, is broad and spacious, while the surrounding buildings are light and airy, and the cellars lofty, regular, and well ventilated. In a large cellier here, where the tuns are ranged side by side between the rows of iron columns supporting the roof, the firm make their *cuvée*; here too the bottling of their wine takes place, and considerable stocks of high-class reserve wines and more youthful growths are stored ready for removal when required by the central establishment. The bulk of Messrs. Heidsieck's reserve wines, however, repose in the outskirts of Reims, near the Porte Dieu-Lumière, in one of the numerous abandoned chalk quarries, which of late years the champagne manufacturers have discovered are capable of being transformed into admirable cellars.

In addition to shipping a rich and a dry variety of the Monopole brand, of which they are sole proprietors, Messrs. Heidsieck export to this country a rich and a dry Grand Vin Royal. It is, however, to their famous Monopole wine, and especially to the dry variety, which must necessarily comprise the finest growths, that the firm owe their principal celebrity.

STATUE OF LOUIS XIII. ON THE REIMS HÔTEL DE VILLE

CHAPTER VII.

THE REIMS ESTABLISHMENTS (CONTINUED).

The Firm of G. H. Mumm and Co.—Their Large Shipments to the United States—Their Establishments in the Rue Andrieux and the Rue Coquebert—Bottle-Washing with Glass Beads—The Cuvée and the Tirage—G.H. Mumm and Co.'s Vendangeoirs at Verzenay—Their Various Wines—The Gate of Mars—The Establishment of M.Gustave Gibert on the Site of the Château des Archevêques—His Cellars in the Vaults of St. Peter's Abbey and beneath the old Hôtel des Fermes in the Place Royale—Louis XV. and Jean Baptiste Colbert—M.Gibert's Wines—Jules Mumm and Co., and Ruinart père et fils—House of the Musicians—The Counts de la Marck—The Brotherhood of Minstrels of Reims—Establishment of Périnet et fils—Their Cellars of Three Stories in Solid Masonry—Their Soft, Light, and Delicate Wines—ARare Still Verzenay—M.Duchâtel-Ohaus's Establishment and Renaissance House—His Cellars in the Cour St. Jacques and Outside the Porte Dieu-Lumière.

Messrs. G. H. Mumm and Co. have their chief establishment in the Rue Andrieux, in an open quarter of the city, facing the garden attached to the premises of M.Werlé, and only a short distance from the grand triumphal arch known as the Gate of Mars, by far the most important Roman remain of which the Champagne can boast. The head of the firm, Mr. G.H. Mumm, is the grandson of the well-known P.A. Mumm, the large shipper of hocks and moselles, and is the only surviving partner in the champagne house of Mumm and Co., established at Reims in 1825, and joined by Mr. G.H. Mumm so far back as the year 1838. The firm not only ship their wine largely to England, but head the list of shipments to the United States, where their brand is held in high repute, with nearly half a million bottles, being more than twice the quantity shipped by M.Louis Roederer—who comes third on the list in question—and a fourth of the entire shipments of champagne to the United States.

The establishment of Messrs. G. H. Mumm and Co., in the Rue Andrieux, is of comparatively modern construction. Alarge *porte-cochère* conducts to a spacious courtyard, bordered with sheds, beneath which huge stacks of new bottles are piled and having a pleasant garden lying beyond. On the left is a large vaulted cellier, where the operations of disgorging, liqueuring, and corking the wine are performed, and which communicates with the vast adjoining packing department. From this cellier entrance is gained to the cellars beneath, containing a million bottles of *vin brut* in various stages of development. This forms, however, merely a portion of the firm's stock, they having another three millions of bottles stored in the cellars of their establishment in the Rue Coquebert, where a scene of great animation presented itself at the time of our visit, several scores of women being engaged in washing bottles for the *tirage*, which, although it was early in May, had already commenced. The bottles, filled with water, and containing a certain quantity of glass beads in lieu of the customary shot, which frequently leave minute particles of lead—deleterious alike to health and the flavour of the wine—adhering to the inside surface of the glass, are placed horizontally in a frame, and by means of four turns of a handle are made to perform sixty-four rapid revolutions. The beads are then transferred to other bottles, which are subjected in their turn to the same revolving process.

The *cuvée*, commonly composed of from two to three thousand casks of wine from various vineyards, with a due proportion of high-class vintages, is made in a vat holding 4,400 gallons. The *tirage* or bottling is effected by means of two large tuns placed side by side, and holding twelve hogsheads of wine each. Pipes from these tuns communicate with a couple of small reservoirs, each of them provided with half-a-dozen self-acting syphon taps, by means of which a like number of bottles are simultaneously filled. Only one set of these taps are set running at a time, as while the wine is being drawn off from one tun the other is being refilled from the casks containing the *cuvée* by means of a pump and leathern hose, which empties a cask in little more than a couple of minutes. Three gangs of eight men each can fill, cork, and secure with *agrafes* from 35,000 to 40,000 bottles during the day. The labour is performed partly by men regularly employed by the house and partly by hands engaged for the purpose, who work, however, under the constant inspection of overseers appointed by the firm.

**THE TIRAGE OR BOTTLING OF CHAMPAGNE
AT THE ESTABLISHMENT OF MESSRS. G.H. MUMM & CO.**

At Messrs. G. H. Mumm's the champagne destined for shipment has the heads of the corks submerged in a kind of varnish, with the object of protecting them from the ravages of insects, and preventing the string and wire from becoming mouldy for several years. In damp weather, when this varnish takes a long time to dry, after the bottles have been placed in a rack with their heads downwards to allow of any superfluous varnish draining from the corks, the latter are subjected to a moderate heat in a machine pierced with sufficient holes to contain 500 bottles, and provided with a warming apparatus in the centre. Here the bottles remain for about twenty minutes.

Messrs. G. H. Mumm and Co. have a capacious vendangeoir at Verzenay, near the entrance to the village when approaching it from Reims. The building contains four presses, three of which are worked with large fly-wheels requiring several men to turn them, while the fourth acts with a screw applied by means of a long pole. At the vintage 3,600 kilogrammes, or nearly 8,000lbs., of grapes are put under each press, aquantity sufficient to yield eight to ten hogsheads of wine of forty-four gallons each, suitable for sparkling wine, besides three or four hogsheads of inferior wine given to the workmen to drink. The pressing commences daily at six in the morning, and lasts until midnight; yet the firm are often constrained to keep their grapes in the baskets under a cool shed for a period of two days. This cannot, however, be done when they are very ripe, as the colouring matter from the skins would become extracted and give a dark and objectionable tint to the wine.

MESSRS. G. H. MUMM & CO.'S VENDANGEOIR AT VERZENAY.

Messrs. G. H. Mumm and Co. ship four descriptions of champagne—Carte Blanche, apale, delicate, fragrant wine of great softness and refined flavour; aperfectly dry variety of the foregoing, known as their Extra Dry; also an Extra Quality and a First Quality—both high-class wines, though somewhat lower in price than the two preceding.

Within a few minutes' walk of Messrs. G. H. Mumm's—past the imposing

Gate of Mars, in the midst of lawns, parterres, and gravel-walks, where coquettish nursemaids and their charges stroll, accompanied by the proverbial *piou-piou*—is the principal establishment of M.Gustave Gibert, whose house claims to-day half a century of existence. On this spot formerly stood the feudal castle of the Archbishops of Reims, demolished nearly three centuries ago. By whom this stronghold was erected is somewhat uncertain. The local chronicles state that a château was built at Reims by Suelf, son of Hincmar, in 922, and restored by Archbishop Henri de France two and a half centuries later. War or other causes, however, seems to have rendered the speedy rebuilding of this castle necessary, as a new Château des Archevêques appears to have been erected at Reims by Henri de Braine between 1228 and 1230. The circumstance of the Archbishops of Reims being dukes and peers as well as primates of the capital of the Champagne accounts for their preference for a fortified place of residence at this turbulent epoch.

On the investiture of a new archbishop it was the custom for him to proceed in great pomp from the château to the church of Saint Remi, with a large armed guard and a splendid retinue of ecclesiastical, civil, and military dignitaries escorting him. The pride of the newly-created "duke and peer" having been thus gratified, the "prelate" had to humble himself, and on the morrow walked barefooted from the church of St. Remi to the cathedral. After the religious wars the château was surrendered to Henri IV., and in 1595 the Remois, anxious to be rid of so formidable a fortress, which, whether held by king or archbishop, was calculated to enforce a state of passive obedience galling to their pride, purchased from the king the privilege to demolish it for the sum of 8,000 crowns. Tradition asserts that the Remish Bastille was destroyed in a single day, but this is exceedingly improbable. Its ruins certainly were not cleared away until the close of the century.

THE CELLIERS AND CELLARS OF M. GUSTAVE GIBERT.
(Near the Porte de Mars, Reims.)

When the old fortress was razed to the ground its extensive vaults were not interfered with, but many long years afterwards were transformed into admirable cellars for the storage of champagne. Above them are two stories of capacious celliers where the wine is blended, bottled, and packed, the vaults themselves comprising two tiers of cellars which contain wine both in cask and bottle. M.Gibert's remaining stocks are stored in the ancient vaults of the abbey of St. Peter, in the heart of the city, and in the roomy cellars which underlie the old Hôtel des Fermes in the Place Royale, where in the days of the *ancien régime* the farmers-general of the province used to receive its revenues. On the pediment of this edifice is a bas-relief with Mercury, the god of commerce, seated beside a nymph and surrounded by children engaged with the vintage and with bales of wool, and evidently intended to symbolise the staple trades of the capital of the Champagne. Abronze statue rises in the centre of the Place which from its Roman costume and martial bearing might be taken for some hero of antiquity did not the inscription on the pedestal apprise us that it is intended for the "wise, virtuous, and magnanimous Louis XV.," amisuse of terms which has caused a transatlantic Republican to characterise the monument as a brazen lie. Leading out of the Place Royale is the Rue de Cérès, in which there is a modernised 16th-century house claiming to be the birthplace of Jean Baptiste Colbert, son of a Reims wool-merchant, and the famous minister who did so much to consolidate the finances which the royal voluptuary, masquerading at Reims in Roman garb, afterwards made such dreadful havocof.

**THE PLACE ROYALE AT REIMS,
SHOWING THE ENTRANCE TO THE CELLARS OF M.GUSTAVE GIBERT.**

M. Gustave Gibert possesses pressing-houses at Ay and Bouzy, and has moreover at both these places accommodation for large reserve stocks of wine in wood. As all the wines which he sends into the market are vintaged by himself, he can ensure their being of uniform high quality. His *Vin du Roi* is notable for perfume, delicacy, perfect effervescence, and that fine flavour of the grape which characterises the grand wines of the Champagne. It is a great favourite with the King of Sweden and Norway, and the labels on the bottles bear his name and arms. M.Gibert's brand has acquired a high reputation in the North of Europe, and having of late years been introduced into England, is rapidly making its way there. The merits of the wines have been again and again publicly recognised, no less than ten medals having been successively awarded M.Gibert at the Exhibitions of Toulouse in 1858, Bordeaux in 1859, Besançon in 1860, Metz and Nantes in 1861, London in 1862, Bayonne and Linz in 1864, and Oporto and Dublin in 1865. This long list of awards has led to the wines being placed *"hors concours,"* nevertheless M.Gibert continues to submit them to competition whenever any Exhibition of importance takes place. The wines are shipped to England, Germany, Russia, and Northern Europe, Spain and Portugal, Calcutta, Java, Melbourne, and Hong-Kong, besides being largely in request for the Paris market.

On quitting M. Gibert's central establishment we proceed along the winding, ill-paved Rue de Mars, past the premises of Messrs. Jules Mumm and Co., an offshoot from the once famous firm of P.A. Mumm and Co., to the Place de l'Hôtel de Ville, in one corner of which stands a massive and somewhat pretentious-looking house, dating back to the time of Louis Quatorze. Here are the offices of Ruinart père et fils, who claim to rank as the oldest existing house in the Champagne. The head of the firm, the Vicomte de Brimont, is a collateral descendant of the Dom Ruinart, whose remains repose nigh to those of the illustrious Dom Perignon in the abbey church of Hautvillers. From the Place de l'Hôtel de Ville we proceed through the narrow Rue du Tambour, originally a Roman thoroughfare, and during the Middle Ages the locality where the nobility of Reims principally had their abodes. Half-way up this street, in the direction of the Place des Marchés, stands the famous House of the Musicians, one of the most interesting architectural relics of which the capital of the Champagne can boast. It evidently dates from the early part of the fourteenth century, but by whom it was erected is unknown. Some ascribe it to the Knights Templars, others to the Counts of Champagne, while others suppose it to have been the residence of the famous Counts de la Marck, who in later times diverged into three separate branches, the first furnishing Dukes of Cleves and Julich to Germany and Dukes of Nevers and Counts of Eu to France, while the second became Dukes of Bouillon and Princes of Sedan, titles which passed to the Turennes when Henri de la Tour d'Auvergne, Vicomte de Turenne, married the surviving heiress of the house. The third branch comprised the Barons of Lumain, allied to the Hohenzollerns. Their most famous member slew Louis de Bourbon, Archbishop of Liège, and flung his body into the Meuse, and subsequently became celebrated as the Wild Boar of the Ardennes, of whom all readers of *Quentin Durward* will retain a lively recollection.

To return, however, to the House of the Musicians. A probable conjecture ascribes the origin of the quaint mediæval structure to the Brotherhood of Minstrels of Reims, who in the thirteenth century enjoyed a considerable reputation, not merely in the Champagne, but throughout the North of France. The house takes its present name from five seated statues of musicians, larger than life-size, occupying the Gothic niches between the first-floor windows, and resting upon brackets ornamented with grotesque heads. It is thought that the partially-damaged figure on the left-hand side was originally playing a drum and a species of clarionet. The next one evidently has the remnants of a harp in his raised hands. The third or central figure is supposed merely to have held a hawk upon his wrist; whilst the fourth seeks to extract harmony from a dilapidated bagpipe; and the fifth, with crossed legs, strums complacently away upon the fiddle. The ground floor of the quaint old tenement is to-day an oil and colour shop, the front of which is covered with chequers in all the tints of the rainbow.

Leading from the Rue du Tambour is the Rue de la Belle Image, thus named from a handsome statuette of the Virgin which formerly decorated a corner niche; and beyond is the Rue St. Hilaire, where Messrs. Barnett et fils, trading under the designation of Périnet et fils, and the only English house engaged in the manufacture of champagne, have an establishment which is certainly as perfect as any to be found in Reims. Aboveground are several large store-rooms, where vintage casks and the various utensils common to a champagne establishment are kept, and a capacious cellier, upwards of 150 feet in length, with its roof resting on huge timber supports. Here new wine is stored preparatory to being blended and bottled, and in the huge tun, holding nearly 3,000 gallons, standing at the further end, the firm make their *cuvée*, while adjacent is a room where stocks of corks and labels, metal foil, and the like are kept.

There are three stories of cellars—an exceedingly rare thing anywhere in the Champagne—all constructed in solid masonry on a uniform plan—namely, two wide galleries running parallel with each other and connected by means of transverse passages. Spite of the great depth to which these cellars descend they are perfectly dry; the ventilation, too, is excellent, and their different temperatures render them especially suitable for the storage of champagne, the temperature of the lowest cellar being 6° Centigrade (43° Fahrenheit), or one degree Centigrade below the cellar immediately above, which, in its turn is two degrees below the uppermost one of all. The advantage of this is that when the wine develops an excess of effervescence any undue proportion of breakages can be checked by removing the bottles to a lower cellar and consequently into a lower temperature.

THE CELLIER AND CELLARS OF PÉRINET ET FILS AT REIMS.

The first cellars we enter are closely stacked with wine in bottle, which is gradually clearing itself by the formation of a deposit, while in an adjoining cellar on the same level the operations of disgorging, liqueuring, and corking are going on.

In the cellars immediately beneath bottles of wine repose in solid stacks ready for the *dégorgeur*, while others rest in racks in order that they may undergo their daily shaking. In the lowest cellars reserved wine in cask is stored, as it best retains its natural freshness and purity in a very cool place. All air is carefully excluded from the casks, any ullage is immediately checked, and as evaporation is continually going on the casks are examined every fortnight, when any deficiency is at once replenished. At Messrs. Périnet et fils', as at all the first-class establishments, the *vin brut* is a *mélange* comprising the produce of some of the best vineyards, and has every possible attention paid to it during its progressive stages of development.

Champagnes of different years were here shown to us, all of them soft, light, and delicate, and with that fine flavour and full perfume which the best growths of the Marne alone exhibit. Among several curiosities submitted to us was a still Verzenay of the year 1857, one of the most delicate red wines it was ever our fortune to taste. Light in body, rich in colour, of a singularly novel and refined flavour, and with a magnificent yet indefinable bouquet, the wine was in every respect perfect. Not only was the year of the vintage a grand one, but the wine must have been made with the greatest possible care and from the most perfect grapes for so delicate a growth to have retained its flavour in such perfection, and preserved its brilliant ruby colour for such a length of time.

From the samples shown to us of Périnet et fils' champagne, we were prepared to find that at some recent tastings in London, the particulars of which have been made public, their Extra Sec took the first place at each of the three severe competitions to which it was subjected.

M. Duchâtel-Ohaus's central establishment is in the Rue des Deux Anges, one of the most ancient streets of Reims, running from the Rue des Élus to the Rue de Vesle, and having every window secured by iron gratings, and every door thickly studded with huge nails. These prison-like façades succeed each other in gloomy monotony along either side of the way, the portion of M.Duchâtel-Ohaus's residence which faces the street being no exception to the general rule. Once within its court, however, and quite a different scene presents itself. Before us is a pleasant little flower-garden with a small but charming Renaissance house looking on to it, the windows ornamented with elaborate mouldings, and surmounted by graceful sculptured heads, while at one corner rises a tower with a sun-dial displayed on its front. Here and in an adjoining house the canons of the Cathedral were accustomed to reside in the days when four-fifths of Reims belonged to the Church.

From the garden we enter a capacious cellier where the blending and bottling of the wine takes place, and in the neighbouring packing-room encounter a score of workpeople filling, securing, and branding a number of cases about to be despatched by rail. From the cellier we pass to the cellars situated immediately underneath, and which, capacious though they are, do not suffice for M.Duchâtel's stock, portions of which are stored in some ancient vaults near the market-place, and in the Rue de Vesle behind the church of St. Jacques. This church, originally built at the close of the twelfth century, is hemmed in on all sides by old houses, above which rises its tapering steeple surmounted by a medieval weathercock in the form of an angel. Alife-size statue of the patron saint decorates the Gothic gateway leading to the church, from which a troop of Remish urchins in the charge of some Frères de la Doctrine Chrétienne emerge as we passby.

The Cour St. Jacques, where M. Duchâtel's cellars are situated, may be reached by passing through the church, the interior of which presents a curious jumble of architectural styles from early Gothic to late Renaissance. One noteworthy object of art which it contains is a life-size crucifix carved by Pierre Jacques, aRemish sculptor of the days of the Good King Henri, and from an anatomical point of view a perfect *chef-d'œuvre*. The cellars we have come to inspect are two stories deep, and comprise numerous ancient cavernous compartments, such as are found in all the older quarters of Reims, and usually in the vicinity of some church, convent, or clerical abode. It has been suggested that they were either crypts for sacred retire-ment and prayer, dungeons for the punishment of recreant brethren, or tombs for the dead; but it is far more probable that in the majority of instances they served then as now simply for the storage of the choice vintages of the Marne, for we all know the monks of old were tipplers of no ordinary capacity, who usually con-trived to secure the best that the district provided. These vaults of M.Duchâtel's, in which a considerable stock of the fine wine of 1874 is stored, are from two to three centuries old, and probably belonged to the curés of St. Jacques. They are of considerable extent, are well ventilated, and are walled and roofed with stone. M.Duchâtel's remaining stock reposes in some new cellars—certain transformed chalk quarries outside the Porte Dieu-Lumière, comprising broad lofty galleries and vast circular chambers—fifty feet or so in height and well lighted from above.

At M. Duchâtel-Ohaus's we tasted a variety of fine samples of his brand, in-cluding a beautiful wine of 1868 and an almost equally good one of 1870, with some of the excellent vintage of 1874, which was then being prepared for ship-ment.

CHAPTER VIII.

THE REIMS ESTABLISHMENTS (CONTINUED).

M. Ernest Irroy's Cellars, Vineyards, and Vendangeoirs—Recognition by the Reims Agricultural Association of his Plantations of Vines—His Wines and their Popularity at the best London Clubs—Messrs. Binet fils and Co.'s Establishment—Wines Sold by the Firm to Shippers—Their Cellars—Samples of Fine Still Ay and Bouzy—Their Still Sillery, Vintage 1857, and their Creaming Vin Brut, Vintage 1865—The Offices and Cellars of Messrs. Charles Farre and Co.—Testing the Wine before Bottling—A Promenade between Bottles in Piles and Racks—Repute in which these Wines are held in England and on the Continent—The New Establishment of Fisse, Thirion, and Co. in the Place de Betheny—Its Construction exclusively in Stone, Brick, and Iron—The Vast Celliers of Two Stories—Bottling the Wine by the Aid of Machinery—The Cool and Lofty Cellars—Ingenious Method of Securing the Corks, rendering the Uncorking exceedingly simple—The Wines Shipped by the Firm.

Few large manufacturing towns like Reims—one of the most important of those engaged in the woollen manufacture in France—can boast of such fine promenades and such handsome boulevards as the capital of the Champagne. As the ancient fortifications of the city were from time to time razed, their site was levelled and generally planted with trees, so that the older quarters of Reims are almost encircled by broad and handsome thoroughfares, separating the city, as it were, from its outlying suburbs. In or close to the broad Boulevard du Temple, which takes its name from its proximity to the site of the ancient Commanderie of the Templars, various champagne manufacturers, including M.Louis Roederer, M.Ernest Irroy, and M.Charles Heidsieck, have their establishments, while but a few paces off, in the neighbouring Rue Coquebert, are the large and handsome premises of Messrs. Krug andCo.

M. ERNEST IRROY'S ESTABLISHMENT AT REIMS.

The offices of M. Ernest Irroy, who is known in Reims not merely as a large champagne grower and shipper, but also as a distinguished amateur of the fine arts, taking a leading part in originating local exhibitions and the like, are attached to his private residence, ahandsome mansion flanked by a large and charming garden in the Boulevard du Temple. The laying out of this sylvan oasis is due to M.Vadré, the head gardener of the city of Paris, who contributed so largely to the picturesque embellishment of the Bois de Boulogne. M.Irroy's establishment, which comprises a considerable range of buildings grouped around two court-yards, is immediately adjacent, although its principal entrance is in the Rue de la Justice. The vast celliers, covering an area of upwards of 3,000 square yards, and either stocked with wine in cask or used for packing and similar purposes, afford the requisite space for carrying on a most extensive business. The cellars beneath comprise three stories, two of which are solidly roofed and lined with masonry, while the lowermost one is excavated in the chalk. They are admirably constructed on a symmetrical plan, and their total surface is very little short of 7,000 square yards. Spite of the great depth to which these cellars descend they are perfectly dry, the ventilation is good, and their temperature moreover is remarkably cool, one result of which is that M.Irroy's loss from breakage never exceeds four per cent. per annum. M.Irroy holds a high position as a vineyard-proprietor in the Champagne, his vines covering an area of nearly 86 acres. At Mareuil and Av-enay he owns some twenty-five acres, at Verzenay and Verzy about fifteen, and at Ambonnay and Bouzy forty-six acres. His father and his uncle, whose properties he inherited or purchased, commenced some thirty years ago to plant vines on certain slopes of Bouzy possessing a southern aspect, and he has followed their example with such success both at Bouzy and Ambonnay that in 1873 the Reims Agricultural Association conferred upon him a silver-gilt medal for his plantations of vines. M.Irroy owns *vendangeoirs* at Verzenay, Avenay, and Ambonnay; and at Bouzy, where his largest vineyards are, he has built some excellent cottages for his labourers. He has also constructed a substantial bridge over the ravine which, formed by winter torrents from the hills, intersects the principal vineyard slopes of Bouzy.

M. Ernest Irroy's wines, prepared with scrupulous care and rare intelligence, have been known in England for some years past, and are steadily increasing in popularity. They are emphatically connoisseurs' wines. The best West-end clubs, such as White's, Arthur's, the old Carlton, and the like, lay down the *cuvées* of this house in good years as they lay down their vintage ports and finer clarets, and drink them, not in a crude state, but when they are in perfection—that is, in five to ten years' time. M.Irroy exports to the British colonies and to the United States the same fine wines which he ships to England.

LABOURERS AT WORK IN M. ERNEST IRROY'S BOUZY VINEYARDS.

From M. Irroy's we proceeded to Messrs. Binet fils and Co., whose establishment in the Rue de la Justice is separated from that of M.Irroy merely by a narrow path, and occupies the opposite side of the way to the principal establishment of M.Louis Roederer. The firm of Binet fils and Co. was founded many years ago, but for a long time they sold their wines principally to other shippers on the Reims and Epernay markets, where their cuvées were held in high repute, and only of recent years have they applied themselves to the shipping trade. Their establishment has two entrances, one in the Rue de la Justice, and the other in the Boulevard du Champ de Mars. On passing through the former we find ourselves in a courtyard of considerable area, with a range of celliers in the rear and a low building on the left, in which the offices are installed. In the first cellier we encounter cases and baskets of champagne all ready to be despatched by rail, with women and men busily engaged in labelling and packing other bottles which continue to arrive from the cellars below in baskets secured to an endless chain. Beyond this range of celliers is another courtyard of smaller dimensions where there are additional celliers in which wines of recent vintages in casks are stored.

The vaults, which are reached by a winding stone staircase, are spacious, and consist of a series of parallel and uniform galleries hewn in the chalk without either masonry supports or facings. Among the solid piles of bottles which here hem us in on all sides are a considerable number of magnums and imperial pints reserved for particular customers—the former more especially for certain military messes, at which the brand of Binet fils and Co. is held in deserved esteem. We tasted here—in addition to several choice sparkling wines, including a grand *vin brut*, vintage 1865—astill Ay of the year 1870, and some still Bouzy of 1874. The former, aremarkably light and elegant wine, was already in fine condition for drinking, while the latter, which was altogether more vinous, deeper in colour, and fuller in body needed the ripening influence of time to bring it to perfection. Through their agents, Rutherford, Drury, and Co., Messrs. Binet fils and Co. achieved a great success in England with their still Sillery, vintage 1857, and subsequently with their superb creaming *vin brut*, vintage 1865, of which we have just spoken, and which is still to be met with at London clubs of repute.

Some short distance from and parallel with the Rue de la Justice is the Rue Jacquart, where Messrs. Charles Farre and Co., of whose establishment at Hautvillers we have already spoken, have their offices and cellars. We enter a large courtyard, where several railway vans are being laden with cases of wine from the packing-hall beyond, and in the tasting-room adjoining find wine being tested prior to bottling, to ascertain the amount of saccharine it contains. This was accomplished by reducing a certain quantity of wine by boiling down to one-sixth, when the saccharometer should indicate 13° of sugar to ensure each bottle containing the requisite quantity of compressed carbonic acid gas.

Messrs. Farre's cellars, comprising eighteen parallel galleries disposed in two stories, are both lofty and commodious, and are mainly of recent construction, the upper ones being solidly walled with masonry, while those below are simply excavated in the chalk. Here, as elsewhere, one performed a lengthened promenade between piles after piles of bottles of the finer vintages and a seemingly endless succession of racks, at which workmen were engaged in dislodging the sediment in the wine by the dim light of a tallow candle. It was here that we were assured the more experienced of these men were capable, when working with both hands, of shaking the enormous number of 50,000 bottles a day, or at the rate of seventy to the minute.

The fine wines of Messrs. Charles Farre and Co. have long enjoyed a well-deserved celebrity, and at the Paris Exhibition of 1855 the firm secured the highest medal awarded to champagnes. The high repute in which the brand is held on the Continent is evidenced by the fact that the Prussian and other courts are consumers of Messrs. Farre's wines. The firm not only number England, Germany, Austria, Russia, and Northern Europe, and, as a matter of course, France, among their customers, but also several of the British colonies and North and South America as well.

The new establishment of Messrs. Fisse, Thirion, and Co., in the erection of which they have largely profited by their experience and the various resources of modern science, is situated in the Place de Betheny, in the vicinity of the railway goods station and the local shooting range, largely resorted to at certain seasons of the year, when the crack shots of the Champagne capital compete with distinguished amateurs from different parts of France and the other side of the Channel.

MESSRS. FISSE, THIRION & CO.'S ESTABLISHMENT AT REIMS.

On entering the courtyard through the iron gate to the right of the dwelling-houses of the resident partners—flanked by gardens brilliant with flowers and foliage—we first reach the offices and tasting-rooms, and then the entrance to the cellars. Aspeciality of this important pile of building is that everything employed in its construction is of stone, brick, or iron, wood having been rigorously excluded from it. In the rear of the courtyard, which presents that aspect of animation common to flourishing establishments in the Champagne, is the principal cellier, with a small building in front, where a steam-pump for pumping up water from the chalk is installed, while at right angles with the cellier are the stables and bottle-sheds. The large cellier, which is 20 feet high and 80 feet broad, will be no less than 260 feet in length when completed. It contains two stories, the floors of both of which are cemented, the lower story being roofed with small brick arches connected by iron girders, and the upper one with tiles resting on iron supports. The cement keeps the temperature remarkably cool in the lower cellier where wine in cask is stored, the upper cellier being appropriated to wine in racks *sur pointe*, bales of corks, and the wicker-baskets and cases in which the wine is packed.

The preparation of the wines in cask and the bottling take place in the lower of the two celliers, amere lad being enabled, by the aid of the mechanism provided, to bottle from six to eight thousand bottles a day. Asingle workman can cork about 4,500 bottles, which a second workman secures with metal agrafes before they are lowered into the cellars. The latter are of two stories, each being divided into three long parallel galleries 20 feet high and 23 feet wide, vaulted with stone and floored with cement. Bordering the endless stacks of bottles are small gutters, into which the wine flows from the exploded bottles. Lofty, well ventilated, and beautifully cool, the temperature invariably ranging from 45° to 47° Fahrenheit, these capitally-constructed cellars combine all that is required for a champagne establishment of the first class. The breakage has never exceeded 3per cent., whereas in some old cellars which the firm formerly occupied in the centre of the city, their breakage on one occasion amounted to ten times this quantity.

At Fisse, Thirion, and Co.'s, after the wine has been disgorged and liqueured, the corks are secured neither with string nor wire, but a special metal fastener is employed for the purpose. This consists of a triple-branched agrafe, provided with a kind of hinge. Atiny toy needle-gun suspended to the agrafe is pulled outwards and turned over the top of the bottle, whereupon the fastening becomes instantly disengaged, and anything like trouble, uncleanliness, or annoyance is entirely avoided. The operation is so easy that a mere child can open a bottle of champagne, secured by this patent fastener, as easily and rapidly as a grown-up man.

The firm of Fisse, Thirion, and Co. succeeded that of Fisse, Fraiquin, and Co.—established originally at Reims in 1821—in 1864, when the brand of the house was already well known on the Continent, more especially in Belgium and Holland. Since that time the wines have been largely introduced into England and the United States, and the firm, who have secured medals at many of the recent exhibitions, to-day have agents in the English and Dutch Indies and the various European settlements in China. Several descriptions of wine are shipped by the house, the finest being their dry Cuvée Reservèe and their fragrant soft-tasting Cachet d'Or.

OLD HOUSE IN THE RUE DES ANGLAIS, REIMS.

CHAPTER IX.

THE REIMS ESTABLISHMENTS (CONCLUDED).

La Prison de Bonne Semaine — Mary Queen of Scots at Reims — Messrs.
Pommery and Greno's Offices — A Fine Collection of Faïence — The
Rue des Anglais a former Refuge of English Catholics — Remains
of the Old University of Reims — Ancient Roman Tower and Cu-
rious Grotto — The handsome Castellated Pommery Establish-
ment — The Spacious Cellier and Huge Carved Cuvée Tun — The
Descent to the Cellars — Their Great Extent — These Lofty Subter-
ranean Chambers Originally Quarries — Ancient Places of Refuge
of the Early Christians and the Protestants — Madame Pommery's
Splendid Cuvée of 1868 — Messrs. de St. Marceaux and Co.'s New
Establishment in the Avenue de Sillery — Its Garden-Court and
Circular Shaft — Animated Scene in the Large Packing Hall —
Lowering Bottled Wine to the Cellars — Great Depth and Extent of
these Cellars — Messrs. de St. Marceaux and Co.'s Various Wines.

Nigh the cathedral of Reims and in the rear of the archiepiscopal palace there
runs a short narrow street known as the Rue Vauthier le Noir, and frequently

mentioned in old works relating to the capital of the Champagne. The discovery of various pillars and statues, together with a handsome Gallo-Roman altar, whilst digging some foundations in 1837, points to the fact that a Pagan temple formerly occupied the site. The street is supposed to have taken its name, however, from some celebrated gaoler, for in mediæval times here stood "la prison de bonne semaine." On the site of this prison a château was subsequently built where Mary Queen of Scots is said to have resided in the days when her uncle, Cardinal Charles de Lorraine, was Lord Archbishop of Reims. Temple, prison, and palace have alike disappeared, and where they stood there now rises midway between court and garden a handsome mansion, the residence of Madame Pommery, head of the well-known firm of Pommery and Greno. To the left of the courtyard, which is entered through a monumental gateway, are some old buildings bearing the sculptured escutcheon of the beautiful and luckless Stuart Queen, while to the right are the offices, with the manager's sanctum, replete with artistic curiosities, the walls being completely covered with remarkable specimens of faïence, including Rouen, Gien, Palissy, Delft, and majolica, collected in the majority of instances by Madame Pommery in the villages around Reims. Here we were received by M.Vasnier, who at once volunteered to accompany us to the cellars of the firm outside the city. Messrs. Pommery and Greno originally carried on business in the Rue Vauthier le Noir, where there are extensive cellars, but their rapidly-increasing connection long since compelled them to emigrate beyond the walls of Reims.

In close proximity to the Rue Vauthier le Noir is the Rue des Anglais, so named from the English Catholic refugees who, flying from the persecutions of our so-called Good Queen Bess, here took up their abode and established a college and a seminary. They rapidly acquired great influence in Reims, and one of their number, William Gifford, was even elected archbishop. At the end of this street, nigh to Madame Pommery's, there stands an old house with a corner tower and rather handsome Renaissance window, which formerly belonged to some of the clergy of the cathedral, and subsequently became the "Bureau Général de la Loterie de France," abolished by the National Convention in 1793.

The Rue des Anglais conducts into the Rue de l'Université, where a few remnants of the old University, founded by Cardinal Charles de Lorraine (1538-74), attract attention, notably a conical-capped corner tower, the sculptured ornaments at the base of which have crumbled into dust beneath the corroding tooth of Time. From the Rue de l'Université our way lies along the Boulevard du Temple to the Porte Gerbert, about a mile beyond which there rises up the curious castellated structure in which the Pommery establishment is installed, and whose tall towers command a view of the whole of Reims and its environs. As we drive up the Avenue Gerbert we espy on the right an isolated crumbling Roman tower, aremnant of the days when Reims disputed with Trèves the honour of being the capital of Belgic Gaul. Close at hand, and almost under the walls of the old fortifications, is a grotto to which an ancient origin is likewise ascribed. In another minute we reach the open iron gates of Messrs. Pommery's establishment, flanked by a picturesque porter's lodge, and proceeding up a broad drive alight under a Gothic portico at the entrance to the spacious and lofty cellier. Iron columns support the roof of this vast hall, at one end of which is the office and tasting-room, provided with a telegraphic apparatus by means of which communication is carried on with the Reims bureaux. Stacked up on every side of the cellier, and when empty often in eight tiers, are rows upon rows of casks, 4,000 of which contain wine of the last vintage, sufficient for a million bottles of champagne. The temperature of this hall is carefully regulated; the windows are high up near the roof, the sun's rays are rigidly excluded, so that a pleasant coolness pervades the apartment. On the left-hand side stands the huge tun, capable of containing 5,500 gallons of wine, in which the firm make their *cuvée*, with the monogram P and G, surmounting the arms of Reims, carved on its head. Aplatform, access to which is gained by a staircase in a side aisle, runs round this tonneau; and boys stand here when the wine is being blended, and by means of a handle protruding above the cask work the paddle-wheels placed inside, thereby securing the complete amalgamation of the wine, which has been hoisted up in casks and poured through a metal trough into the tonneau. Adjoining are the chains and lifts worked by steam by means of which wine is raised and lowered from and to the cellars beneath, one lift raising or lowering eight casks, whether full or empty, in the space of a minute.

THE POMMERY ESTABLISHMENT, IN THE OUTSKIRTS OF REIMS.

At the farther end of the hall a Gothic door, decorated with ornamental iron-work, leads to the long broad flight of steps 116 in number and nearly twelve feet in width, conducting to the suite of lofty subterranean chambers where bottles of *vin brut* repose in their hundreds of thousands in slanting racks or solid piles, passing leisurely through those stages of development necessary to fit them for the *dégorgeur*. Altogether there are thirty large shafts, which were originally quarries, and are now connected by spacious galleries. This side of Reims abounds with similar quarries, which are believed to have served as places of refuge for the Protestants at the time of the League and after the revocation of the Edict of Nantes, and it is even conjectured that the early Christians, the followers of St. Sixtus and St. Sinicus, here hid themselves from their persecutors. Since the cellars within the city have no longer sufficed for the storage of the immense stocks required through the development of the champagne trade, these vast subterranean galleries have been successfully utilised by various firms. Messrs. Pommery, after pumping out the water with which the chambers were filled, proceeded to excavate the intersecting tunnels, shore up the cracking arches, and repair the flaws in the chalk with masonry, finally converting these abandoned quarries into magnificent cellars for the storage of champagne. No less than £60,000 was spent upon them and the castellated structure aboveground. The underground area is almost 240,000 square feet, and a million bottles of champagne can be stored in these capacious vaults.

**HEAD OVERSEER AT
POMMERY AND GRENO'S.**

Madame Pommery made a great mark with her splendid *cuvée* of 1868, and since this time her brand has become widely popular, the Pommery Sec especially being highly appreciated by connoisseurs.

On leaving Messrs. Pommery's we retrace our steps down the Avenue Gerbert, bordered on either side with rows of plane-trees, until we reach the treeless Avenue de Sillery, where Messrs. de Saint Marceaux and Co.'s new and capacious establishment is installed. The principal block of building is flanked by two advanced wings inclosing a garden-court, set off with flowers and shrubs, and from the centre of which rises a circular shaft, covered in with glass, admitting light and air to the cellars below. In the building to the left the wine is received on its arrival from the vineyard, and here are ranged hundreds of casks replete with the choice *crûs* of Verzenay, Ay, Cramant, and Bouzy, while some thousands of bottles ready for labelling are stocked in massive piles at the end of the packing-hall in the corresponding wing of the establishment. Here, too, atribe of workpeople are arraying the bottles with gold and silver headdresses and robing them in pink paper, while others are filling, securing, marking, and addressing the cases or baskets to Hong-Kong, San Francisco, Yokohama, Bombay, London, New York, St. Petersburg, Berlin, or Paris.

THE PACKING HALL OF MESSRS. DE SAINT-MARCEAUX AT REIMS.

The wine in cask, stored in the left-hand wing, after having been duly blended in a vast vat holding over 2,400 gallons, is drawn off into bottles, which are then lowered down a shaft to the second tier of cellars by means of an endless chain, on to which the baskets of bottles are swiftly hooked. The workman engaged in this duty, in order to prevent his falling down the shaft, has a leather belt strapped round his waist, by means of which he is secured to an adjoining iron column. We descend into the lower cellars down a flight of ninety-three broad steps—adepth equal to the height of an ordinary six-storied house—and find no less than four-and-twenty galleries excavated in the chalk, without any masonry supports, and containing upwards of a million bottles of champagne. The length of these galleries varies, but they are of a uniform breadth, allowing either a couple of racks with wine *sur pointe*, or stacks of bottles, in four rows on either side, with an ample passage down the centre.

The upper range of cellars comprises two large arched galleries of considerable breadth, one of which contains wine in wood and wine *sur pointe*, while the other is stocked with bottles of wine heads downward, ready to be delivered into the hands of the *dégorgeur*.

**BAS-RELIEF NEAR THE
PORTE DIEU-LUMIÈRE.**

MM. de St. Marceaux and Co. have the honour of supplying the King of the Belgians, the President of the French Republic, and several German potentates, with an exceedingly delicate champagne known as the Royal St. Marceaux. The same wine is popular in Russia and other parts of Europe, just as the Dry Royal of the firm is much esteemed in the United States. The brand of the house most appreciated in this country is its Carte d'Or, avery dry wine which, in conjunction with the firm's Extra Quality, secured the first place at a recent champagne competition in England.

In the neighbourhood of the Pommery and de St. Marceaux establishments numerous other champagne manufacturers have their cellars formed from the abandoned quarries so numerous on this side of the city. Of some of these firms we have already spoken, but there remain to be mentioned Messrs. Kunklemann and Co., Ruinart père et fils, George Goulet, Jules Champion, Théophile Roederer, &c. The cellars of the three last-named are immediately outside the Porte Dieu-Lumière, near which is a house with a curious bas-relief on its face, the subject of which has been a source of much perplexity to local antiquaries.

JEAN REMI MOET.

CHAPTER X.

EPERNAY CHAMPAGNE ESTABLISHMENTS.

Early Records of the Moët Family at Reims and Epernay—Jean Remi Moët Founder of the Commerce in Champagne Wines—Extracts from the Old Account-Books of the Moëts—First Sales of Sparkling Wines—Sales to England in 1788—"Milords" Farnham and Findlater—Jean Remi Moët receives the Emperor Napoleon, Josephine, and the King of Westphalia—The Firm of Moët and Chandon Constituted—Their Establishment in the Rue du Commerce—Delivering and Washing the New Bottles—The Numerous Vineyards and Vendangeoirs of the Firm—Making the Cuvée in Vats of 12,000 Gallons—The Bottling of the Wine by 200 Hands—AHundred Thousand Bottles Completed Daily—20,000 Francs' worth of Broken Glass in Two Years—ASubterranean City, with miles of Streets, Cross Roads, Open Spaces, Tramways, and Stations—The Ancient Entrance to these Vaults—Tablet Commemorative of the Visit of NapoleonI.—Millions of Bottles of Champagne in Piles and Racks—The Original Vaults known as Siberia—Scene in the Packing Hall—Messrs. Moët and Chandon's Large and Complete Staff—Provision for Illness and Old Age—Annual Fête Given by the Firm—Their Famous "Star" Brand—M.Perrier-Jouët, the lucky Grandson of a little Epernay Grocer—His Offices and Cellars—His Wine Classed according to its Deserts—Messrs. Roussillon and Co.'s Establishment—The Recognition accorded to their Wines— Their Stock of Old Vintages—The Extensive Establishment of Messrs. Pol Roger and Co.— Their Large Stock of the Fine 1874 Vintage—Preparations for the Tirage—Their Vast Fireproof Cellier and its Admirable Temperature—Their Lofty and Capacious Cellars of Two Stories.

Those magnates of the champagne trade, Messrs. Moët and Chandon, whose famous "star" brand is familiar in every part of the civilised globe, and whose half-score miles of cellars contain as many million bottles of champagne as there are millions of inhabitants in most of the secondary European states, have their head-quarters at Epernay in a spacious château—in that street of châteaux named the Rue du Commerce, but commonly known as the Faubourg de la Folie—which is approached through handsome iron gates, and has beautiful gardens in the rear extending in the direction of the River Marne. The existing firm dates from the year 1833, but the family of Moët—conjectured to have originally come from the Low Countries—had already been associated with the champagne wine trade for well-nigh a century previously. If the Moëts came from Holland they must have established themselves in the Champagne at a very early date, for the annals of Reims record that in the fifteenth century Jean and Nicolas Moët were *échevins* of the city. AMoët was present in that capacity at the coronation of Charles VII. in 1429, when Joan of Arc stood erect by the principal altar of the cathedral with her sacred banner in her hand, and for having contributed to repulse an attempt on the part of the English to prevent the entrance of the Royal party into the city, the Moëts were subsequently ennobled by the same monarch. Amural tablet in the church of St. Remi records the death of D.G. Moët, Grand Prior, in 1554, and nine years later we find Nicol Moët claiming exemption at Epernay from the payment of *tailles* on the ground of his being a noble. An old commercial book preserved in the family archives shows that in the year 1743—at the epoch when the rashness of the Duc de Grammont saved the English army under GeorgeII. from being cut to pieces at Dettingen—adescendant of the foregoing, one Claude Louis Nicolas Moët, who owned considerable vineyard property in the vicinity of Epernay, decided upon embarking in the wine trade. It is his son, however, Jean Remi Moët, born in 1758, who may be looked upon as the veritable founder of the present commerce in Champagne wines, which, thanks to his efforts, received a wonderful impulse, so that instead of the consumption of the vintages of the Marne being limited as heretofore to the privileged few, it spread all over the civilised world.

At Messrs. Moët and Chandon's we had the opportunity of inspecting some of the old account-books of the firm, and more particularly those recording the transactions of Jean Remi Moët and his father. The first sales of sparkling wine, on May 23rd, 1743, comprised 301 bottles of the vintage of 1741 to Pierre Joly, wine-merchant, *bon des douze chez le Roi*, whatever that may mean, at Paris; 120 bottles to Pierre Gabriel Baudoin, also *bon des douze*, at Paris; and a similar quantity to the Sieur Compoin, keeping the "hotellerie ditte la pestitte Escurie," Rue du Port Maillart, at Nantes in Brittany. The entry specifies that the wine for Nantes is to be left at Choisy-le-Roi, and taken by land to Orleans by the carters of that town, who are to be found at the Ecu d'Orléans, Porte St. Michel, Paris, the carriage as far as Choisy being 4livres 10 deniers (about 4francs) for the two half-baskets, and to Paris 3livres 15 deniers the basket.

Between 1750 and '60, parcels of wine were despatched to Warsaw, Vienna, Berlin, Königsberg, Dantzig, Stettin, Brussels, and Amsterdam; but one found no mention of any sales to England till the year 1788, when the customers of the firm included "Milord" Farnham, of London, and Messrs. Felix Calvert and Sylvin, who had a couple of sample bottles sent to them, for which they were charged five shillings. In the same year Messrs. Carbonnell, Moody, and Walker (predecessors of the well-known existing firm of Carbonnell and Co.) wrote in French for two baskets, of ten dozens each, of *vin de champagne* "of good body, not too charged with liqueur, but of excellent taste, and *not at all sparkling!*" while the Chevalier Colebrook, writing from Bath, requests that 72 bottles of champagne may be sent to his friend the Hon. John Butler, Molesworth Street, Dublin, "who if contented with the wine will become a good customer, he being rich, keeping a good house, and receiving many amateurs of *vin de champagne.*" Shortly afterwards the chevalier himself receives 50 bottles of still wine, vintage 1783. In 1789 120 bottles of champagne, vintage 1788, are supplied to "Milord" Findlater, of London—an ancestor, no doubt, of the wine-merchants of the same name carrying on business to-day, and whom the Moëts in their simplicity dubbed a "Milord"—and in 1790 the customers of the house include Power and Michel, of 44, Lamb Street, London, and Manning, of the St. Alban Tavern, the latter of whom is supplied on March 30th with 130 bottles of champagne at three livres, or two "schillings," per bottle; while a month later Mr. Lockart, banker, of 36, Pall Mall, is debited with 360 bottles, vintage 1788, at three shillings.

WASHING BOTTLES AT MESSRS. MOËT & CHANDON'S, EPERNAY.

In this same year M. Moët despatches a traveller to England named Jeanson, and his letters, some two hundred in number, are all preserved in the archives of the house. On the 17th May, 1790, he writes from London as follows:—"As yet I have only gone on preparatory and often useless errands. Ihave distributed samples of which I have no news. Patience is necessary, and I endeavour to provide myself with it. How the taste of this country has changed since ten years ago! Almost everywhere they ask for dry wine, but at the same time require it so vinous and so strong that there is scarcely any other than the wine of Sillery which can satisfy them.... To-morrow I dine five miles from here, at M.Macnamara's. We shall uncork four bottles of our wine, which will probably be all right." In May, 1792, Jean Remi Moët is married, and thenceforward assumes the full management of the house. On December 20 of the year following, when the Reign of Terror was fairly inaugurated, we find the accounts in the ledger opened to this or the other "citoyen." The orthodox Republican formula, however, did not long continue, and "sieur" and "monsieur" resumed their accustomed places, showing that Jean Remi Moët had no sympathy with the Jacobin faction of the day. In 1805 he became Mayor of Epernay, and between this time and the fall of the Empire received Napoleon several times at his residence, as well as the Empress Josephine and the King of Westphalia. The Emperor, after recapturing Reims from the Allies, came on to Epernay, on which occasion he presented M.Moët with the cross of the Legion of Honour. In 1830 the latter was arbitrarily dismissed from his mayoralty by Charles X., but was speedily reinstated by Louis Philippe, though he did not retain his office for long, his advanced age compelling him to retire from active life in the course of 1833. At this epoch the firm, which, since 1807 had been known as Moët and Co., was remodelled under the style of Moët and Chandon, the two partners being M.Victor Moët, son of the outgoing partner, and M.P.G. Chandon, the descendant of an old ennobled family of the Mâconnais, who had married M.Jean Remi Moët's eldest daughter. The descendants of these gentlemen are to-day at the head of the business, the partners being on the one hand M.Victor Moët-Romont and M.C.J.V. Auban Moët-Romont; and on the other, MM.Paul and Raoul Chandon de Briailles.

Facing Messrs. Moët and Chandon's offices at Epernay is a range of comparatively new buildings, with its white façade ornamented with the well-known monogram M.andC., surmounted by the familiar star. It is here that the business of blending and bottling the wine is carried on. Passing through the arched gateway access is obtained to a spacious courtyard, where carts laden with bottles are being expeditiously lightened of their fragile contents by the busy hands of numerous workmen. Another gateway on the left leads into the spacious bottle-washing room, which from the middle of May until the middle of July presents a scene of extraordinary animation. Bottle-washing apparatus, supplied by a steam-engine with 20,000 gallons of water per diem, are ranged in fifteen rows down the entire length of this hall, and nearly 200 women strive to excel each other in diligence and celerity in their management, apractised hand washing from 900 to 1,000 bottles in the course of the day. To the right of this *salle de rinçage*, as it is styled, bottles are stacked in their tens of thousands, and lads furnished with barrows, known as *diables*, hurry to and fro, conveying these to the washers, or removing the clean bottles to the adjacent courtyard, where they are allowed to drain, prior to being taken to the *salle de tirage* or bottling room.

MESSRS. MOËT & CHANDON'S VENDANGEOIR AT BOUZY.

Before, however, the washing of bottles on this gigantic scale commences, the "marrying" or blending of the wine is accomplished in a vast apartment, 250 feet in length and 100 feet broad, during the early spring. The casks of newly-vintaged wine which have been stowed away during the winter months, in the extensive range of cellars hewn out of the chalk underlying Epernay, where they have slowly fermented, are mixed together in due proportions in huge vats, each holding upwards of 12,000 gallons. Some of this wine is the growth of Messrs. Moët and Chandon's own vineyards, of which they possess as many as 900 acres (giving constant employment to 800 labourers and vinedressers) at Ay, Avenay, Bouzy, Cramant, Champillon, Chouilly, Dizy, Epernay, Grauves, Hautvillers, Le Mesnil, Moussy, Pierry, Saran, St. Martin, Verzy, and Verzenay, and the average annual cost of cultivating which is about £40 per acre. At Ay the firm own 210 acres of vineyards; at Cramant and Chouilly, nearly 180 acres; at Verzy and Verzenay, 120 acres; at Pierry and Grauves, upwards of 100 acres; at Hautvillers, 90 acres; at Le Mesnil, 80 acres; at Epernay, nearly 60 acres; and at Bouzy, 55 acres. Messrs. Moët and Chandon, moreover, possess vendangeoirs, or pressing-houses, at Ay, Bouzy, Cramant, Epernay, Hautvillers, Le Mesnil, Pierry, Saran, and Verzenay, in which the large number of 40 presses are installed. At these vendangeoirs no less than 5,450 pièces of fine white wine, sufficient for 1,360,000 bottles of champagne, are annually made—that is, 1,200 pièces at Ay, 1,100 at Cramant and Saran, 800 at Verzy and Verzenay, and smaller quantities at the remaining establishments. All these establishments have their celliers and their cellars, together with cottages for the accommodation of the numerous vinedressers in the employment of the firm.

BOTTLING CHAMPAGNE AT MESSRS. MOËT & CHANDON'S, EPERNAY.

Extensive as are the vineyards owned by Messrs. Moët and Chandon, the yield from them is utterly inadequate to the enormous demand which the great Epernay firm are annually called upon to supply, and large purchases have to be made by their agents from the growers throughout the Champagne. The wine thus secured, as well as that grown by the firm, is duly mixed together in such proportions as will ensure lightness with the requisite vinosity, and fragrance combined with effervescence, athorough amalgamation being effected by stirring up the wine with long poles provided with fan-shaped ends. If the vintage be indifferent in quality the firm have scores of huge tuns filled with the yield of more favoured seasons to fall back upon to ensure any deficiencies of character and flavour being supplied.

The casks of wine to be blended are raised from the cellars, half a dozen at a time, by means of a lift provided with an endless chain, and worked by the steam-engine of which we have already spoken. They are emptied, through traps in the floor of the room above, into the huge vats which, standing upon a raised platform, reach almost to the ceiling. From these vats the fluid is allowed to flow through hose into rows of casks stationed below. Before being bottled the wine reposes for a certain time, is next duly racked and again blended, and is eventually conveyed through silver-plated pipes into oblong reservoirs, each fitted with a dozen syphon-taps, so arranged that directly the bottle slipped on to one of them becomes full the wine ceases to flow.

Upwards of 200 workpeople are employed in the *salle de tirage* at Messrs. Moët and Chandon's, which, while the operation of bottling is going on, presents a scene of bewildering activity. Men and lads are gathered round the syphon-taps briskly removing the bottles as they become filled, and supplanting them by empty ones. Other lads hasten to transport the filled bottles on trucks to the corkers, whose so-called "guillotine" machines send the corks home with a sudden thud. The corks being secured with *agrafes* the bottles are placed in large flat baskets called *manettes*, and wheeled away on tracks, the quarts being deposited in the cellars by means of lifts, while the pints slide down an inclined plane by the aid of an endless chain, which raises the trucks with the empty baskets at the same time the full ones make their descent into the cellars. What with the incessant thud of the corking machines, the continual rolling of iron-wheeled trucks over the concrete floor, the rattling and creaking of the machinery working the lifts, the occasional sharp report of a bursting bottle, and the loudly-shouted orders of the foremen, who display the national partiality for making a noise to perfection, the din becomes at times all but unbearable. The number of bottles filled in the course of the day naturally varies, still Messrs. Moët and Chandon reckon that during the month of June a daily average of 100,000 are taken in the morning from the stacks in the *salle de rinçage*, washed, dried, filled, corked, wired, lowered into the cellars and carefully arranged in symmetrical order. This represents a total of two and a half million bottles during that month alone.

The bottles on being lowered into the cellars, either by means of the incline or the lifts, are placed in a horizontal position, and with their uppermost side daubed with white chalk, are stacked in layers from two to half-a-dozen bottles deep with narrow oak laths between. The stacks are usually about six or seven feet high and 100 feet and upwards in length. Whilst the wine is thus reposing in a temperature of about 55° Fahrenheit, fermentation sets in, and the ensuing month is one of much anxiety. Thanks, however, to the care bestowed, Messrs. Moët and Chandon's annual loss from bottles bursting rarely exceeds three per cent., though fifteen was once regarded as a respectable and satisfactory average. The broken glass is a perquisite of the workmen, the money arising from its sale, which at the last distribution amounted to no less than 20,000 francs, being divided amongst them every couple of years.

The usual entrance to Messrs. Moët and Chandon's Epernay cellars—which, burrowed out in all directions, are of the aggregate length of nearly seven miles, and have usually between 11,000,000 and 12,000,000 bottles and 25,000 casks of wine stored therein—is through a wide and imposing portal, and down a long and broad flight of steps. It is, however, by the ancient and less imposing entrance, through which more than one crowned head has condescended to pass, that we set forth on our lengthened tour through these intricate underground galleries—this subterranean city with its miles of streets, crossroads, open spaces, tramways, and stations devoted solely to champagne. Agilt inscription on a black marble tablet testifies that "on the 26th July, 1807, Napoleon the Great, Emperor of the French, King of Italy, and Protector of the Confederation of the Rhine, honoured commerce by visiting the cellars of Jean Rémi Moët, Mayor of Epernay, President of the Canton, and Member of the General Council of the Department," within three weeks of the signature of the treaty of Tilsit. Passing down the flight of steep slippery steps traversed by the victor of Eylau and Jena, access is gained to the upper range of vaults, brilliantly illuminated by the glare of gas, or dimly lighted by the flickering flame of tallow-candles, upwards of 60,000lbs. of which are annually consumed. Here group after group of the small army of 350 workmen employed in these subterranean galleries are encountered engaged in the process of transforming the *vin brut* into champagne. At Messrs. Moët and Chandon's the all-important operation of liqueuring the wine is effected by aid of machines of the latest construction, which regulate the quantity administered to the utmost nicety. The corks are branded by being pressed against steel dies heated by gas, by women who can turn out 3,000 per day apiece, the quantity of string used to secure them amounting to nearly ten tons in the course of the year.

There is another and a lower depth of cellars to be explored to which access is gained by trapholes in the floor—through which the barrels and baskets of wine are raised and lowered—and by flights of steps. From the foot of the latter there extends an endless vista of lofty and spacious passages hewn out of the chalk, the walls of which, smooth as finished masonry, are lined with thousands of casks of raw wine, varied at intervals by gigantic vats. Miles of long, dark-brown, dampish-looking galleries stretch away to the right and left, and though devoid of the picturesque festoons of fungi which decorate the London Dock vaults, exhibit a sufficient degree of mouldiness to give them an air of respectable antiquity. These multitudinous galleries, lit up by petroleum-lamps, are mostly lined with wine in bottles stacked in compact masses to a height of six or seven feet, only room enough for a single person to pass being left. Millions of bottles are thus arranged, the majority on their sides, in huge piles, with tablets hung up against each stack to note its age and quality; and the rest, which are undergoing daily evolutions at the hands of the twister, at various angles of inclination. In these cellars there are nearly 11,000 racks in which the bottles of *vin brut* rest *sur pointe*, as many as 600,000 bottles being commonly twisted daily.

The way runs on between regiments of bottles of the same size and shape, save where at intervals pints take the place of quarts; and the visitor, gazing into the black depths of the transverse passages to the right and left, becomes conscious of a feeling that if his guide were suddenly to desert him he would feel as hopelessly lost as in the catacombs of Rome. There are two galleries, each 650 feet in length, containing about 650,000 bottles, and connected by 32 transverse galleries, with an aggregate length of 4,000 feet, in which nearly 1,500,000 bottles are stored. There are, further, eight galleries, each 500 feet in length, and proportionably stocked; also the extensive new vaults, excavated some five or six years back, in the rear of the then-existing cellarage, and a considerable number of smaller vaults. The different depths and varying degrees of moisture afford a choice of temperature of which the experienced owners know how to take advantage. The original vaults, wherein more than a century ago the first bottles of champagne made by the infant firm were stowed away, bear the name of Siberia, on account of their exceeding coldness. This section consists of several roughly-excavated low winding galleries, resembling natural caverns, and affording a striking contrast to the broad, lofty, and regular-shaped corridors of more recent date.

THE PACKING HALL AT MESSRS. MOËT AND CHANDON'S, EPERNAY.

When the proper period arrives for the bottles to emerge once more into the upper air they are conveyed to the packing-room, aspacious hall 180 feet long and 60 feet broad. In front of its three large double doors waggons are drawn up ready to receive their loads. The seventy men and women employed here easily foil, label, wrap, and pack up some 10,000 bottles a day. Cases and baskets are stacked in different parts of this vast hall, at one end of which numerous trusses of straw used in the packing are piled. Seated at tables ranged along one side of the apartment women are busily occupied in pasting on labels or encasing the necks of bottles in gold or silver foil, whilst elsewhere men, seated on three-legged stools in front of smoking caldrons of molten sealing-wax of a deep green hue, are coating the necks of other bottles by plunging them into the boiling fluid. When labelled and decorated with either wax or foil the bottles pass on to other women, who swathe them in pink tissue-paper and set them aside for the packers, by whom, after being deftly wrapped round with straw, they are consigned to baskets or cases, to secure which last no less than 10,000lbs. of nails are annually used. England and Russia are partial to gold foil, pink paper, and wooden cases holding a dozen or a couple of dozen bottles of the exhilarating fluid, whereas other nations prefer waxed necks, disdain pink paper, and insist on being supplied in wicker baskets containing fifty bottles each.

Some idea of the complex character of so vast an establishment as that of Messrs. Moët and Chandon may be gathered from a mere enumeration of their staff, which, in addition to twenty clerks and 350 cellarmen proper, includes numerous agrafe-makers and corkcutters, packers and carters, wheelwrights and saddlers, carpenters, masons, slaters and tilers, tinmen, firemen, needlewomen, &c., while the inventory of objects used by this formidable array of workpeople comprises no fewer than 1,500 distinct heads. Amedical man attached to the establishment gives gratuitous advice to all those employed, and a chemist dispenses drugs and medicines without charge. While suffering from illness the men receive half-pay, but should they be laid up by an accident met with in the course of their work full salary is invariably awarded to them. As may be supposed, so vast an establishment as this is not without a provision for those past work, and all the old hands receive liberal pensions from the firm upon retiring. Every year Messrs. Moët and Chandon give a banquet or a ball to the people in their employ—usually after the bottling of the wine is completed—when the hall in which the entertainment takes place is handsomely decorated and illuminated with myriads of coloured lamps.

It is needless to particularise Messrs. Moët and Chandon's wines, which are familiar to all drinkers of champagne. Their famous "star" brand is known in all societies, figures equally at clubs and mess-tables, at garden parties and picnics, dinners and *soirées*, and has its place in hotel *cartes* all over the world. One of the best proofs of the wine's universal popularity is found in the circumstance that as many as 1,000 visitors from all parts of the world come annually to Epernay and make the tour of Messrs. Moët and Chandon's spacious cellars.

A little beyond Messrs. Moët and Chandon's, in the broad Rue du Commerce, we encounter a heavy, ornate, pretentious-looking château, the residence of M.Perrier-Jouët, which presents a striking contrast to the almost mean-looking premises opposite, where the business of the firm is carried on. M.Perrier-Jouët is the fortunate grandson of the Sieur Perrier Fissier, alittle Epernay grocer, who some eighty years or so ago used to supply corks, candles, and string to the firm of Moët and Co., and who, when the profits arising from this connection warranted his doing so, discarded his grocer's sleeves and apron and blossomed forth as a competitor in the champagne trade. Perrier-Jouët and Co.'s offices are situated on the left-hand side of a courtyard surrounded by low buildings, which serve as celliers, store-houses, packing-rooms, and the like. From an inner courtyard where piles of bottles are stacked under open sheds, the cellars themselves are reached. Previous to descending into these we passed through the various buildings, in one of which a party of men were engaged in disgorging and preparing wine for shipment. In another we noticed one of those heavy beam presses for pressing the grapes which the more intelligent manufacturers regard as obsolete, while in a third was the *cuvée* vat, holding no more than 2,200 gallons. In making their *cuvée* the firm commonly mix one part of old wine to three parts of new. An indifferent vintage, however, necessitates the admixture of a larger proportion of the older growth. The cellars, like all the more ancient ones at Epernay, are somewhat straggling and irregular, still they are remarkably cool, and on the lower floor remarkably damp as well. This, however, would appear to be no disadvantage, as the breakage in them is calculated never to exceed 2½ per cent.

The firm have no less than five qualities of champagne, and at one of the recent champagne competitions at London, where the experts engaged had no means of identifying the brands submitted to their judgment, Messrs. Perrier-Jouët's First Quality got classed below a cheaper wine of their neighbours Messrs. Pol Roger and Co., and very considerably below the Extra Sec of Messrs. Périnet et fils, and inferior even to a wine of De Venoge's, the great Epernay manufacturer of common class champagnes.

Champagne establishments, combined with the handsome residences of the manufacturers, line both sides of the long, imposing Rue du Commerce at Epernay. On the left hand is a succession of fine châteaux, commencing with one belonging to M.Auban Moët, whose terraced gardens overlook the valley of the Marne, and command views of the vine-clad heights of Cumières, Hautvillers, Ay, and Mareuil, and the more distant slopes of Ambonnay and Bouzy, while on the other side of the famous Epernay thoroughfare we encounter beyond the establishments of Messrs. Moët and Chandon and Perrier-Jouët the ornate monumental façade which the firm of Piper and Co.—of whom Messrs. Kunkelmann and Co. are to-day the successors—raised some years since above their extensive cellars. Alittle in the rear of the Rue du Commerce is the well-ordered establishment of Messrs. Roussillon and Co., the extension of whose business of late has necessitated their removal to these capacious premises. The wines of the firm enjoy a high reputation in England, France, and Russia, and have secured favourable recognition at the Paris, Philadelphia, and other Exhibitions. Their stock includes considerable quantities of the older vintages, it being a rule of the house never to ship crude young wines. It is on their dry varieties that Messrs. Roussillon and Co. especially pride themselves, and some of the fine wine of 1874 that was here shown to us was as remarkable for its delicacy as for its fragrance.

COURTYARD OF MESSRS. POL ROGER'S ESTABLISHMENT AT EPERNAY.

In a side street at the farther end of the Rue du Commerce stands a château of red brick, overlooking on the one side an extensive pleasure-garden, and on the other a spacious courtyard, bounded by celliers, stables, and bottle-sheds, all of modern construction and on a most extensive scale. These form the establishment of Messrs. Pol Roger and Co., settled for many years at Epernay, and known throughout the Champagne for their large purchases at the epoch of the vintage.

From the knowledge they possess of the best crûs, and their relations with the leading vineyard proprietors, they are enabled whenever the wine is good to acquire large stocks of it. Having bottled a considerable quantity of the fine wine of 1874, they resolved to profit by the exceptional quality of this vintage to commence shipping champagne to England, where their agents, Messrs. Reuss, Lauteren, and Co., have successfully introduced the new brand.

Passing through a large open gateway we enter the vast courtyard of the establishment, which, with arriving and departing carts—the first loaded with wine in cask or with new bottles, and the others with cases of champagne—presents rather an animated scene. Under a roof projecting from the wall of the vast cellier on the right hand a tribe of "Sparnaciennes"—as the feminine inhabitants of Epernay are termed—are occupied in washing bottles in readiness for the coming tirage. The surrounding buildings, most substantially constructed, are not destitute of architectural pretensions.

The extensive cellier, the area of which is 23,589 square feet, is understood to be the largest single construction of the kind in the Champagne district. Built entirely of iron, stone and brick, its framework is a perfect marvel of lightness. The roof, consisting of rows of brick arches, is covered above with a layer of Portland cement, in order to keep it cool in summer and protect it against the winter cold, two most desirable objects in connection with the manipulation of champagne. Here an endless chain of a new pattern enables wine in bottle to be lowered and raised with great rapidity to or from the cellars beneath—lofty and capacious excavations of two stories, the lowest of which is reached by a flight of no less than 170 steps.

Epernay, unlike Reims, has little of general interest to attract the stranger. Frequently besieged and pillaged during the Middle Ages, and burnt to the ground by the dauphin, son of FrançoisI., the town, although of some note as far back as the time of Clovis, exhibits to-day no evidence whatever of its great antiquity. The thoroughfare termed the Rempart de la Tour Biron recalls a memorable incident which transpired during the siege of the town by Henri IV. While the king was reconnoitring the defences a cannon-ball aimed at his waving white plume took off the head of the Maréchal Biron at the moment Henri's hand was resting familiarly on the maréchal's shoulder. Strange to say, the king himself escaped unhurt.

THE VENDANGEOIR OF HENRI QUATRE.

CHAPTER XI.

CHAMPAGNE ESTABLISHMENTS AT AY AND MAREUIL.

The Establishment of Deutz and Geldermann—Drawing off the Cuvée—Mode of Excavating Cellars in the Champagne—The Firm's New Cellars, Vineyards, and Vendangeoir—The old Château of Ay and its Terraced Garden—The Gambling Propensities of Balthazar Constance Dangé-Dorçay, aformer Owner of the Château—The Picturesque Situation and Aspect of Messrs. Ayala's Establishment—APromenade through their Cellars—M.Duminy's Cellars and Wines—His new Model Construction—The House Founded in 1814—Messrs. Bollinger's Establishment—Their Vineyard of La Grange—The Tirage in Progress—The Fine Cellars of the Firm—Messrs. Pfungst's frères and Co.'s Cellars—Their Dry Champagnes of 1868, '70, '72, and '74—The Old Church of Ay and its Decorations of Grapes and Vineleaves—The Vendangeoir of Henri Quatre—The Montebello Establishment at Mareuil—The Château formerly the Property of the Dukes of Orleans—ATitled Champagne Firm—The Brilliant Career of Marshal Lannes—

APromenade through the Montebello Establishment— The Press House, the Cuvée Vat, the Packing-Room, the Offices, and the Cellars—Portraits and Relics at the Château—The Establishment of Bruch-Foucher and Co.—The handsome Carved Gigantic Cuvée Tun—The Cellars and their Lofty Shafts—The Wines of the Firm.

The historic *bourgade* of Ay is within a short walk of the station on the line of railway connecting Epernay with Reims. The road lies across the light bridge spanning the Marne canal, the tall trees fringing which hide for a time the clustering houses; still we catch sight of the tapering steeple of the antique church rising sharply against the green vine-covered slopes and the fleecy-clouded summer sky. We soon reach the Place de l'Hôtel de Ville, and continuing onward in the direction of the steep hills which shelter the town on the north, come to a massive-looking corner house in front of the broad *porte-cochère* of which some railway carts laden with cases of champagne are standing. Passing through the gateway we find ourselves in an open court, with a dwelling-house to the right and a range of buildings in front where the offices of Messrs. Deutz and Geldermann are installed. This is the central establishment of the firm, whose Extra Dry "Gold Lack" and "Cabinet" champagnes have long been favourably known in England. Here are spacious celliers for disgorging and finishing off the wine, alarge packing-hall, and rooms where bales of corks and other accessories of the trade are stored, the operations of making the *cuvées* and bottling being accomplished in an establishment some little distance off.

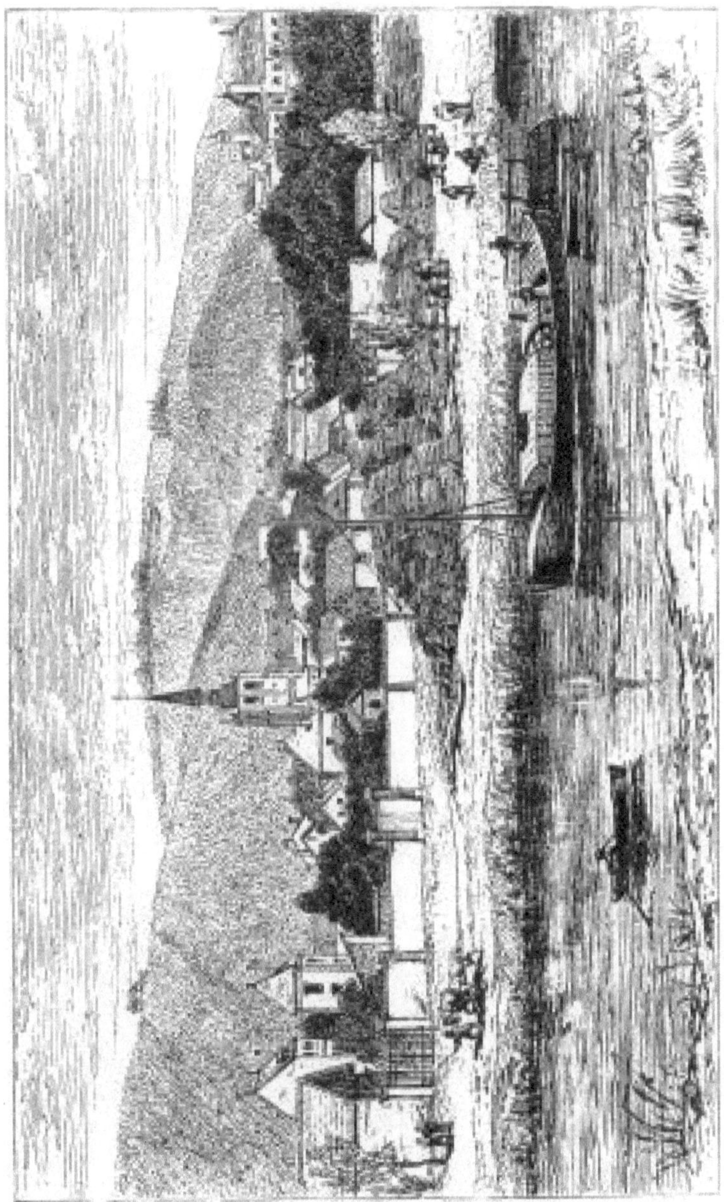

VIEW OF AY FROM THE BANKS OF THE MARNE CANAL.

Proceeding thither, we find an elegant château with a charming terraced garden, lying at the very foot of the vine-clad slopes, and on the opposite side of the road some large celliers where wine in wood is stored, and where the *cuvées* of the firm, consisting usually of upwards of 50,000 gallons each, are made in a vat of gigantic proportions, furnished with a raised platform at one end for the accommodation of the workman who agitates the customary paddles. When the wine is completely blended it is drawn off into casks disposed for the purpose in the cellar below, as shown in the accompanying engraving, and after being fined it rests for about a month to clear itself. To each of these casks of newly-blended wine a portion of old wine is added separately, and at the moment of bottling the whole is newly amalgamated.

DRAWING OFF THE CUVÉE AT DEUTZ & GELDERMANN'S, AY.

Adjoining M. Deutz's château is the principal entrance to the extensive cellars of the firm, to which, at the time of our visit, considerable additions were being made. In excavating a gallery the workmen commence by rounding off the roof, and then proceed to work gradually downwards, extracting the chalk, whenever practicable, in blocks suitable for building purposes, which being worth from three to four shillings the square yard help to reduce the cost of the excavation. When any serious flaws present themselves in the sides or roof of the galleries, they are invariably made good with masonry.

EXCAVATING DEUTZ & GELDERMANN'S NEW CELLARS, AY.

This range of cellars now comprises eight long and lofty galleries no less than 17 feet wide, and the same number of feet in height, and of the aggregate length of 2,200 yards. These spacious vaults, which run parallel with each other, and communicate by means of cross passages, underlie the street, the château, the garden, and the vineyard slopes beyond, and possess the great advantage of being always dry. They are capable, we were informed, of containing several million bottles of champagne in addition to a large quantity of wine in cask.

Messrs. Deutz and Geldermann possess vineyards at Ay, and own a large vendangeoir at Verzenay, where in good years they usually press 500 pièces of wine. They, moreover, make large purchases of grapes at Bouzy, Cramant, Le Mesnil, Pierry, &c, and invariably have these pressed under their own superintendence. Beyond large shipments to England, Messrs. Deutz and Geldermann transact a considerable business with other countries, and more especially with Germany, where their brand has been for years one of the most popular, and is to-day the favourite at numerous regimental messes and the principal hotels.

The old château of Ay, which dates from the early part of the last century, belongs to-day to the Count de Mareuil, amember of the firm of Ayala and Co., one of the leading establishments of the famous Marne-side crû. Perched half-way up the slope, covered with "golden plants," which rises in the rear of the village, the château, with its long façade of windows, commands the valley of the Marne for miles, and from the stately terraced walk, planted with ancient lime-trees, geometrically clipped in the fashion of the last century, asplendid view of the distant vineyards of Avize, Cramant, Epernay, and Chouilly is obtained. The château formed one of a quartette of seignorial residences which at the commencement of the present century belonged to Balthazar Constance Dangé-Dorçay, whose ancestors had been lords of Chouilly under the *ancien régime*. Dorçay had inherited from an aunt the châteaux of Ay, Mareuil, Boursault, and Chouilly, together with a large patrimony in land and money; but a mania for gambling brought him to utter ruin, and he dispossessed himself of money, lands, and châteaux in succession, and was reduced, in his old age, to earn a meagre pittance as a violin-player at the Paris Opera House. The old château of Boursault, which still exists contiguous to the stately edifice raised by Mme. Clicquot on the summit of the hill, was risked and lost on a single game at cards by this pertinacious gamester, whose pressing pecuniary difficulties compelled him to sell the remaining châteaux one by one. That of Ay was purchased by M.Froc de la Boulaye, and by him bequeathed to his cousin the Count de Mareuil, whose granddaughter became the wife of one of the Messrs. Ayala, and whose son is to-day their partner.

MESSRS. AYALA & CO.'S ESTABLISHMENT AT AY.

The offices of the firm adjoin the château, and rather higher up the hill is their very complete establishment, picturesquely situated in a hollow formed by some excavations, with the thickly-planted vine-slopes rising above its red-tiled roof. The boldly-designed basement, the ascending sweep conducting to the extensive celliers and the little centre belfry give a character of originality to the building. Carts laden with cases of champagne are leaving for the railway station, casks of wine are being transferred from one part of the establishment to another, bottles are being got ready for the approaching tirage, and in the packing department, installed in one of the three celliers into which the story aboveground is divided, quite an animated scene presents itself. Iron columns support the roofs of this and its companion celliers, where the firm make their *cuvée*, and the bottling of the wine takes place. On descending into the basement beneath, the popping of corks and the continual clatter of machinery intimate that the disgorging and re-corking of the wine are being accomplished, and in the dim light we discern groups of workmen engaged in the final manipulation which champagne has to undergo, while fresh relays of wine are arriving from the cellars by the aid of endless chains. There are two stories of these cellars which, excavated in the chalk, extend under the road and wind round beneath the château, the more modern galleries being broad, lofty, and admirably ventilated, and provided with supports of masonry wherever the instability of the chalk rendered this requisite. After a lengthened promenade through them we come to the ancient vaults extending immediately under the grounds of the château, where every particle of available space is utilised, and some difficulty is found in passing between the serried piles of bottles of *vin brut*—mostly the fine wine of 1874—which rise continuously on either side.

Within a hundred yards of the open space, surrounded by houses of different epochs and considerable diversity of design, where the Ay market is weekly held, and in one of the narrow winding streets common to the town, an escutcheon, with a bunch of grapes for device, surmounting a lofty gateway, attracts attention. Within, atrim courtyard, girt round with orange-trees in bright green boxes, and clipped in orthodox fashion, affords access to the handsome residence and offices of M.Duminy, well-known in England and America as a shipper of high-class champagnes, and whose Parisian connection is extensive. On the right-hand side of the courtyard is the packing-room, and through the cellars, which have an entrance here, one can reach the celliers in an adjoining street, where the *cuvée* is made and the bottling of the wine accomplished.

M. Duminy's cellars are remarkably old, and consequently of somewhat irregular construction, being at times rather low and narrow, as well as on different levels. In addition, however, to these venerable vaults, packed with wines of 1869, '70, '72, and '74, M.Duminy has various subterranean adjuncts in other parts of

Ay, and is at present engaged in constructing, at the foot of his vineyards up the mountain slope, anoble establishment which includes a vast court, upwards of a thousand square yards in extent, wherein are installed capacious bottle-racks and bottle-washing machines of the latest improved manufacture. Here are also handsome and extensive celliers, together with immense underground cellars, comprising broad and lofty galleries of regular design, the whole being constructed with a completeness and studied regard for convenience which bid fair to render this establishment when finished the model one of the Champagne district.

The house was originally founded so far back as 1814 by M.Taverne-Richard, who was intimately connected with the principal vineyard proprietors of the district. In 1842 this gentleman took his son-in-law, M.Duminy, father of the present proprietor of the establishment, into partnership, and after the retirement of M.Taverne he gave a great impetus to the business, and succeeded in introducing his light and delicate wines into the principal Paris hotels and restaurants. During its two-thirds of a century of existence the house has invariably confined itself to first-class wines, taking particular pride in shipping fully-matured growths. Besides its own large reserve of these, it holds considerable stocks long since disposed of, and now merely awaiting the purchasers' orders to be shipped.

A few paces beyond M. Duminy's we come upon an antiquated, decrepit-looking timber house, with its ancient gable bulging over as though the tough oak brackets on which it rests were at last grown weary of supporting their unwieldy burthen. Judging from the quaint carved devices, this house was doubtless the residence of an individual of some importance in the days when the principal European potentates had their commissioners installed at Ay to secure them the finest vintages. Continuing our walk along the same narrow winding street, we soon reach the establishment of Messrs. Bollinger, whose house, founded in the year 1829, claims to be the first among the Ay firms who shipped wines to foreign countries generally, including England, where the brand has long been held in high repute. Messrs. Bollinger, besides being shippers of champagne, are extensive vineyard proprietors, owning vinelands at Bouzy, Verzenay, and Dizy. Avineyard of theirs at the latter place, known as "La Grange," is said to have formerly belonged to the monks who founded the abbey of St. Peter at Hautvillers, the legend connected with which we have already related.

A couple of large gateways offer access to the spacious courtyard of Messrs. Bollinger's establishment; ahandsome dwelling-house standing on the right, and a small pavilion, in which the offices are installed, while on the left hand and in the rear of the courtyard rises a range of buildings of characteristic aspect, appropriated to the business of the firm. In one of the celliers, which has its open-raftered roof supported by slim metal columns, we found the tirage going on, the gang of workmen engaged in it filling, corking, and lowering into the cellars some 20,000 bottles a day. In one corner of the apartment stood the large *cuvée* tun—capable of holding some 50 hogsheads—in which the blending of the wine is effected, and in an adjoining cellier women were briskly labelling and wrapping up the completed bottles of champagne. The cellars, constructed some fifty years ago at a cost of nearly £12 the superficial yard, are faced entirely with stone, and are alike wide and lofty; this is especially the case with four of the more modern galleries excavated in 1848, and each 160 feet in length. Besides the foregoing, Messrs. Bollinger possess other cellars in Ay, where they store their reserve wines both in bottle and in the wood.

On the northern side of Ay, some little distance from the vineyard owned by them, the firm of Pfungst frères & Cie. have their cellars, the entrance to which lies just under the lofty vine-clad ridge. Messrs. Pfungst frères lay themselves out exclusively for the shipment of high-class champagnes, and the excellent growths of the Ay district necessarily form an important element in their carefully-composed *cuvées*. Aconsiderable portion of their stock consists of reserves of old wine, and we tasted here a variety of samples of finely-matured champagnes of 1868 and '70, as well as the vintages of 1872 and '74. All of these wines were of superior quality, combining delicacy and fragrance with dryness, the latter being their especial feature. In addition to their business with England, Messrs. Pfungst frères ship largely to India and the United States.

It is on this side of the town that the fine old Gothic church, dating as far back as the twelfth century, is situated. Many of the mouldings and the capitals of the columns both inside and outside the building are covered over with grape-laden vine-branches, and the sculptured figure of a boy bearing a basket of grapes upon his head surmounts the handsome Renaissance doorway, seemingly to indicate the honour in which the vine—the source of all the prosperity of the little town—was held both by the mediæval and later architects of the edifice. Nigh to the church stands the old house with its obliterated carved escutcheons, known traditionally as the Vendangeoir of Henri Quatre. This monarch loved the wine of the place almost as well as his favourite vintage of Arbois, and dubbed himself, as

we have already mentioned, Seigneur of Ay, whose inhabitants he sought to grati-
fy by confirming the charter which centuries before had been granted to the town.

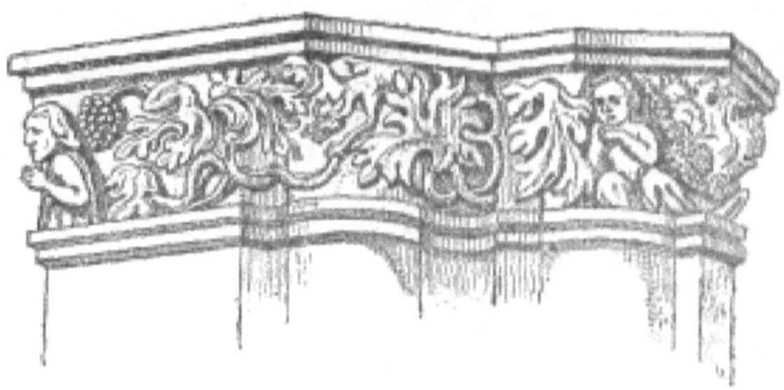

Within half-an-hour's walk of Ay, in an easterly direction, is the village of
Mareuil, along straight street of straggling houses, bounded by trees and gar-
den-plats, with vine-clad hills rising abruptly behind on the one side, and the
Marne canal flowing placidly by on the other. The archaic church, amixture of
the Romanesque and Early Gothic, stands at the farther end of the village, and
some little distance on this side of it is a massive-looking eighteenth-century building, spacious enough to accommodate a regiment of horse, but conventual rather
than barrack-like in aspect, from the paucity of windows looking on to the road.
Abroad gateway leads into a spacious courtyard to the left of which stands a grand
château, while on the right there rises an ornate round tower of three stories, from
the gallery on the summit of which a fine view over the valley of the Marne is
obtained. The buildings inclosing the court on three sides comprise press-houses,
celliers, and packing-rooms, an antiquated sundial marking the hour on the blank
space above the vines that climb beside the entrance gateway. The more ancient of
these tenements formed the vendangeoir of the Dukes of Orleans at the time they
owned the château of Mareuil, purchased in 1830 by the Duke de Montebello, son
of the famous Marshal Lannes, and minister and ambassador of Louis Philippe
and Napoleon III.

THE MONTEBELLO ESTABLISHMENT AT MAREUIL.

The acquisition of this property, to which were attached some important vineyards, led, several years later, to the duke's founding, in conjunction with his brothers, the Marquis and General Count de Montebello, achampagne firm, whose brand speedily acquired a notable popularity. To-day the business is carried on by their sons and heirs, for all the original partners in the house have followed their valiant father to the grave. Struck down by an Austrian cannon-ball in the zenith of his fame, the career of Marshal Lannes, brief as it was, furnishes one of the most brilliant pages in French military annals. Joining the army of Italy as a volunteer in 1796, he was made a colonel on the battle-field in the gorges of Millesimo, when Augereau's bold advance opened Piedmont to the French. He fought at Bassano and Lodi, took part in the assault of Pavia and the siege of Mantua, and at Arcola, when Napoleon dashed flag in hand upon the bridge, Lannes was seriously wounded whilst shielding his general from danger. He afterwards distinguished himself in Egypt, and led the van of the French army across the Alps, displaying his accustomed bravery both at Montebello and Marengo. At Austerlitz, where he commanded the right wing of the army, he greatly contributed to the victory, and at Jena, Friedland, and Eylau his valour was again conspicuous. Sent to Spain, he defeated the Spaniards at Tudela, and took part in the operations against Saragossa. Wounded at the battle of Essling, when the Archduke Charles inflicted upon NapoleonI. the first serious repulse he had met with on the field of battle, the valiant Lannes expired a few days afterwards in the Emperor's arms.

CHÂTEAU OF MAREUIL, BELONGING TO THE DUKE OF MONTEBELLO.

We were met at Mareuil, on the occasion of our visit, by Count Alfred Ferdinand de Montebello, the present manager of the house, and conducted by him over the establishment. In the press-house, to the left of the courtyard, were two of the ponderous presses used in the Champagne, for, like all other large firms, the house makes its own wine. Grapes grown in the Mareuil vineyards arrive here in baskets slung across the backs of mules, muzzled so that while awaiting their loads they may not devour the fruit within reach. In a cellier adjoining the press-house stands a large vat, capable of holding 50 pièces of wine, with a crane beside it for hauling up the casks when the *cuvée* is made. Here the tirage likewise takes place, and in the range of buildings, roofed with glass, in the rear of the tower, the bottled wine is labelled, capped with foil, and packed in cases for transmission to Paris, England, and other places abroad.

A double flight of steps, decorated with lamps and vases, leads to the handsome offices of the firm, situated on the first floor of the tower, while above is an apartment with a panelled ceiling, gracefully decorated with groups of Cupids engaged in the vintage and the various operations which the famous wines of the Mountain and the River undergo during their conversion into champagne. On the ground floor of the tower a low doorway conducts to the spacious cellars, which, owing to the proximity of the Marne, are all on the same level as well as constructed in masonry. The older vaults, where the Marquis de Pange, aformer owner of the château, stored the wine which he used to sell to the champagne manufacturers, are somewhat low and tortuous compared with the broad and lofty galleries of more recent date, which have been constructed as the growing connection of the firm obliged them to increase their stocks. Spite, however, of numerous additions, portions of their reserves have to be stored in other cellars in Mareuil. Considerable stocks of each of the four qualities of wine supplied by the firm are being got ready for disgorgement, including Cartes Noires and Bleues, with the refined Carte Blanche and the delicate Crêmant, which challenge comparison with brands of the highest repute.

In the adjacent château, the gardens of which slope down to the Marne canal, there are various interesting portraits, with one or two relics of the distinguished founder of the Montebello family, notably Marshal Lannes's gold-embroidered velvet saddle trappings, his portrait and that of Marshal Gerard, as well as one of NapoleonI., by David, with a handsome clock and candelabra of Egyptian design, abust of Augustus Cæsar, and a portrait of the Regent d'Orléans.

Another champagne house of standing at Mareuil is that of Bruch-Foucher and Co., whose establishment is situated near the village mairie. Entering by a lofty porte-cochère, we notice on the left hand a spacious packing-room, where men and women are expeditiously completing some shipping order, while beyond are the offices, looking on to a terraced garden whence a pleasant view is gained of the verdant valley of the Marne. From the packing-room a broad staircase leads to the cellars beneath, which can also be reached from a venerable range of buildings on the opposite side of the road, where young wines and old cognac spirit, used in the preparation of the liqueur, are stored in the wood.

In one of these ancient celliers is a vast tun, capable of containing nearly 5,000 gallons, carved over with an elaborate device of vineleaves and bunches of grapes entwined around overflowing cornucopia and bottles of champagne. This handsome cask, in which the firm make their *cuvée*, is a worthy rival of the sole antique ornamental tun that still reposes in the Royal cellars at Wurzburg. In Messrs. Bruch-Foucher and Co.'s capacious cellars, faced and vaulted with stone, from eight to nine hundred thousand bottles of wine are stored. The cellars form a single story, and extend partly under the adjacent vineyard slopes, deriving light and ventilation from numerous shafts which are occasionally no less than 150 feet in height. Messrs. Bruch-Foucher and Co., who are owners of vineyards at Mareuil, ship three qualities of champagne, the finest being their Carte d'Or and their Monogram Carte Blanche. Their chief business is with England, Germany, and the United States, where their brands enjoy considerable repute.

DOORWAY OF AVIZE CHURCH.

CHAPTER XII.

CHAMPAGNE ESTABLISHMENTS AT AVIZE AND RILLY.

Avize the Centre of the White Grape District—Its Situation and Aspect—The Establishment of Giesler and Co.—The Tirage and the Cuvée—Vin Brut in Racks and on Tables—The Packing-Hall, the Extensive Cellars, and the Disgorging Cellier—Bottle Stores and Bottle-Washing Machines—Messrs. Giesler's Wine-Presses at Avize and Vendangeoir at Bouzy—Their Vineyards and their Purchases of Grapes—Reputation of the Giesler Brand—The Establishment of M.Charles de Cazanove—ATame Young Boar—Boar-Hunting in the Champagne—M.de Cazanove's Commodious Cellars and Carefully-Selected Wines—Vineyards Owned by Him and His Family—Reputation of his Wines in Paris and their Growing Popularity in England—Interesting View from M.de Cazanove's Terraced Garden—The Vintaging of the White Grapes in the Champagne—Roper frères' Establishment at Rilly-la-Montagne—Their Cellars Penetrated by Roots of Trees—Some Samples of Fine Old Champagnes—The Principal Châlons Establishments—Poem on Champagne by M.Amaury de Cazanove.

Avize, situated in the heart of the Champagne white grape district, may be reached from Epernay by road through Pierry and Cramant or by the Châlons Railway to Oiry Junction, between which station and Romilly there runs a local line, jocularly termed the *chemin de fer de famille*, from the general disregard displayed by the officials for anything approaching to punctuality. Avize can scarcely be styled a town, and yet its growing proportions are beyond those of an ordinary village. It lies pleasantly nestled among the vines, sheltered by bold ridges on the north-west, with the monotonous plains of La Champagne pouilleuse, unsuited to the cultivation of the vine, stretching away eastward in the direction of Châlons. Avize cannot pretend to the same antiquity as its neighbour Vertus, and lacks the many picturesque vestiges of which the latter can boast. Its church dates back only to the 15th century, although the principal doorway in the Romanesque style evidently belongs to a much earlier epoch. There is a general air of trim prosperity about the place, and the villagers have that well-to-do appearance common to the inhabitants of the French wine districts. Only at vintage time, however, are there any particular outdoor signs of activity, although half a score of champagne firms have their establishments here, giving employment to the bulk of the population, and sending forth their two or three million bottles of the sparkling wine of the Marne annually.

MAKING THE CUVÉE AT MESSRS. GIESLER'S, AT AVIZE.

Proceeding along the straight level road leading from the station to the village we encounter on our right hand the premises of Messrs. Giesler and Co., the reputation of whose brand is universal. When M.Giesler quitted the firm of P.A. Mumm, Giesler, and Co., at Reims, in 1838, he removed to Avize and founded the present extensive establishment. Entering through a large open gateway we find ourselves within a spacious courtyard with a handsome dwelling-house in the rear, and all the signs of a champagne business of magnitude apparent. Aspiral staircase conducts to the counting-house on the first story of a range of buildings on the left hand, the ground floor of which is divided into celliers. Passing through a door by the side of this staircase we enter a large hall where the operation of bottling the wine is going on. Four tuns, each holding five ordinary pièces of wine, and raised upon large blocks of wood, are standing here, and communicating with them are bottling syphons of the type commonly employed in the Champagne. Messrs. Giesler do not usually consign the newly-bottled wine at once to the cellars, but retain it aboveground for about a fortnight in order that it may develop its effervescent qualities more perfectly. We find many thousands of these bottles stacked horizontally in the adjoining celliers, in one of which stands the great *cuvée* tun wherein some fifty hogsheads of the finest Champagne growths are blended together at one time, two hundred hogsheads being thus mingled daily while the *cuvées* are in progress. The casks of wine having been hoisted from the cellars to the first floor by a crane, and run on to a trough, their bungs are removed, and the wine flows through an aperture in the floor into the huge tun beneath, its amalgamation being accomplished by the customary fan-shaped appliances, set in motion by the turning of a wheel. In an adjacent room is the machine used for mixing the liqueur which Messrs. Giesler add so sparingly to their light and fragrant wines.

There are a couple of floors above these celliers, the uppermost of which is used as a general store, while in the one beneath many thousands of bottles of *vin brut* repose *sur pointe*, either in racks or on tables as at the Clicquot-Werlé establishment. This latter system requires ample space, for as the *remueur*, or workman who shakes the bottles, is only able to use one hand, the operation of dislodging the sediment necessarily occupies a much longer time than is requisite when the bottles rest in racks.

PREPARING THE LIQUEUR AT MESSRS. GIESLER'S.

The buildings on the opposite side of the courtyard comprise a large packing-hall, celliers where the wine is finished off, and rooms where corks and such-like things are stored. Here, too, is the entrance to the cellars, of which there are three tiers, all lofty and well-ventilated galleries, very regular in their construction, and faced with either stone or brick. In these extensive vaults are casks of fine reserved wines for blending with youthful vintages, and bottles of *vin brut*, built up in solid stacks, that may be reckoned by their hundreds of thousands. At Messrs. Giesler's the disgorging of the wine is accomplished in a small cellier partially underground, and the temperature of which is very cool and equable. The *dégorgeurs*, isolated from the rest of the workpeople, are carrying on their operations here by candlelight. So soon as the sediment is removed the bottles are raised in baskets to the cellier above, where the liqueuring, re-corking, stringing, and wiring are successively accomplished. By pursuing this plan the loss sustained by the disgorgement is believed to be reduced to a minimum.

Extensive as these premises are they are still insufficient for the requirements of the firm, and across the road is a spacious building where new bottles are stored and the washing of the bottles in preparation for the tirage takes place. By the aid of the machinery provided, sixteen women, assisted by a couple of men, commonly wash some fifteen or sixteen thousand bottles in the course of a day. Here, too, stands one of the two large presses with which at the epoch of the vintage a hundred pièces of wine are pressed every four-and-twenty hours. The remaining press is installed in a cellier at the farther end of the garden on the other side of the road. Messrs. Giesler possess additional presses at their vendangeoir at Bouzy, and during the vintage have the command of presses at Ay, Verzenay, Vertus, Le Mesnil, &c., it being a rule of theirs always to press the grapes within a few hours after they are gathered to obviate their becoming bruised by their own weight and imparting a dark colour to the wine, acontingency difficult to guard against in seasons when the fruit is over-ripe. The firm own vineyards at Avize, and have agreements with vine-proprietors at Ay, Bouzy, Verzenay, and elsewhere, to purchase their crops regularly every year. Messrs. Giesler's brand has secured its existing high repute solely through the fine quality of the wines shipped by the house—wines which are known and appreciated by all real connoisseurs of champagne.

From Messrs. Giesler's it is merely a short walk to the establishment of M.Charles de Cazanove, situated in the principal street of Avize. On entering the court we encountered a tame young boar engaged in the lively pursuit of chasing some terrified hens, while a trio of boarhounds, basking on the sunny flagstones, contemplated his proceedings with lazy indifference. Boars abound in the woods hereabouts, and hunting them is a favourite pastime with the residents, and the young boar we had noticed proved to be one of the recent captures of the sons of M.de Cazanove, who are among the warmest partisans of the exciting sport. Many of the boars found in the woods around Reims journey thither, it is said, by night from the famous forest of the Ardennes—the scene of Rosalind's wanderings and Touchstone's eccentricities as set forth in *As You Like It*, and whose gloomy depths and tangled glens shelter to-day not merely boars but wolves as well.

In the Champagne it is no longer the fashion

"With javelin's point a churlish swine to gore,"

nor to hunt the boar on horseback, as is still the case in Burgundy. When the presence of one or more of these animals is signalled in the neighbourhood, aparty starts off accompanied by dogs and armed with double-barrelled rifles. Acircle having been formed round the boar's lair the dogs are set to draw him out, while the *chasseurs* keep on the alert so as not to allow him to escape through their circle alive. In this manner a few score of boars are killed every year in the woods round about Reims and Epernay.

VINEYARDS OF AVIZE AND CRAMANT FROM THE GARDEN OF M. C. DE CAZANOVE.

The house of M. Charles de Cazanove was established in 1843 by its present proprietor on the foundation of a business which had been in existence since 1811. Compared with the monumental grandeur of some of the great Reims and Epernay establishments the premises present a simple and modest aspect, nevertheless they are capacious and commodious, besides which the growing business of the house has led to the acquisition of additional cellarage in other parts of Avize. More important than all, however, is the quality of the wine with which these cellars are stocked, and following the rule observed by champagne firms of the highest repute, it has been a leading principle with M.de Cazanove always to rely upon the choicer growths—those light, delicate, and fragrant wines of the Marne which throw out the true aroma of the flower of the vine. M.de Cazanove, who is distinguished for his knowledge of viticulture, occupies an influential position at Avize, being Vice-President of the Horticultural Society of the Marne, and a member of the committee charged with guarding the Champagne vineyards against the invasion of the phylloxera. His own vines include only those fine varieties to which the crûs of the Marne owe their great renown. He possesses an excellent vineyard at Grauves, near Avize, and his mother-in-law, Madame Poultier, of Pierry, is one of the principal vine-growers of the district.

M. de Cazanove's wines are much appreciated in Paris, where his business is very extensive. His shipments to England are also considerable, but from the circumstance of some of his principal customers importing the wine under special brands of their own, the brand of the house is not so widely known as we should have expected.

From M. de Cazanove's terraced garden in the rear of his establishment a fine view is obtained of one of the most famous viticultural districts of the Champagne, yielding wines of remarkable delicacy and exquisite bouquet. On the left hand rises up the mountain of Avize, its summit fringed with dense woods, where in winter the wild boar has his lair. In front stretch the long vine-clad slopes of Cramant, with orchards at their base, and the housetops of the village and the spire of the quaint old church just peeping over the brow of the hill. To the right towers the bold forest-crowned height of Saran with M.Moët's château perched half-way up its north-eastern slope, and fading away in the hazy distance are the monotonous plains of the Champagne.

We have already explained that the wines of Avize and Cramant rank as *premiers crûs* of the white grape district, and that every champagne manufacturer of repute mingles one or the other in his *cuvée*. The white grapes are usually gathered a fortnight or three weeks later than the black varieties, but in other respects the vintaging of them is the same. The grapes undergo the customary minute examination by the *éplucheuses*, and all unripe, damaged, and rotten berries being thrown aside, the fruit is conveyed with due care to the press-houses in the large baskets known as *paniers mannequins*. The pressing takes place under exactly the same conditions as the pressing of the black grapes; the must, too, is drawn off into hogsheads to ferment, and by the end of the year, when the active fermentation has terminated, the wine is usually clear and limpid.

At Rilly-la-Montagne, on the line of railway between Reims and Epernay, Roper frères & Cie., late of Epernay, now have their establishment. Starting from the latter place we pass Ay and Avenay, and then the little village of Germaine in the midst of the forest, and nigh the summit of the mountain of Reims, with its "Rendezvous des Chasseurs" in immediate proximity to the station. Finally we arrive at Rilly, which, spite of its isolated situation, has about it that aspect of prosperity common to the more favourable wine districts of France. This is scarcely surprising when the quality of its wines is taken into consideration. The still red wine of Rilly has long enjoyed a high local reputation, and to-day the Rilly growths are much sought after for conversion into champagne. White wine of 1874 from black grapes fetched, we were informed, as much as from 600 to 700 francs the pièce, while the finer qualities from white grapes realised from 300 to 400 francs. Messrs. Roper frères & Cie. are the owners of some productive vineyards situated on the high road to Chigny and Ludes.

The establishment of Roper frères is adjacent to a handsome modern house standing back from the road in a large and pleasant garden, bounded by vineyards on two of its sides. In the celliers all the conveniences pertaining to a modern champagne establishment are to be found, while extending beneath the garden are the extensive cellars of the firm, comprising two stories of long and spacious galleries excavated in the chalk, their walls and roofs being supported whenever necessary by masonry. A curious feature about these cellars is that the roots of the larger trees in the garden above have penetrated through the roof of the upper story and hang pendent overhead like innumerable stalactites. Here after the comparatively new wine of 1874 had been shown to us — including samples of the *Vin Brut* or natural champagne of which the firm make a speciality at a moderate price — some choice old champagnes were brought forth, including the fine vintages of 1865, 1857, and 1846. The latter wine had of course preserved very little of its effervescence, still its flavour was exceedingly fine, being soft and delicate to a degree. At the Vienna Exhibition of 1873 and the London Exhibition of 1874 the collection of champagnes exhibited by Roper frères met with favourable recognition from the international juries.

Our tour through the Champagne vineyards and wine-cellars here comes to an end. It is true there are important establishments at Châlons, notably those of Jacquesson et fils, the Perriers, Freminet et fils, and Jacquard frères, the cellars of the first-named being, perhaps, unrivalled in the Champagne. As, however, any description of these establishments would be little else than a recapitulation of something we have already said, we content ourselves with merely notifying their existence, and bring our Facts about Champagne to a close with the translation of a poem from the pen of M.Amaury de Cazanove of Avize:—

CHAMPAGNE.

Less for thy grace and glory, land of ours,
Than for thy dolour, dear;
Let the grief go, and here—
Here's to thy skies, thy women and thy flowers!
France! take the toast, thy women and thy roses,
France! to thy wine, more wealth unto thy store!
And let the lips a grievous memory closes
Smile their proud smile once more!

Swarthy Falernian, Massica the Red,
Were ye the nectars poured
At the great gods' broad board?
No, poor old wines, all but in name long dead,
Nectar's Champagne, the sparkling soul of mirth,
That bubbling o'er with laughing gas,
Flashes gay sunbeams in the glass,
And like our flag goes proudly round the earth.

"I am the blood Burgundian sunshine makes;
A fine old feudal knight
Of bluff and boisterous might,
Whose casque feels—ah, so heavy when one wakes!"
"And I, the dainty Bordeaux, violets'
Perfume, and whose rare rubies gourmets prize.
My subtile savour gets
In partridge wings its daintiest allies."

Ah, potent chiefs, Bordeaux and Burgundy.
If we must answer make,
This sober counsel take:
Messeigneurs, sing your worth less haughtily,
For 'tis Champagne, the sparkling soul of mirth,
That bubbling o'er with laughing gas,
Flashes gay sunbeams in the glass,
And like our flag goes proudly round the earth.

Aye, 'tis the true, the typic wine of France;
Aye, 'tis our heart that sparkles in our eyes,
And higher beats for every dire mischance;
It was the wit that made our fathers wise,
That made their valour gallant, gay,
When plumes were stirr'd by winds of waving swords,
And chivalry's defiance spoke the words:
"À vous, Messieurs les Anglais, les premiers!"

Let the dull beer-apostle till he's hoarse

Vent his small spleen and spite,
Fate fill his sleepless night
With nightmares of invincible remorse!
We sing Champagne, the sparkling soul of mirth,
That bubbling o'er with laughing gas,
Flashes gay sunbeams in the glass,
And like our flag goes proudly round the earth.

PEASANT WOMEN OF THE ENVIRONS OF SAUMUR.

CHAPTER XIII.

SPARKLING SAUMUR AND SPARKLING SAUTERNES.

The Sparkling Wines of the Loire often palmed off as Champagnes—
The Finer qualities Improve with Age—Anjou the Cradle of the
Plantagenet Kings—Saumur and its Dominating Feudal Château
and Antique Hôtel de Ville—Its Sinister Rue des Payens and Steep
Tortuous Grande Rue—The Vineyards of the Coteau of Saumur—
Abandoned Stone Quarries converted into Dwellings—The Vin-
tage in Progress—Old-fashioned Pressoirs—The Making of the
Wine—The Vouvray Vineyards—Balzac's Picture of La Vallée
Coquette—The Village of Vouvray and the Château of Moncon-
tour—Vernou with its Reminiscences of Sully and Pépin-le-Bref—
The Vineyards around Saumur—Remarkable Ancient Dolmens—
Ackerman-Laurance's Establishment at Saint-Florent—Their
Extensive Cellars, Ancient and Modern—Treatment of the New-
ly-Vintaged Wine—The Cuvée—Proportions of Wine from Black
and White Grapes—The Bottling and Disgorging of the Wine
and Finishing Operations—The Château of Varrains and the Es-

tablishment of M.Louis Duvau aîné—His Cellars a succession of Gloomy Galleries—The Disgorging of the Wine accomplished in a Melodramatic-looking Cave—M.Duvau's Vineyard—His Sparkling Saumur of Various Ages—Marked Superiority of the more Matured Samples—M.Alfred Rousteaux's Establishments at Saint-Florent and Saint-Cyr—His convenient Celliers and extensive Cellars—Mingling of Wine from the Champagne with the finer Sparkling Saumur—His Vineyard at La Perrière—M.E.Normandin's Sparkling Sauternes Manufactory at Châteauneuf—Angoulême and its Ancient Fortifications—Vin de Colombar—M. Normandin's Sparkling Sauternes Cuvée—His Cellars near Châteauneuf—High recognition accorded to the Wine at the Concours Régional d'Angoulême.

After the Champagne Anjou is the French province which ranks next in importance for its production of sparkling wines. Vintaged on the banks of the Loire, these are largely consigned to the English and other markets, labelled Crême de Bouzy, Sillery and Ay Mousseux, Cartes Noires and Blanches, and the like, while their corks are branded with the names of phantom firms, supposed to be located at Reims and Epernay. As a rule these wines come from around Saumur, but they are not necessarily the worse on that account, for the district produces capital sparkling wines, the finer qualities of which improve greatly by being kept for a few years. One curious thing shown to us at Saumur was the album of a manufacturer of sparkling wines containing examples of the many hundred labels ticketed with which his produce had for years past been sold. Not one of these labels assigned to the wines the name of their real maker or their true birthplace, but introduced them under the auspices of mythical dukes and counts, as being manufactured at châteaux which are so many "castles in Spain," and as coming from Ay, Bouzy, Châlons, Epernay, Reims, and Verzenay, but never by any chance from Saumur.

THE VINEYARDS OF THE COTEAU DE SAUMUR.

Being produced from robuster growths than the sparkling wines of the Department of the Marne, sparkling saumur will always lack that excessive lightness which is the crowning grace of fine champagne, still it has only to be kept for a few years instead of being drunk shortly after its arrival from the wine-merchant for its quality to become greatly improved and its intrinsic value to be considerably enhanced. We have drunk sparkling saumur that had been in bottle for nearly twenty years, and found the wine not only remarkably delicate, but, singular to say, with plenty of effervescence.

To an Englishman Anjou is one of the most interesting of the ancient provinces of France. It was the cradle of the Plantagenet Kings, and only ten miles from Saumur still repose the bones of Henry, the first Plantagenet, and Richard of the Lion Heart, in the so-called Cimetière des Rois of the historic abbey of Fontevrault. The famous vineyards of the Coteau de Saumur, eastward of the town and bordering the Loire, extend as far as here, and include the communes of Dampierre, Souzay, Varrains, Chacé, Parnay, Turquant, and Montsoreau, the last-named within three miles of Fontevrault, and chiefly remarkable through its seigneur of ill-fame, Jean de Chambes, who instigated his wife to lure Boissy d'Amboise to an assignation in order that he might more surely poignard him. Saumur is picturesquely placed at the foot of this bold range of heights near where the little river Thouet runs into the broad and rapid Loire. Amassive-looking old château perched on the summit of an isolated crag stands out grandly against the clear sky and dominates the town, the older houses of which crouch at the foot of the lofty hill and climb its steepest sides. The restored antique Hôtel de Ville, in the pointed style, with its elegant windows, graceful belfry, and florid wrought-iron balconies, stands back from the quay bordering the Loire. In the rear is the Rue des Payens, whither the last of the Huguenots of this "metropolis of Protestantism," as it was formerly styled, retired, converting their houses into so many fortresses to guard against being surprised by their Catholic adversaries. Adjacent is the steep tortuous Grande Rue, of which Balzac—himself a Tourangeau—has given such a graphic picture in his *Eugénie Grandet*, the scene of which is laid at Saumur. To-day, however, only a few of its ancient carved timber houses, quaint overhanging corner turrets, and fantastically-studded massive oak doors have escaped demolition.

The vineyards of the Coteau de Saumur, yielding the finest wines, are reached by the road skirting the river, the opposite low banks of which are fringed with willows and endless rows of poplars, which at the time of our visit were already golden with the fading tints of autumn. Numerous fantastic windmills crown the heights, the summit of which is covered with vines, varied by dense patches of woodland. Here, as elsewhere along the banks of the Loire, the many abandoned quarries along the face of the hill have been turned by the peasants into cosy dwellings by simply walling-up the entrances while leaving, of course, the necessary apertures for doors and windows. Dampierre, the first village reached, has many of these cave-dwellings, and numbers of its houses are picturesquely perched up the sides of the slope. The holiday costumes of the peasant women encountered in the neighbourhood of Saumur are exceedingly quaint, their elaborate and varied head-dresses being counterparts of *coiffures* in vogue so far back as three and four centuries ago.

Quitting the banks of the river, we ascend a steep tortuous road shut in on either side by high stone walls—for hereabouts all the best vineyards are scrupulously inclosed—and finally reach the summit of the heights, whence a view is gained over what the Saumurois proudly style the grand valley of the Loire. Everywhere around the vintage is going on. The vines are planted rather more than a yard apart, and those yielding black grapes are trained, as a rule, up tall stakes, although some few are trained espalier fashion. Women dexterously detach the bunches with pruning-knives and throw them into the *seilles*—small squat buckets with wooden handles—the contents of which are emptied from time to time into baskets—the counterpart of the chiffonnier's *hotte*, and coated with pitch inside so as to close all the crevices of the wickerwork—which the *portes-bastes* carry slung to their backs. When white wine is being made from black grapes for sparkling saumur the grapes are conveyed in these baskets forthwith to the underground pressoirs in the neighbouring villages before their skins get at all broken in order that the wine may be as pale as possible in colour.

The black grape yielding the best wine in the Saumur district is the breton, said to be the same as the carbinet-sauvignon, the leading variety in the grand vineyards of the Médoc. Other species of black grapes cultivated around Saumur are the varennes, yielding a soft and insipid wine of no kind of value, and the liverdun, or large gamay, the prevalent grape in the Mâconnais, and the same which in the days of Philippe-le-Hardi the *parlements* of Metz and Dijon interdicted the planting and cultivation of. The prevalent white grapes are the large and small pineau blanc, the bunches of the former being of an intermediate size, broad and pyramidal in shape, and with the berries close together. These have fine skins, are oblong in shape, and of a transparent yellowish-green hue tinged with red, are very sweet and juicy, and as a rule ripen late. As for the small pineau, the bunches are less compact, the berries are round and of a golden tint, are finer as well as sweeter in flavour, and ripen somewhat earlier than the fruit of the larger variety.

We noticed as we drove through the villages of Champigny and Varrains—the former celebrated for its fine red wines, and more especially its crû of the Clos des Cordeliers—that hardly any of the houses had windows looking on to the narrow street, but that all were provided with low openings for shooting the grapes into the cellar where, when making red wine, they are trodden, but when making white wine, whether from black or white grapes, they are invariably pressed. Each of the houses had its ponderous porte-cochère and low narrow portal leading into the large inclosed yard at its side, and over the high blank walls vines were frequently trained and pleasantly varied their dull grey monotony.

The grapes on being shot into the openings just mentioned fall through a kind of tunnel into a reservoir adjacent to the heavy press, which is invariably of wood and of the old-fashioned cumbersome type. They are forthwith placed beneath the press and usually subjected to five separate squeezes, the must from the first three being reserved for sparkling wine, while that from the two latter, owing to its being more or less deeply tinted, only serves for table wine. The must is at once run off into casks in order that it may not ferment on the grape-skins and imbibe any portion of their colouring matter. Active fermentation speedily sets in and lasts for a fortnight or three weeks according to whether the temperature chances to be high or low.

The vintaging of the white grapes takes place about a fortnight later than the black grapes, and is commonly a compound operation, the best and ripest bunches being first of all gathered just as the berries begin to get shrivelled and show symptoms of approaching rottenness. It is these selected grapes that yield the best wine. The second gathering, which follows shortly after the first, includes all the grapes remaining on the vines, and yields a wine perceptibly inferior in quality. The grapes on their arrival at the press-house are generally pressed immediately and the must is run off into tuns to ferment. At the commencement these tuns are filled up every three or four days to replace the fermenting must which has flowed over; afterwards any waste is made good at the interval of a week, and then once a fortnight, the bungholes of the casks being securely closed towards the end of the year, by which time the first fermentation is over.

It should be noted that the Saumur sparkling wine manufacturers draw considerable supplies of the white wine required to impart lightness and effervescence to their *vin préparé* from the Vouvray vineyards. Vouvray borders the Loire a few miles from the pleasant city of Tours, which awakens sinister recollections of truculent Louis XI., shut up in his fortified castle of Plessis-lez-Tours, around which Scott has thrown the halo of his genius in his novel of *Quentin Durward*. On proceeding to Vouvray from Tours we skirt a succession of poplar-fringed meadows stretching eastward in the direction of Amboise along the right bank of the Loire; and after a time a curve in the river discloses to view a range of vine-clad heights extending some distance beyond the village of Vouvray. Our route lies past the picturesque ruins of the abbey of Marmoûtier and the Château des Roches—one of the most celebrated castles of the Loire—the numerous excavations in the soft limestone ridge on which they are perched being converted as usual into houses, magazines, and wine-cellars. We proceed through the village of Rochecorbon, and along a road winding among the spurs of the Vouvray range, past hamlets, half of whose inhabitants live in these primitive dwellings hollowed out of the cliff, and finally enter the charming Vallée Coquette, hemmed in on all sides with vine-clad slopes. Here a picturesque old house, half château half homestead, was pointed out to us as a favourite place of sojourn of Balzac, who speaks of this rocky ridge as "inhabited by a population of vine-dressers, their houses of several stories being hollowed out in the face of the cliff, and connected by dangerous staircases hewn in the soft stone. Smoke curls from most of the chimneys which peep above the green crest of vines, while the blows of the cooper's hammer resound in several of the cellars. A young girl trips to her garden over the roofs of these primitive dwellings, and an old woman, tranquilly seated on a ledge of projecting rock, supported solely by the thick straggling roots of the ivy which spreads itself over the disjointed stones, leisurely turns her spinning-wheel regardless of her dangerous position." The picture sketched by the author of *La Comédie Humaine*, some forty years ago, has scarcely changed at the present day.

At the point where the village of Vouvray climbs half-way up the vine-crested ridge the rapid-winding Cise throws itself into the Loire, and on crossing the bridge that spans the tributary stream we discern on the western horizon, far beyond the verdant islets studding the swollen Loire, the tall campaniles of Tours Cathedral, which seem to rise out of the water like a couple of Venetian towers. Vouvray is a trim little place, clustered round about with numerous pleasant villas in the midst of charming gardens. The modern château of Moncontour here dominates the slope, and its terraced gardens, with, their fantastically-clipped trees and geometric parterres, rise tier above tier up the face of the picturesque height that overlooks the broad fertile valley, with its gardens, cultivated fields, patches of woodland, and wide stretches of green pasture which, fringed with willows and poplars, border the swollen waters of the Loire. Where the river Brenne empties itself into the Cise the Coteau de Vouvray slopes off towards the north, and there rise up the vine-clad heights of Vernou, yielding a similar but inferior wine to that of Vouvray. The village of Vernou is nestled under the hill, and near the porch of its quaint little church a venerable elm tree is pointed out as having been planted by Sully, Henry IV.'s able Minister. Here, too, an ancient wall, pierced with curious arched windows, and forming part of a modern building, is regarded by popular tradition as belonging to the palace in which Pépin-le-Bref, father of Charlemagne, lived at Vernou.

The communes of Dampierre, Souzay, and Parnay, in the neighbourhood of Saumur, produce still red wines rivalling those of Champigny, besides which all the finest white wines are vintaged hereabouts—in the Perrière, the Poilleux, and the Clos Morain vineyards, and in the Rotissans vineyard at Turquant. Wines of very fair quality are also grown on the more favourable slopes extending southwards along the valley of the Thouet, and comprised in the communes of Varrains, Chacé, St. Cyr-en-Bourg, and Brézé. The whole of this district, by the way, abounds with interesting archæological remains. While visiting the vineyards of Varrains and Chacé we came upon a couple of dolmens—vestiges of the ancient Celtic population of the valley of the Loire singularly abundant hereabouts. Brézé, the marquisate of which formerly belonged to Louis XVI.'s famous grand master of the ceremonies—immortalized by the rebuff he received from Mirabeau— boasts a noble château on the site of an ancient fortress, in connection with which there are contemporary excavations in the neighbouring limestone, designed for a garrison of 500 or 600 men. Beyond the vineyards of Saint-Florent, westward of Saumur and on the banks of the Thouet, is an extensive plateau partially overgrown with vines, where may be traced the remains of a Roman camp. Moreover, in the southern environs of Saumur, in the midst of vineyards producing exclusively white wines, is one of the most remarkable dolmens known. This imposing structure, perfect in all respects save that one of the four enormous stones which roof it in has been split in two, and requires to be supported, is no less than 65 feet in length, 23 feet in width, and 10 feet high.

DOLMEN AT BAGNEUX, NEAR SAUMUR.

At Saint-Florent, the pleasant little suburb of Saumur, skirting the river Thouet, and sheltered by steep hills formed of soft limestone, offering great facilities for the excavation of extensive cellars, the largest manufacturer of Saumur sparkling wines has his establishment. Externally this offers but little to strike the eye. Acouple of pleasant country houses, half hidden by spreading foliage, stand at the two extremities of a spacious and well-kept garden, beyond which one catches a glimpse of some outbuildings sheltered by the vine-crowned cliff, in which a labyrinth of gloomy galleries has been hollowed out. Here M.Ackerman-Laurance, the extent of whose business ranks him as second among the sparkling wine manufacturers of the world, stores something like 10,000 casks and several million bottles of wine.

At the commencement of the present century, in the days when, as Balzac relates in his *Eugénie Grandet*, the Belgians bought up entire vintages of Saumur wine, then largely in demand with them for sacramental purposes, the founder of the Saint-Florent house commenced to deal in the ordinary still wines of the district. Nearly half a century ago he was led to attempt the manufacture of sparkling wines, but his efforts to bring them into notice failed, and he was on the point of abandoning his enterprise when an order for one hundred cases revived his hopes, and led to the foundation of the present vast establishment. As already mentioned, for many miles all the heights along the Loire have been more or less excavated for stone for building purposes, so that every one hereabouts who grows wine or deals in it has any amount of cellar accommodation ready to hand. It was the vast extent of the galleries which M.Ackerman *père* discovered already excavated at Saint-Florent that induced him to settle there in preference to Saumur. Extensive, however, as the original vaults were, considerable additional excavations have from time to time been found necessary; and to-day the firm is still further increasing the area of its cellars, which already comprise three principal avenues, each the third of a mile long, and no fewer than sixty transverse galleries, the total length of which is several miles. One great advantage is that the whole are on the ordinary level.

Ranged against the black uneven walls of the more tortuous ancient vaults which give access to these labyrinthine corridors are thousands of casks of wine—some in single rows, others in triple tiers—forming the reserve stock of the establishment. As may be supposed, apowerful vinous odour permeates these vaults, in which the fumes of wine have been accumulating for the best part of a century. After passing beneath a massive stone arch which separates the old cellars from the new, aseries of broad and regularly-proportioned galleries are reached, having bottles stacked in their tens of thousands on either side. Overhead the roof is perforated at regular intervals with circular shafts, affording both light and ventilation, and enabling the temperature to be regulated to a nicety. In these lateral and transverse galleries millions of bottles of wine in various stages of preparation are stacked.

THE CELLARS OF M. ACKERMAN-LAURANCE AT SAINT-FLORENT. LA-BELLING AND PACKING SPARKLING SAUMUR.

We have explained that in the Champagne it is the custom for the manufacturers of sparkling wine to purchase considerable quantities of grapes from the surrounding growers, and to press these themselves, or have them pressed under their own superintendence. At Saumur only those firms possessing vineyards make their own *vin brut*, the bulk of the wine used for conversion into sparkling wine being purchased from the neighbouring growers. On the newly-expressed must arriving at M.Ackerman-Laurance's cellars it is allowed to rest until the commencement of the ensuing year, when half of it is mixed with wine in stock belonging to last year's vintage, and the remaining half is reserved for mingling with the must of the ensuing vintage. The blending is accomplished in a couple of colossal vats hewn out of the rock, and coated on the inside with cement. Each of these vats is provided with 200 paddles for thoroughly mixing the wine, and with five pipes for drawing it off when the amalgamation is complete. Usually the *cuvée* will embrace 1,600 hogsheads, or 80,000 gallons of wine, almost sufficient for half a million bottles. Afourth of this quantity can be mixed in each vat at a single operation, and this mixing is repeated again and again until the last gallon run off is of precisely the same type as the first. For the finer qualities of sparkling saumur the proportion of wine from the black grapes to that from white is generally at the rate of three or four to one. For the inferior qualities more wine from white than from black grapes is invariably used. Only in the wine from white grapes is the effervescent principle retained to any particular extent; but, on the other hand, the wine from black grapes imparts both quality and vinous character to the blend.

The blending having been satisfactorily accomplished, the wine is stored in casks, never perfectly filled, yet with their bungholes tightly closed, and slowly continues its fermentation, eating up its sugar, purging itself, and letting fall its lees. Three months later it is fined. It is rarely kept in the wood for more than a year, though sometimes the superior qualities remain for a couple of years in cask. Occasionally it is even bottled in the spring following the vintage; still, as a rule, the bottling of sparkling saumur takes place during the ensuing summer months, when the temperature is at the highest as this insures to it a greater degree of effervescence. At the time of bottling its saccharine strength is raised to a given degree by the addition of the finest sugar-candy, and henceforward the wine is subjected to precisely the same treatment as is pursued with regard to champagne.

It is in a broad but sombre gallery of the more ancient vaults—the roughly-hewn walls of which are black from the combined action of alcohol and carbonic acid gas—that the processes of disgorging the wine of its sediment, adding the syrup, filling up the bottles with wine to replace that which gushes out when the disgorging operation is performed, together with the re-corking, stringing, and wiring of the bottles, are carried on. The one or two adjacent shafts impart very little light, but a couple of resplendent metal reflectors, which at a distance one might fancy to be some dragon's flaming eyes, combined with the lamps placed near the people at work, effectually illuminate the spot.

THE CELLARS OF M. LOUIS DUVAU AÎNÉ AT THE CHÂTEAU OF VAR-RAINS.

Another considerable manufacturer of sparkling saumur is M.Louis Duvau aîné, owner of the château of Varrains, in the village of the same name, at no great distance from the Coteau de Saumur. His cellars adjoin the château, apicturesque but somewhat neglected structure of the last century, with sculptured medallions in high relief above the lower windows, and florid vases surmounting the man-sards in the roof. In front is a large rambling court shaded with acacia and lime trees, and surrounded by outbuildings, prominent among which is a picturesque dovecote, massive at the base as a martello tower, and having an elegant open stone lantern springing from its bell-shaped roof. The cellars are entered down a steep incline under a low stone arch, the masonry above which is overgrown with ivy in large clusters and straggling creeping plants. We soon come upon a deep recess to the right, wherein stands a unique cumbersome screw-press, needing ten or a dozen men to work the unwieldy capstan which sets the juice flowing from the crushed grapes into the adjacent shallow trough. On our left hand are a couple of ancient reservoirs, formed out of huge blocks of stone, with the en-trance to a long vaulted cellar filled with wine in cask. We advance slowly in the uncertain light along a succession of gloomy galleries with moisture oozing from their blackened walls and roofs, picking our way between bottles of wine stacked in huge square piles and rows of casks ranged in tiers. Suddenly a broad flood of light shooting down a lofty shaft throws a Rembrandtish effect across a spacious and most melodramatic-looking cave, roughly hewn out of the rock, and towards which seven dimly-lighted galleries converge. On all sides a scene of bustling animation presents itself. From one gallery men keep arriving with baskets of wine ready for the disgorger; while along another bottles of wine duly dosed with syrup are being borne off to be decorated with metal foil and their distinctive labels. Groups of workmen are busily engaged disgorging, dosing, and re-corking the newly-arrived bottles of wine; corks fly out with a succession of loud reports suggestive of the irregular fire of a party of skirmishers; afizzing, spurting, and spluttering of the wine next ensues, and is followed by the incessant clicking of the various apparatus employed in the corking and wiring of the bottles.

Gradual inclines conduct to the two lower tiers of galleries, for the cellars of M.Duvau consist of as many as three stories. Down below there is naturally less light, and the temperature, too, is sensibly colder. Advantage is taken of this latter circumstance to remove the newly-bottled wine to these lower vaults whenever an excessive development of carbonic acid threatens the bursting of an undue proportion of bottles, acasualty which among the Saumur sparkling wine manufacturers ranges far higher than with the manufacturers of champagne. For the economy of time and labour a lift, raised and lowered by means of a capstan worked by horses, is employed to transfer the bottles of wine from one tier of cellars to another.

The demand for sparkling saumur is evidently on the increase, for M.Duvau, at the time of our visit, was excavating extensive additional cellarage. The subsoil at Varrains being largely composed of marl, which is much softer than the tufa of the Saint-Florent coteau, necessitated the roofs of the new galleries being worked in a particular form in order to avoid having recourse to either brickwork or masonry. Tons of this excavated marl were being spread over the soil of M.Duvau's vineyard in the rear of the château, greatly, it was said, to the benefit of the vines, whose grapes were all of the black variety; indeed, scarcely any wine is vintaged from white grapes in the commune of Varrains.

At M. Duvau's we went through a complete scale of sparkling saumurs, commencing with the younger and less matured samples, and ascending step by step to wines a dozen and more years old. Every year seemed to produce an improvement in the wine, the older varieties gaining greatly in delicacy and softening very perceptibly in flavour.

Another sparkling saumur manufacturer of note is M. Alfred Rousteaux, to-day the sole proprietor of the well-known brand of Morlet and Rousteaux, afirm established for many years at Saint-Florent. M.Rousteaux's cellars here are excavated in the tufa cliff which rises behind the little suburban village, and are all on one level. The galleries, though somewhat winding and irregular, are broad and roomy, and in them about 400,000 bottles of wine undergoing the necessary treatment are piled up in stacks or placed *sur pointe*. The original firm had only been in existence a few years when they found that their Saint-Florent establishment was inadequate to the requirements of a largely-increasing business, and they started the branch establishment of La Perrière at Saint-Cyr, near Tours, but on the opposite bank of the Loire. Here are a handsome residence and gardens, aspacious court, and convenient celliers where the bottling of the wine is effected, together with extensive and well-constructed cellars in which a like quantity of wine to that contained in the cellars at Saint-Florent is stored. With his finer sparkling wines M.Rousteaux mixes a certain proportion of wine from the Champagne district, and thus secures a degree of lightness unattainable when the *cuvée* is exclusively composed of Saumur vintages. At La Perrière M.Rousteaux has a vineyard of upwards of sixty acres, yielding the best wine of the district, which is noted, by the way, for its excellent growths. Hereabouts a succession of vineyard slopes stretch from one to another of the many historic châteaux along this portion of the Loire, the romantic associations of which render the Touraine one of the most interesting provinces of France. Near Tours besides the vineyards of Saint-Cyr are those of Joué and Saint-Avertin; the two last situate on the opposite bank of the Cher, where the little town of Joué, perched on the summit of a hill in the midst of vineyards, looks over a vast plain known by the country people as the Landes de Charlemagne, the scene, according to local tradition, of Charles Martel's great victory over the Saracens. The Saint-Avertin vineyards extend towards the east, stretching almost to the forest of Larçay, on the borders of the Cher, where Paul Louis Courier, the famous vigneron pamphleteer of the Restoration, noted alike for his raillery, wit, and satire, fell beneath the balls of an assassin. Anoticeable crû in the neighbourhood of Tours is that of Cinq Mars, the ruined château of which survives as a memorial of the vengeance of Cardinal Richelieu, who, after having sent its owner to the scaffold, commanded its massive walls and towers to be razed "*à hauteur d'infamie*" as we see them now.

Finding that sparkling wines were being made in most of the wine-producing districts of France, where the growths were sufficiently light and of the requisite quality, Messrs. E.Normandin and Co. conceived the idea of laying the famous Bordeaux district under contribution for a similar purpose, and, aided by a staff of experienced workmen from Epernay, they have succeeded in producing a sparkling sauternes. Sauternes, as is well known, is one of the finest of white wines, soft, delicate, and of beautiful flavour, and its transformation into a sparkling wine has been very successfully accomplished. Messrs. Normandin's head-quarters are in the thriving little town of Châteauneuf, in the pleasant valley of the Charente, and within fifteen miles of Angoulême, afamous old French town, encompassed by ancient ramparts and crumbling corner towers, and which, dominated by the lofty belfry of its restored semi-Byzantine cathedral, rising in a series of open arcades, spreads itself picturesquely out along a precipitous height, watered at its base by the rivers Anguienne and Charente. Between Angoulême and Châteauneuf vineyard plots dotted over with walnut trees, or simple rows of vines divided by strips of ripening maize, and broken up at intervals by bright green pastures, line both banks of the river Charente. The surrounding country is undulating and picturesque. Poplars and elms fringe the roadsides, divide the larger fields and vineyards, and screen the cosy-looking red-roofed farmhouses, which present to the eyes of the passing tourist a succession of pictures of quiet rural prosperity.

Châteauneuf communicates with the Sauternes district by rail, so that sup-plies of wine from there are readily obtainable. Vin de Colombar—afamous white growth which English and Dutch cruisers used to ascend the Charente to obtain cargoes of when the Jerez wines were shut out from England by the Spanish War of Succession—vintaged principally at Montignac-le-Coq, also enters largely into Messrs. Normandin and Co.'s sparkling sauternes *cuvée*. This colombar grape is simply the semillon—one of the leading varieties of the Sauternes district—trans-ported to the Charente. The remarkably cool cellars where the firm store their wine, whether in wood or bottle, have been formed from some vast subterranean galleries whence centuries ago stone was quarried, and which are situated about a quarter of an hour's drive from Châteauneuf, in the midst of vineyards and corn-fields. The wine is invariably bottled in a cellier at the head establishment, but it is in these cellars where it goes through the course of careful treatment similar to that pursued with regard to champagne.

In order that the delicate flavour of the wine may be preserved the liqueur is prepared with the finest old sauternes, without any addition of spirit, and the dose is administered with the most improved modern appliance, constructed of silver, and provided with crystal taps. At the Concours Régional d'Angoulême of 1877, the jury, after recording that they had satisfied themselves by the aid of a chemical analysis that the samples of sparkling sauternes submitted to their judgment were free from any foreign ingredient, awarded to Messrs. Normandin and Co. the only gold medal given in the Group of Alimentary Products.

Encouraged, no doubt, by the success obtained by Messrs. Normandin and Co. with their sparkling sauternes, the house of Lermat-Robert and Co., of Bordeaux, have recently introduced a sparkling barsac, samples of which were submitted to the jury at the Paris Exhibition of 1878.

CHAPTER XIV.

THE SPARKLING WINES OF BURGUNDY AND THE JURA.

Sparkling Wines of the Côte d'Or at the Paris Exhibition—Chambertin, Romanée, and Vougeot—Burgundy Wines and Vines formerly the Presents of Princes—Vintaging Sparkling Burgundies—Their After-Treatment in the Cellars—Excess of Breakage—Similarity of Proceeding to that followed in the Champagne—Principal Manufacturers of Sparkling Burgundies—Sparkling Wines of Tonnerre, the birthplace of the Chevalier d'Eon—The Vin d'Arbanne of Bar-sur-Aube—Death there of the Bastard de Bourbon—Madame de la Motte's Ostentatious Display and Arrest there—Sparkling Wines of the Beaujolais—The Mont-Brouilly Vineyards—Ancient Reputation of the Wines of the Jura—The Vin Jaune of Arbois beloved of Henri Quatre—Rhymes by him in its Honour—Lons-le-Saulnier—Vineyards yielding the Sparkling Jura Wines—Their Vintaging and Subsequent Treatment—Their High Alcoholic Strength and General Drawbacks.

Sparkling wines are made to a considerable extent in Burgundy, notably at

Beaune, Nuits, and Dijon, and though as a rule heavier and more potent than the subtile and delicate-flavoured wines of the Marne, still some of the higher qualities, both of the red and white varieties, exhibit a degree of refinement which those familiar only with the commoner kinds can scarcely form an idea of. At the Paris Exhibition of 1878 we tasted, among a large collection of the sparkling wines of the Côte d'Or, samples of Chambertin, Romanée, and Vougeot of the highest order. Although red wines, they had the merit of being deficient in that body which forms such an objectionable feature in sparkling wines of a deep shade of colour. M.Regnier, the exhibitor of sparkling red vougeot, sent, moreover, awhite sparkling wine from the species of grape known locally as the clos blanc de Vougeot. These wines, as well as the Chambertin, came from the Côte de Nuits, the growths of which are generally considered of too vigorous a type for successful conversion into sparkling wine, preference being usually given to the produce of the Côte de Beaune. Among the sparkling burgundies from the last-named district were samples from Savigny, Chassagne, and Meursault, all famous for their fine white wines.

Burgundy ranks as one of the oldest viticultural regions of Central Europe, and for centuries its wines have been held in the highest renown. In the Middle Ages both the wines and vines of this favoured province passed as presents from one royal personage to another, just as grand *cordons* are exchanged between them now-a-days. The fabrication of sparkling wine, however, dates no further back than some sixty years or so. The system of procedure is much the same as in the Champagne, and, as there, the wine is mainly the produce of the pineau noir and pineau blanc varieties of grape. At the vintage, in order to avoid bruising the ripened fruit and to guard against premature fermentation, the grapes are conveyed to the pressoirs in baskets instead of the large oval vats termed *balonges*, common to the district. They are placed beneath the press as soon as possible, and for superior sparkling wines only the juice resulting from the first pressure and known as the *mère goutte*, or mother drop, is employed. For the ordinary wines that expressed at the second squeezing of the fruit is mingled with the other. The must is at once run off into casks which have been previously sulphured to check, in a measure, the ardour of the first fermentation and lighten the colour of the newly-made wine. Towards the end of October, when this first fermentation is over, the wine is removed to the cellars, or to some other cool place, and in December it is racked into other casks. In the April following it is again racked to insure its being perfectly clear at the epoch of bottling in the month of May. The sulphuring of the original casks having had the effect of slightly checking the fermentation and retaining a certain amount of saccharine in the wine, it is only on exceptional occasions that the latter is artificially sweetened previous to being bottled.

A fortnight after the tirage the wine commonly attains the stage known as *grand mousseux*, and by the end of September the breakage will have amounted to between 5 and 8 per cent., which necessitates the taking down the stacks of bottles and piling them up anew. The wine as a rule remains in the cellars for fully a couple of years from the time of bottling until it is shipped. Posing the bottles *sur pointe*, agitating them daily, together with the disgorging and liqueuring of the wine, is accomplished precisely as in the Champagne.

Among the principal manufacturers of sparkling burgundies are Messrs. André and Voillot, of Beaune, whose sparkling white Romanée, Nuits, and Volnay are well and favourably known in England; M.Louis Latour, also of Beaune, and equally noted for his sparkling red Volnay, Nuits, and Chambertin, as for his sparkling white varieties; Messrs. Maire et fils, likewise of Beaune; M.Labouré-Goutard and Messrs. Geisweiller et fils, of Nuits; Messrs. Marey and Liger-Belair, of Nuits and Vôsne; and M.Regnier, of Dijon.

In the department of the Yonne—that is, in Lower Burgundy—sparkling wines somewhat alcoholic in character have been made for the last half-century at Tonnerre, where the Chevalier d'Eon, that enigma of his epoch, was born. The Tonnerre vineyards are of high antiquity, and for sparkling wines the produce of the black and white pineau and the white morillon varieties of grape is had recourse to. The vintaging is accomplished with great care, and only the juice which flows from the first pressure is employed. This is run off immediately into casks which are hermetically closed when the fermentation has subsided. The after-treatment of the wine is the same as in the Champagne. Sparkling wines are likewise made at Epineuil, avillage in the neighbourhood of Tonnerre, and at Chablis, so famous for its white wines, about ten miles distant.

An effervescing wine known as the Vin d'Arbanne is made at Bar-sur-Aube, some fifty miles north-east of Tonnerre, on the borders of Burgundy, but actually in the province of Champagne, although far beyond the limits to which the famed viticultural district extends. It was at Bar-sur-Aube where the Bastard de Bourbon, chief of the sanguinary gang of *écorcheurs* (flayers), was sewn up in a sack and flung over the parapet of the old stone bridge into the river beneath by order of Charles VII.; and here, too, Madame de la Motte, of Diamond Necklace notoriety, was married, and in after years made a parade of the ill-gotten wealth she had acquired by successfully fooling that infatuated libertine the Cardinal Prince de Rohan, until her ostentatious display was cut short by her arrest. This Vin d'Arbanne is produced from pineaux and white gamay grapes, which, after being gathered with care at the moment the dew falls, are forthwith pressed. The wine is left on its lees until the following February, when it is racked and fined, the bottling taking place when the moon is at the full in March.

Red and white sparkling wines are made to a small extent at Saint-Lager, in the Beaujolais, from wine vintaged in the Mont-Brouilly vineyards, one of the best known of the Beaujolais crûs. Mont-Brouilly is a lofty hill near the village of Cercie, and is covered from base to summit on all its sides with vines of the gamay species, rarely trained at all, but left to trail along the ground at their own sweet will. At the vintage, as we witnessed it, men and women—young, middle-aged, and old—accompanied by troops of children, were roaming all over the slopes dexterously nipping off the bunches of grapes with their thumb and finger nails and flinging them into the little wooden tubs with which they were provided. The pressing of the grapes and the after-treatment of the wine destined to become sparkling are the same in the Beaujolais as in Upper and Lower Burgundy.

The red, straw, and yellow wines of the Jura have long had a high reputation in the East of France, and the *vin jaune* of Arbois, an ancient fortified town on the banks of the Cuisance, besieged and sacked in turn by Charles of Amboise, Henri IV., and Louis XIV., was one of the favourite beverages of the tippling Béarnais who styled himself Seigneur of Ay and Gonesse, and who acquired his liking for it while sojourning during the siege of Arbois at the old Château des Arsures. In one of Henri Quatre's letters to his minister Sully we find him observing, "Isend you two bottles of Vin d'Arbois, for I know you do not detest it." Acouple of other bottles of the same wine are said to have cemented the king's reconciliation with Mayenne, the leader of the League, and the lover of La Belle Gabrielle is moreover credited with having composed at his mistress's table some doggrel rhymes in honour of the famous Jura crû:—

> "Come, little page, serve us aright,
> The crown is often heavy to bear;
> So fill up my goblet large and light
> Whenever you find a vacancy there.
> This wine is surely no Christian wight,
> And yet you never complaint will hear
> That it's not baptised with water clear.
>
> Down my throat I pour
> The old Arbois;
>
> And now, my lords, let us our voices raise,
> And sing of Silenus and Bacchus the praise!"

In more modern times the Jura, not content with the fame of the historic yellow wines of Arbois and the deservedly-esteemed straw wines of Château-Châlon, has produced large quantities of sparkling wine, the original manufacture of which commenced as far back as a century ago. To-day the principal seats of the manufacture are at Arbois and Lons-le-Saulnier, the latter town the capital of the department and one of the most ancient towns of France. Originally founded by the Gauls on the banks of the Vallière, in a little valley bordered by lofty hills, which are to-day covered with vines, it was girded round with fortifications by the Romans. Subsequently the Huns and the Vandals pillaged it; then the French and the Burgundians repeatedly contested its possession, and it was only definitively acquired by France during the reign of Louis XIV. Rouget de l'Isle, the famous author of the "Marseillaise," was born at Lons-le-Saulnier, and here also Marshal Ney assembled and harangued his troops before marching to join Napoleon, whom he had promised Louis XVIII. to bring back to Paris in an iron cage.

The vineyards whence the principal supplies for these sparkling wines are derived are grouped at varying distances around Lons-le-Saulnier at L'Etoile, Quintigny, Salins, Arbois, St. Laurent-la-Roche, and Pupillin, with the Jura chain of mountains rising up grandly on the east. The best vineyards at L'Etoile—which lies some couple of miles from Lons-le-Saulnier, surrounded by hills, planted from base to summit with vines—are La Vigne Blanche, Montmorin, and Montgenest. At Quintigny, the wines of which are less potent than those of Arbois, and only retain their effervescent properties for a couple of years, the Paridis, Prémelan, and Montmorin vineyards are held in most repute, while at Pupillin, where a soft agreeable wine is vintaged, the principal vineyards are the Faille and the Clos. The vine cultivated for the production of sparkling wines are chiefly the savagnin, or white pineau, the melon of Poligny, and the poulsard, ablack variety of grape held locally in much esteem.

At the vintage, which commences towards the end of October and lasts until the middle of the following month, all the rotten or unripe grapes are carefully set aside and the sound ones only submitted to the action of a screw-press. After the must has flowed for about half-an-hour the grapes are newly collected under the press and the screw again applied. The produce of this double operation is poured into a vat termed a *sapine*, where it remains until bubbles are seen escaping through the *chapeau* that forms on the surface of the liquid. The must is then drawn off—sometimes after being fined—into casks, which the majority of wine-growers previously impregnate with the fumes of sulphur. When in cask the wine is treated in one of two ways; either the casks are kept constantly filled to the bunghole, causing the foam which rises to the surface during the fermentation to flow over, and thereby leave the wine comparatively clear, or else the casks are not completely filled, in which case the wine requires to be racked several times before it is in a condition for fining. This latter operation is effected about the commencement of February, and a second fining follows if the first one fails to render the wine perfectly clear. At the tirage, which invariably takes place in April, the Jura wines rarely require any addition of sugar to insure an ample effervescence. After bottling they are treated in exactly the same manner as the vintages of the Marne are treated by the great champagne manufacturers. In addition to white sparkling wine a pink variety, with natural effervescent properties, is made by mixing with the savagnin and melon grapes a certain proportion of the poulsard species, from which the best red wines of the Jura are produced.

One of the principal sparkling wine establishments at Lons-le-Saulnier is that of M.Auguste Devaux, founded in the year 1860. He manufactures both sweet and dry wines, which are sold largely in France and elsewhere on the Continent, and have lately been introduced into England. Their alcoholic strength is equivalent to from 25° to 26° of proof spirit, being largely above the dry sparkling wines of the Champagne, which the Jura manufacturers regard as a positive advantage rather than an obvious drawback. M.Devaux's principal brand is the Fleur de l'Etoile, of which, he has white, pink, and amber-coloured varieties, quoted by him at merely three francs the bottle for the grand years.

Besides being too spirituous, the sparkling wines of the Jura are deficient in refinement and delicacy. The commoner kinds, indeed, frequently have a pronounced unpleasant flavour, due to the nature of the soil, to careless vinification, or to the inferior quality of liqueur with which the wines have been dosed. Out of some fifty samples of all ages and varieties which in my capacity of juror I tasted at the Paris Exhibition I cannot call to mind one that a real connoisseur of sparkling wines would care to admit to his table.

CONVEYING GRAPES TO THE PRESS AT SAINT-PÉRAY.

CHAPTER XV.

THE SPARKLING WINES OF THE SOUTH OF FRANCE.

Sparkling Wines of Auvergne, Guienne, Dauphiné, and Langued-oc—Sparkling Saint-Péray the Champagne of the South—Valence with its Reminiscences of Pius VI. and NapoleonI.—The "Horns of Crussol" on the Banks of the Rhône—Vintage Scene at Saint-Péray—The Vines and Vineyards Producing Sparkling Wine—Manipulation of Sparkling Saint-Péray—Its Abundance of Natural Sugar—The Cellars of M.de Saint-Prix and Samples of his Wines—Sparkling Côte-Rotie, Château-Grille, and Hermitage—Annual Production and Principal Markets of Sparkling Saint-Péray—Clairette de Die—The Porte Rouge of Die Cathedral—How the Die Wine is Made—The Sparkling White and Rose-Coloured Muscatels of Die—Sparkling Wines of Vercheny and Lagrasse—Barnave and the Royal Flight to Varennes—Narbonne formerly a Miniature Rome, now Noted merely for its Wine and Honey—Fête of the Black Virgin at Limoux—Preference given to the New Wine over the Miraculous Water—Blanquette of Limoux and How it is Made—Characteristics of this Overrated Wine.

Sparkling wines are made after a fashion in several of the southern provinces of France—in Auvergne, at Clermont-Ferrand, under the shadow of the lofty Puy de Dôme; in Guienne, at Astaffort, the scene of a bloody engagement during the Wars of Religion in which the Protestant army was cut to pieces when about to cross the Garonne; at Nérac, where frail Marguerite de Valois kept her dissolute Court, and Catherine de Médicis brought her flying squadron of fascinating maids of honour to gain over the Huguenot leaders to the Catholic cause; and at Cahors, the Divina, or divine fountain of the Celts, and the birthplace of Pope John XXII., of Clement Marot, the early French poet, and of Léon Gambetta; in Dauphiné, at Die, Saint-Chef, Saint-Péray, and Largentière, so named after some abandoned silver mines, and where the vines are cultivated against low walls rising in a series of terraces from the base to the summit of the lofty hills; and in Languedoc, at Brioude, where St. Vincent, the patron saint of the vinedressers, suffered martyrdom, and where it is the practice to expose the must of the future sparkling wine for several nights to the dew in order to rid it of its reddish colour; also at Linardie, and, more southward still, at Limoux, whence comes the well-known effervescing Blanquette.

Principal among the foregoing is the excellent wine of Saint-Péray, commonly characterised as the champagne of the South of France. The Saint-Péray vineyards border the Rhône some ten miles below the Hermitage coteau—the vines of which are to-day well-nigh destroyed by the phylloxera—but are on the opposite bank of the river. Our visit to Saint-Péray was made from Valence, in which dull southern city we had loitered in order to glance at the vast Hôtel du Gouvernement—where octogenarian Pius VI., after being spirited away a prisoner from Rome and hurried over the Alps in a litter by order of the French Directory, drew his last breath while silently gazing across the rushing river at the view he so much admired—and to discover the house in the Grande Rue, numbered4, in an attic of which history records that NapoleonI., when a sub-lieutenant of artillery in garrison at Valence, resided, and which he quitted owing three and a-half francs to his pastrycook.

We crossed the Rhône over one of its hundred flimsy suspension bridges, on the majority of which a notice warns you neither to smoke nor run, and were soon skirting the base of a lofty, bare, precipitous rock, with the "horns of Crussol," as the peasants term two tall pointed gables of a ruined feudal château, perched at the dizzy edge, and having a perpendicular fall of some five or six hundred feet below. The château, which formerly belonged to the Dukes of Uzès, recognised by virtue of the extent of their domains as *premiers pairs de France*, was not originally erected in close proximity to any such formidable precipice. The crag on which it stands had, it seems, been blasted from time to time for the sake of the stone, until on one unlucky occasion when too heavy a charge of powder was employed, the entire side of the rock, together with a considerable portion of the château itself, were sent flying into the air. The authorities, professing to regard what remained of the edifice as an historical monument of the Middle Ages, hereupon stepped in and prohibited the quarry being worked for the future.

Passing beneath the cliff, one wound round to the left and dived into a picturesque wooded dell at the entrance to a mountain pass, then crossed the rocky bed of a dried-up stream and drove along an avenue of mulberry-trees, which in a few minutes conducted us to Saint-Péray, where one found the vintage in full operation. Carts laden with tubs filled with white and purple grapes, around which wasps without number swarmed, were arriving from all points of the environs and crowding the narrow streets. Any quantity of grapes were seemingly to be had for the asking, for all the pretty girls in the place were gorging themselves with the luscious-looking fruit. In the coopers' yards bran-new casks were ranged in rows in readiness for the newly-made wine, and through open doorways, and in all manner of dim recesses, one caught sight of sturdy men energetically trampling the gushing grapes under their bare feet, and of huge creaking wine-presses reeking with the purple juice. It was chiefly common red wine, of an excellent flavour, however, that was being made in these nooks and corners, the sparkling white wine, known as Saint-Péray, being manufactured in larger establishments, and on more scientific principles. It is from a white species of grape known as the petite and grosse rousette—the same which yields the white Hermitage—that the champagne of the south is produced, and the vineyards where they are cultivated occupy all the more favourable slopes immediately outside the village, the most noted being the Coteau-Gaillard, Solignaes, Thioulet, and Hungary.

Although there is a close similarity between the manufacture of champagne and the effervescing wine of Saint-Péray, there are still one or two noteworthy variations. For a wine to be sparkling it is requisite that it should ferment in the bottle, aresult obtained by bottling it while it contains a certain undeveloped proportion of alcohol and carbonic acid, represented by so much sugar, of which they are the component parts. This ingredient has frequently to be added to the Champagne wines to render them sparkling, but the wine of Saint-Péray in its natural state contains so much sugar that any addition would be deleterious. This excess of saccharine enables the manufacturer to dispense with some of the operations necessary to the fabrication of champagne, which, after fermenting in the cask, requires a second fermentation to be provoked in the bottle, whereas the Saint-Péray wine ferments only once, being bottled immediately it comes from the wine-press.

The deposit in the wine after being impelled towards the neck of the bottle is got rid of by following the same system as is pursued in the Champagne, but no liqueur whatever is subsequently added to the wine. On the other hand, it is a common practice to reduce the over-sweetness of sparkling Saint-Péray in years when the grapes are more than usually ripe by mixing with it some old dry white wine.

At Saint-Péray we visited the cellars of M. de Saint-Prix, one of the principal wine-growers of the district. The samples of effervescing wine which he produced for us to taste were of a pale golden colour, of a slightly nutty flavour, and with a decided suggestion of the spirituous essence known to be concentrated in the wine, one glass of which will go quite as far towards elevating a person as three glasses of champagne. Keeping the wine for a few years is said materially to improve its quality, to the sacrifice, however, of its effervescent properties. M.de Saint-Prix informed us that he manufactured every year a certain quantity of sparkling Côte-Rotie, Château-Grillé, and Hermitage. The principal markets for the Saint-Péray sparkling wines—the production of which falls considerably short of a million bottles per annum—are England, Germany, Russia, Holland, and Belgium.

The other side of the Rhône is fruitful in minor sparkling wines, chief amongst which is the so-called Clairette de Die, made at the town of that name, aplace of some splendour, as existing antiquities show, in the days of the Roman dominion in Gaul. Later on, Die was the scene of constant struggles for supremacy between its counts and bishops, one of the latter having been massacred by the populace in front of the cathedral doorway—ever since known by the sinister appellation of the Porte Rouge—and Catholics and Huguenots alike devastated the town in the troublesome times of the Reform. Clairette de Die is made principally from the blanquette or malvoisie variety of grape, which, after the stalks have been removed, is both trodden with the feet and pressed. The must is run off immediately into casks, and four-and-twenty hours later it is racked into other casks, asimilar operation being performed every two or three days for the period of a couple of months, when the fermentation having subsided the wine is fined and usually bottled in the following March. Newly-made Clairette de Die is a sweet sparkling wine, but it loses its natural effervescence after a couple of years, unless it has been treated in the same manner as champagne, which is rarely the case. The wine enjoys a reputation altogether beyond its merits.

In addition to the well-known Clairette, some of the wine-growers of Die make sparkling white and rose-coloured muscatels of superior quality, which retain their effervescent properties for several years. Asparkling wine is also made some ten miles from Die, on the road to Saillans, in a district bounded on the one side by the waters of the Drôme, and on the other by strange mountains with helmet-shaped crests. The centre of production is a locality called Vercheny, composed of several hamlets, one of which, named Le Temple, was the original home of the family of Barnave. The impressionable young deputy to the National Assembly formed one of the trio sent to bring back the French royal family from Varennes after their flight from Paris. It will be remembered how, under the influence of Marie Antoinette and Madame Elizabeth, Barnave became transformed during the journey into a faithful partisan of their unhappy cause, and that he eventually paid the penalty of his devotion with his life.

In the extreme south of France, and almost under the shadow of the Pyrenees, asparkling wine of some repute is made at a place called Lagrasse, about five-and-twenty miles westward of Narbonne, the once-famous Mediterranean city, the maritime rival of Marseilles, and in its palmy days, prior to the Christian era, aminiature Rome, with its capitol, its curia, its decemvirs, its consuls, its prætors, its questors, its censors, and its ediles, and which boasted of being the birthplace of three Roman Emperors. To-day Narbonne has to content itself with the humble renown derived from its delicious honey and its characterless full-bodied red wines. Limoux, so celebrated for its Blanquette, lies a long way farther to the west, behind the Corbières range of mountains that join on to the Pyrenees, and the jagged peaks, deep barren gorges, and scarred sides of which have been witness of many a desperate struggle during the century and a half when they formed the boundary between France and Spain.

We arrived at Limoux just too late for the famous fête of the Black Virgin, which lasts three weeks, and attracts crowds of southern pilgrims to the chapel of Our Lady of Marseilles, perched on a little hill some short distance from the town, with a fountain half-way up it, whose water issues drop by drop, and has the credit of possessing unheard-of virtues. The majority of pilgrims, however, exhibit a decided preference for the new-made wine over the miraculous water, and for one-and-twenty days something like a carnival of inebriety prevails at Limoux.

Blanquette de Limoux derives its name from the species of grape it is produced from, and which we believe to be identical with the malvoisie, or malmsey. Its long-shaped berries grow in huge bunches, and dry readily on the stalks. The fruit is gathered as tenderly as possible, care being taken that it shall not be in the slightest degree bruised, after which it is spread out upon a floor to admit of the sugar it contains becoming perfect. The bad grapes having been carefully picked out, and the pips extracted from the remaining fruit, the latter is now trodden, when the must, after being filtered through a strainer, is placed in casks, where it remains fermenting for about a week, during which time any overflow is daily replenished by other must reserved for the purpose. The wine is again clarified and placed in fresh casks with the bungholes only lightly closed until all sensible fermentation has ceased, when they are securely fastened up. The bottling takes place in the month of March, and the wine is subsequently treated much after the same fashion as sparkling Saint-Péray, excepting that it is generally found necessary to repeat the operation of *dégorgement* three, if not as many as four times.

Blanquette de Limoux is a pale white wine, the saccharine properties of which have become completely transformed into carbonic acid gas and alcohol. It is, consequently, both dry and spirituous, deficient in delicacy, and altogether proves a great disappointment. At its best it may, perhaps, rank with sparkling Saint-Péray, but unquestionably not with any average champagne.

CHAPTER XVI.

THE SPARKLING WINES OF GERMANY.

Origin of Sparkling Hock and Moselle—Sparkling German Wines
First Made on the Neckar—Heilbronn, and Gotz von Berlichingen of the Iron Hand—Lauteren of Mayence and Rambs of Trèves
turn their attention to Sparkling Wines—Change of late years in
the Character of Sparkling Hocks and Moselles—Difference be-
tween them and Moussirender Rheinwein—Vintaging of Black
and White Grapes for Sparkling Wine—The Treatment which
German Sparkling Wines Undergo—Artificial Flavouring and
Perfuming of Sparkling Moselles—Fine Natural Bouquet of High
Class Sparkling Hocks—Impetus given to the Manufacture of
German Sparkling Wines during the Franco-German War—An-
nual Production—Deinhard and Co.'s Splendid New Cellars at
Coblenz—The Firm's Collection of Choice Rhine and Moselle
Wines—Their Trade in German Sparkling Wines—Their Sources
of Supply—The Vintaging and After-Treatment of their Wines—
Characteristics of their Sparkling Hocks and Moselles.

The reader is by this time aware that sparkling wines are not indebted for their
effervescent properties to any particular variety of vine or quality of soil, although

some species of grapes yield a wine possessing a higher degree of effervescence than others. Any wine, in fact, can be rendered sparkling, although only wines of a certain lightness of body and which are at the same time delicate and clean to the taste—being devoid of anything approaching to a *goût de terroir*—are really suited to the purpose. Given a wine containing sufficient saccharine, either natural or applied, and duly regulate its temperature, and it is easy enough to render it sparkling. The Germans discovered this long ago when they first transformed the acidulous wines of the Rhine into what we term sparkling hocks.

The rise of this industry dates from the epoch of the final downfall of NapoleonI., when the officers of the armies of occupation acquired more than a passing liking for the exhilarating products of Clicquot and Moët, carrying it, in fact, home with them, and so disseminating a taste for the sparkling wines of France throughout the North of Europe. In Germany the wealthy few only were able to indulge in it, and the consumption was for a long time exceedingly limited. When, however, after many years of peace, riches began to accumulate, some shrewd men set themselves to ascertain whether the German wines could not be rendered sparkling like the French. This was satisfactorily and speedily settled in the affirmative; but the great difficulty was to find the requisite capital for the large preliminary investment necessary to the establishment of a manufactory of sparkling wine on even a moderate scale, and from which no return could be counted on for the first three years. Eventually this was overcome; but the new wines, being in the first instance altogether different in character from champagne, found but little favour in the country of their production. It was different, however, in England, where they speedily succeeded in establishing themselves under the designations of sparkling hock and sparkling moselle, and from this time forward they have retained their position in the English market.

It is generally asserted that sparkling wines were first manufactured in Germany more than half a century ago from the inferior Neckar grape both at Esslingen and Heilbronn—the latter rendered memorable by the exploits of Götz von Berlichingen, whose iron hand distributed blows which effectually "cured headache, toothache, and every other human malady." Subsequently, towards 1830, aformer *chef de cave* at Madame Clicquot's establishment at Reims came to Herr Lauteren, of Mayence, and suggested to him to engage in the manufacture of sparkling Rhine wines, aproposal which the latter soon afterwards profited by; and eight years later Herr Rambs, of Trèves, vineyard proprietor and wine-merchant, aided by a French cellarman, made the earliest attempt to manufacture sparkling moselles, their first trials in this direction resulting in a breakage amounting to fifty per cent.

For some years the great anxiety of manufacturers of sparkling hocks was to render their wines as much as possible like champagne, which was only to be accomplished by disguising their true flavour and dosing them largely with syrup. In this form they satisfied, and indeed still satisfy, their German and Russian consumers; but of late years England has set the example of a decided preference for the drier kinds of sparkling wines, the result being that the character of the wines destined for the English market has undergone a complete change.

THE AHR VALLEY.

Next to its sweetness the principal difference between German champagne, or Moussirender Rheinwein as it is usually called, for Continental consumption, and sparkling hocks designed for the English and other markets, consists in the former being made principally from black grapes, pressed immediately they are gathered and not allowed to ferment in their skins, while the latter are made almost exclusively from white grapes. The vineyards yielding the black grapes used for these sparkling wines are mainly situated at Ingelheim, midway between Bingen and Mayence, and in the Ahr valley, between Coblenz and Cologne. At the black grape vintage, which precedes the gathering of the white varieties by some three or four weeks, the fruit is conveyed to the press in high tubs, carried on men's backs, and holding about 40lbs. apiece. The old wooden presses are mostly employed, although of late small transportable presses with iron screws, and of French manufacture, are coming into use. In order that the wine may be pale in colour, the grapes, which, like those of the Champagne, are of the pineau variety, are pressed as soon as possible after the gathering; the pressure applied is, moreover, rapid and not too strong, and the must is separated forthwith from the skins and stalks. On the other hand, the white grapes used in the making of German sparkling wine, and which are almost exclusively of the far-famed riesling species, are treated precisely as when making still Rhine wine—that is, they are crushed in the vineyards by means of grape-mills, and afterwards pressed in the usual way. The must for sparkling wines, whether from black or white grapes, is run at once into casks to ferment. If possible it is conveyed in large casks known as stucks—immediately after the pressing, and before fermentation begins—to the manufacturer's cellars in town; but if this cannot be accomplished it remains in the cellars of the district until the first fermentation is over, which is in December or January. It is then racked off its lees, and the produce of black and white grapes is blended together, only a small proportion of the former entering into the composition of true sparkling hock, which should retain in a marked degree the subtile and fragrant perfume of the riesling grape.

The process pursued in the manufacture of sparkling hocks is the same as that followed with regard to champagnes. The quantity of grape sugar generated in these Northern German latitudes being far from large, both hocks and moselles invariably need a small addition of saccharine, previous to their being put into bottle, to insure the requisite effervescence, whereas in the Champagne the practice of adding sugar with this object is not the uniform rule. After the wine is bottled it remains in a cool cellar for eighteen months or a couple of years, being constantly shaken during this period, in the same way as champagne, in order to force the sediment to deposit itself near to the cork. By this time the added as well as the natural sugar contained in the wine has become converted into alcohol and carbonic acid; and after the sediment has been expelled from the bottle the operation of dosing, or flavouring, the wine takes place.

Sparkling hocks intended both for the German and Russian markets are frequently almost cloying in their sweetness, as much as one-fifth of syrup being often added to four-fifths of wine. The sparkling moselles, too, for Russia, and not unfrequently for England also, are largely dosed with the preparation of elder-flowers, which imparts to them their well-known muscatel flavour and perfume. The manufacturers say they are doing their best to abandon this absurd practice of artificially perfuming sparkling moselles; but many of their customers, and especially those in the English provinces, stipulate for the scented varieties, possibly from an erroneous belief in their superiority. Effervescing Rhine wines of the highest class have a marked and refined flavour, together with a very decided natural bouquet. Moreover, they retain their effervescent properties for a considerable time after being uncorked, and appear to the taste as light, if not precisely as delicate, as the finer champagnes, although in reality such is not the case; for all sparkling hocks possess greater body than even the heaviest champagnes, and cannot, therefore, be drunk with equal freedom.

Great impetus was given to the manufacture of German sparkling wines during the war of 1870, when the Champagne was in a measure closed to the outside world. At this epoch the less scrupulous manufacturers, instigated by dishonest speculators, boldly forged both the brands on the corks and the labels on the bottles of the great Reims and Epernay firms, and sent forth sparkling wines of their own production to the four quarters of the globe as veritable champagnes of the highest class. The respectable houses acted more honestly, and, as it turned out, with better policy, for by maintaining their own labels and brands they extended the market for their produce, causing German sparkling wines to be introduced under their true names into places where they had never penetrated before, the result being a considerable increase in the annual demand, even after the stores of the champagne manufacturers were again open to all the world.

Owing to this increased demand, and the deficient supply of suitable Rhine wines at a moderate price, the manufacturers of sparkling hocks are reduced to buy much of their raw wine at a distance, and are to-day large purchasers of the growths of the Palatinate, which are less delicate than the vintages of the Rheingau, besides being deficient in that fine aroma which distinguishes genuine hock. Aleading manufacturer computes that between four-and-a-half and five million bottles of sparkling wine are made annually in Germany, where there are no fewer than fifty manufacturing establishments. The principal market is Great Britain, which consumes some two millions of bottles annually; amillion bottles are drunk at home; while the remainder is divided among the North of Europe, the United States, India, Australia, China, and Japan. The cheapness of these wines is, no doubt, largely in their favour.

MESSRS. DEINHARD & CO.'S NEW ESTABLISHMENT AT COBLENZ.

At Coblenz, the capital of Rhenish Prussia, and one of the strongest fortresses in the world, the so-called blue Moselle mingles its waters with those of the Rhine, and hence the original Roman name of Confluentia. With so favourable a situation it is not surprising that the city should be the abode of several important firms trading in the wines of the two rivers. At the head of these is the well-known house of Deinhard and Co., dealing extensively both in the magnificent still vintages of the Rheingau and the Moselle, and the higher-class sparkling wines of these districts. In the resident partner, Herr Julius Wegeler, Iwas pleased to meet again my courteous colleague of the Wine Jury of the Vienna Exhibition, and accompanied by him I went over their establishment on the Clemens Platz—one of the most perfect and admirably appointed in Germany. The firm was founded in 1798 by Herr F.Deinhard, who in 1806, when Coblenz was in the hands of the French, secured a ninety-nine years' lease of some cellars under an old convent at the low rental of 30 francs per annum, and to-day this curious document exists amongst the archives of the firm. Rents of wine-cellars were low enough in those days of uncertainty and peril, when commerce was at a standstill and Europe gazed panic-stricken on the course of warlike events; nevertheless, for such a trifle as 30 francs a year of course no very extensive entrepôt could have been rented. To-day Messrs. Deinhard's new cellars on the Clemens Platz alone cover an area of nearly 43,000 square feet, besides which they have several other vaults stored with wine in various quarters of the city, the whole giving employment to upwards of eighty workmen and a score of coopers. Their Clemens Platz establishment was only completed in the autumn of 1875, when it was formally inaugurated in presence of the Empress Augusta, who left behind her the following graceful memento of her visit:—

"In grateful attachment to Coblenz, in full appreciation of a work which does honour to the town and to the firm, Iwish continued prosperity to both.

Augusta,
"German Empress and Queen of Prussia."

MESSRS. DEINHARD & CO.'S NEW CELLARS AT COBLENZ.

The proximity of the establishment to the Rhine did not allow of the cellars being excavated to a greater depth than 30 feet below the surface—amere trifle when compared with the depth of many vaults in the Champagne. Any lower excavation, however, would have been attended with danger, and as it is, when the Rhine rose to an unusual height in March, 1876, the water percolated through the soil and inundated the lower cellars to a height of 5feet. Above these vaults is a corresponding range of buildings of picturesque design and substantial construction, divided like the cellars into three aisles, each 210 feet in length and 23 feet broad. One of the arches of the façade looking on to the courtyard is decorated with a graceful and characteristic bas-relief, an engraving of which is subjoined.

The cellars, containing 1,400 stucks, as they are termed, of still wines—the stuck being equal to 1,500 bottles—present a striking appearance with their long vistas of vaulted arcades, admirably built of brick, and illuminated by innumerable gas jets, aided by powerful reflectors at the extremities of the three aisles. The capacious elliptical-headed casks, ranged side by side in uninterrupted sequence, contain the choicest German vintages, including the grand wines of the Rheingau—Johannisberger, Steinberger, Rudesheimer, Rauenthaler, and the like; the red growths of Assmannshausen and Walporzheim; Deidesheimers, with rare bouquets and of tender tonical flavour; Liebfrauenmilch, of flowery perfume; the finest Moselles from Josefshof and Scharzhofberg, Brauneberg and Berncastel, with other growths too numerous to mention, of grand years, and from the best situations.

The sparkling wines stored in separate vaults form to-day an important item in Messrs. Deinhard's business. In 1843 the firm made their first cuvée, consisting of less than 10,000 bottles. Four years later their cuvée amounted to over 50,000 bottles. A falling off was shown during the revolutionary epoch, and business only recovered its normal condition in 1851, since which time it has gradually increased as the wines have grown in favour, until in 1875 the tirage of 1874 vintage wines exceeded half a million bottles.

VINEYARDS IN THE AHR VALLEY.

Messrs. Deinhard draw their supplies of wine from white grapes, for conversion into sparkling wines, from the Rhine, the Main, the Moselle, and the Palatinate, giving preference to the produce of the riesling grape, as to this the wine is indebted for its natural bouquet. The proportion of wine from black grapes, mingled with the other wines, is vintaged by themselves in the Ahr valley and at Ingelheim on the Rhine. The Ahr, in summer a rippling streamlet and in winter a rushing torrent, falls into the Rhine about twenty miles below Coblenz. The soil of the neighbouring hills seems peculiarly adapted for the growth of black grapes, one of the best of German red wines being produced in the vineyards adjacent to the village of Walporzheim. In order that the wine may be as pale as possible, the black grapes are pressed as soon after gathering as they can be, and only the juice resulting from the first pressure is reserved, the subsequently extracted must being sold to the small growers of the neighbourhood. The newly-made wine is brought in casks to Coblenz, and rests for eight weeks while completing its fermentation. It is then racked into stucks and double stucks, and is blended in casks of the latter capacity during the early part of the following year, great care being taken to preserve the bouquet of the white grapes, with which view, contrary to the practice followed in the Champagne, only a moderate proportion of wine from black grapes enters into the blend.

ON THE BRIDGE AT RECH, AHR VALLEY.

Next comes the fining, and four weeks afterwards the wine is newly racked. The bottling takes place during May or June, when any deficiency of natural saccharine in the wine is supplied by the addition of pure sugar-candy. At Messrs. Deinhard's the wine is bottled at a temperature of 72° Fahr., and the bottles remain resting on large stone tables until the fermentation is completed, and the saccharine is converted into alcohol and carbonic acid gas. This result is commonly obtained in ordinary hot weather in eight days' time, most of the breakage taking place during this interval. If on being tested with a manometer the wine should indicate too high a pressure, it is at once removed to a cool cellar, consequently the average total breakage rarely exceeds 2¼ per cent. The wine is now left quiet for at least a year, and if possible for two years, after which the bottles are placed on stands in the customary inverted position, and shaken daily for a period of six weeks, in order to dislodge the sediment and force it against the cork. German workmen are far less expert at this operation than their fellows in the Champagne, as few of the former can manage more than their four-and-twenty thousand bottles per diem. The disgorgement and liqueuring of the wine is accomplished at Messrs. Deinhard's and other German establishments in precisely the same fashion as is followed in the Champagne.

The dry sparkling hocks we tasted here had the real riesling flavour and the fine natural perfume common to this grape. In preparing them no attempt had been made to imitate champagne; but, on the other hand, every care had been taken to preserve the true hock character with its distinguishing freshness of taste combined with a lightness which wines containing liqueur in excess could never have exhibited. The sparkling moselles, too, depended not on any imparted muscatel flavour and perfume, but on their own natural bouquet and the flavour they derive from the schistous soil in which these wines are grown.

LIEBENSTEIN AND STERRENBERG.

CHAPTER XVII.

THE SPARKLING WINES OF GERMANY (CONTINUED).

From Coblenz to Rüdesheim—Ewald and Co.'s Establishment and its
Pleasant Situation—Their Fine Vaulted Cellars and Convenient
Accessories—Their Supplies of Wine drawn from the most fa-
voured Localities—The Celebrated Vineyards of the Rheingau—
Eltville and the extensive Establishment of Matheus Müller—His
Vast Stocks of Still and Sparkling German Wines—The Vineyards
laid under contribution for the latter—M.Müller's Sparkling Jo-

hannisberger, Champagne, and Red Sparkling Assmannshaus-
er—The Site of Gutenberg's Birthplace at Mayence occupied by the
Offices and Rhine-cellars of Lauteren Sohn—The Sparkling Wine
Establishment of the Firm, and their Fine Collection of Hocks and
Moselles—The Hochheim Sparkling Wine Association—Foundation of the Establishment—Its Superior Sparkling Hocks and
Moselles—The Sparkling Wine Establishments of Stock and Sons
at Creuznach in the Nahe Valley, of Kessler and Co. at Esslingen,
on the Neckar, and of M.Oppmann at Wurzburg—The Historic
Cellars of the King of Bavaria beneath the Residenz—The Estab-
lishment of F.A. Siligmüller.

STOLZENFELS.

Ascending the Rhine from Coblenz—past many an ancient ruined castle,
past restored Stolzenfels, the historic Königs-stuhl, the romantic Liebenstein and

Sterrenberg, the legendary Lurlei, the tribute-exacting Pfalz, and the old town of Bacharach, famous in the Middle Ages for its wine mart—we eventually come to Lorch, where the Wisper brook flows into the Rhine, and the grand wine-producing district known as the Rheingau begins. A few miles higher up are the vineyards of Assmannshausen, dominated by the Niederwald, and yielding the finest red wine in all Germany. Then passing by Bishop Hatto's legendary tower we emerge from the gorge of the Rhine and soon reach Rüdesheim, crouched at the foot of lofty terraced vineyards, which, according to doubtful tradition, were planted with Burgundy and Orleans vines by Charlemagne. Rüdesheim, like other antiquated little Rhine-side towns, boasts its ancient castle with its own poetical legend, while many modern houses have sprung up there of late years, and signs of further development are apparent on all sides. In the outskirts of the town there are a couple of sparkling wine establishments, the one nigh the railway station on the western side belonging to Messrs. Dietrich and Co., while eastwards on a picturesque slope overlooking the Rhine, and in the midst of extensive pleasure-grounds, is the establishment of Messrs. Ewald and Co., who date from the year 1858, and rank to-day amongst the leading shippers of sparkling hocks and moselles to England.

MESSRS. EWALD & CO.'S ESTABLISHMENT AT RÜDESHEIM.

Here are handsome and capacious buildings aboveground, and two floors of cellars comprising five vaults, each 160 feet in length and 30 feet broad. The lower vaults, 40 feet from the surface, are arched over and walled with stone, while the upper ones are faced with brick, both being floored with concrete and slanting towards the centre to allow of the wine from bottles that have burst running off. Each range of cellars is separately ventilated by shafts, generally kept open in winter and closed in the summer so as to maintain a temperature not exceeding 47° Fahr. in the lower cellars and under 52° in those above. Moreover, with the view of conducing to this result the cellars have an ice well communicating with them.

Late in the spring, when the newly-bottled wine indicates a sufficient number of atmospheres to insure a satisfactory effervescence, it is deposited in the lower vaults, the upper ones being devoted to reserve wines in wood and wines awaiting the process of disgorgement, or undergoing their daily shaking in order to force the deposit against the cork. Aboveground there are rooms for storing the liqueur, the corks, and the packing-cases, and in a spacious apartment, provided with three lifts for communicating with the cellars beneath, the wine is blended and bottled, and in due time disgorged and packed. In very warm weather, however, it is found preferable for the disgorging and its attendant operations to be performed in the cooler temperature of the cellars. Messrs. Ewald formerly tested the strength of their bottles with a manometer before using them, but for some time past they have given up the practice, feeling convinced that it was productive of more harm than good. Glass is an amorphous and unelastic substance which, although it will stand a high pressure once, often succumbs when put to a second test by the action of the fermenting wine. The firm calculate their annual breakage at from 2½ to 3 per cent.

Messrs. Ewald being installed almost in the heart or the Rheingau can readily draw their supplies of wine from the most favoured localities. Johannisberg is within a few miles of Rüdesheim, and in those years when, owing to the grapes not having thoroughly ripened, the wine is only of intermediate value as a still wine, it serves admirably for conversion into sparkling wine, retaining as it does its powerful bouquet. Ingelheim, too, noted for its vineyards of black grapes, whose produce is much sought after for blending with the finer sparkling Rhine wines, is only a few miles higher up the river, on the opposite bank. The drier varieties of sparkling hocks and moselles shipped by Messrs. Ewald to England have the merit of retaining all the fine flavour and natural perfume of the higher-class growths from which, as a rule, these wines are prepared.

THE ESTABLISHMENT OF MATHEUS MÜLLER AT ELTVILLE.

Above Rüdesheim the waters of the Rhine expand, the left bank of the river, if still lofty, is no longer precipitous, while the right continues almost flat so soon as the Rochusberg is left behind. Between here and Eltville all the more celebrated vineyards of the Rheingau are passed in rapid succession—Geisenheim-Rothenberg, Johannisberg, Steinberg, Marcobrunn, Kiedrich-Grafenberg, Rauenthal, and others. At Eltville—the former capital of the Rheingau, and where Gunther, of

Schwarzburg, resigned his crown to Charles IV., and died poisoned, it is said, by his successful rival—we find one of the most extensive wine establishments in Germany, that of Matheus Müller, who enjoys a high reputation in England both for his still and sparkling hocks and moselles. His stock ordinarily consists of from 800 to 1,000 stuck—equivalent to a quarter of a million gallons—of still Rhine and Moselle wines, much of it of the best years, and from vineyards of repute, together with nearly a million bottles of sparkling wines stored in his cellars at Eltville and on the road to Erbach, the aggregate length of which is some 3,400 feet. The sparkling wines repose in long cool vaulted galleries similar to many cellars in the Champagne, while the still wines are stored in capacious subterranean halls each 100 yards in length.

For his higher-class sparkling hocks Herr Müller derives his principal supplies from the Rheingau, partly from his own vineyards at Eltville, Rauenthal, and Hattenheim, and partly by purchases at Erbach, Hallgarten, Œstrich, Winkel, Johannisberg, Geisenheim, and Rudesheim; while for his best sparkling moselles, Berncastel, Graach, Trèves, and the Saar districts are laid under contribution. The Palatinate growths of Dürkheim, Deidesheim, Mussbach, Haardt, Rhodt, &c., serve as the basis for the medium and cheaper sparkling hocks, and for sparkling moselles of a corresponding character such wines as Zeltinger, Rachtiger, Erdener, Aldegonder, Winninger, &c., are used. Ingelheim and Heidesheim furnish the wine from black grapes necessary in a subordinate degree to all sparkling hocks, and very freely had recourse to when it is desired to impart a champagne character to the wine, as is commonly the case when this is intended for consumption in Germany. Herr Müller invariably presses the black grapes himself, in order that the wine may be as light in colour as possible. As the house annually lays down large stocks of *vin brut* it is under no necessity of drawing upon them until they have attained the requisite maturity and developed all their finer qualities.

The dry sparkling hocks and moselles, such as are shipped by Herr Müller to England and its colonies, receive a large addition of liqueur when destined for the Russian market. His sparkling Johannisberger and high-class sparkling moselle from Rheingau and Moselle wines of superior vintages are of delicate flavour and great softness, and are frequently shipped without any liqueur whatever. Besides Moussirender Rheinwein of a champagne character, and largely consumed in Ger-

many and Belgium, Herr Müller makes a veritable champagne from wine import-
ed by him from the Champagne district. His shipments also include red sparkling
Assmannshauser—the result of a blend of Assmannshauser, Ingelheimer, and
other red Rhenish wines—aromatic and full-bodied, and dry or moderately sweet
according to the country to which it is intended to be exported.

ENTRANCE TO LAUTEREN SOHN'S ESTABLISHMENT, MAYENCE.

The trade in German sparkling wines has numerous representatives at Mayence—the sec of St. Boniface, the apostle of the Germans, and the birthplace of Gutenberg, whose fame is universal. The pioneer of printing was born in a house at the corner of the Emmerans and Pfandhaus gasse, the site of which is to-day occupied by the residence of three members of the firm of C.Lauteren Sohn, established at Mayence so far back as 1794, and one of the first in Germany to devote itself to the manufacture of sparkling wines. In 1830 the firm profited by an offer made to them by a cellarman who had been for many years in the service of Madame Clicquot at Reims. The Emmerans-gasse, where the chief establishment of the firm is situated, is in the older quarter of Mayence—in the midst of a network of intricate winding streets bordered by picturesque tall gabled houses and edifices of the Spanish type where ornamental oriel windows with quaint supports, medallions, and bas-reliefs of varied design continually catch the eye, and saints look down upon one from almost every corner. Passing under the gateway of the house where Gutenberg was born, and in the rear of which Lauteren Sohn have their offices, cooperage, and cellars for still wines, we notice on our left hand a tablet commemorating the birth of the inventor of printing in these terms:—

"Gensfleisch House. Family residence of the inventor of the art of printing, John Gensfleisch of Gutenberg, who in the year 1398 was here born. Christian Lauteren has dedicated on the site of the ancient house this memorial to the immortal inventor, Jan. 29, 1825."

Messrs. Lauteren's cellars for sparkling wines extend mainly under an old monastery, and comprise a succession of large vaulted galleries connected by narrow passages with arched entrances. Here are stacked some 800,000 bottles of wine in varying conditions of maturity. Messrs. Lauteren bottle their wines in August, instead of fully two months earlier according to the usual practice, in the belief that the system they pursue is more conducive to perfect effervescence, besides being attended with less breakage, owing to the newly-bottled wine escaping the heat of the summer. All the arrangements at this establishment are very complete. There is a place for everything, and everything is to be found in its place. Adjoining the courtyard, where new bottles are stacked beneath open ornamental sheds, are the tasting-room and the apartment where the operations of disgorging, dosing, and re-corking are performed. The liqueur added by the firm to their sparkling wines is kept in bottle from three to five years before being used. In the tasting-room we were shown a variety of sparkling hocks and moselles, the former with all the distinguishing characteristics of fine Rhine wine, the older samples having gained considerably in softness. Adry Cabinet specimen submitted to us exhibited a fine bouquet and much delicacy of flavour. The moselles we found particularly interesting, made as they were of genuine wines from some of the best vineyards of the Moselle district.

The largest German sparkling wine establishment is at Hochheim, which, although, situated on the banks of the Main, and several miles distant from its confluence with the Rhine, has curiously enough supplied us with a generic name under which we inconsistently class the entire produce of the Rhine vineyards. Behind the Hochheim railway station there rises a long low slope, planted from base to summit with vines, aportion of which are screened on the north by a plain-looking church and a weather-stained deanery. The vines thus sheltered yield the famous Dom Dechanei, the finest Hochheimer known. Some short distance off in a westerly direction are the extensive premises of the Hochheim Sparkling Wine Association, whose brands are well known in England. The firm of Burgeff and Co., whose business the association acquired in 1858 and subsequently considerably extended, was founded in 1837. At this establishment all the arrangements are of the most perfect character. The bottles are cleaned by a machine employing ten persons, and turning out several thousand bottles a day. All the bottles moreover, before being used, have their strength tested by an ingenious apparatus which subjects them to three or four times the pressure they are likely to undergo when filled with wine. Pumps, bottle-washing machine, and the revolving casks in which the sugar is dissolved for the liqueur, are all moved by steam, and the association even manufactures the gas used for lighting up the establishment. We tasted here several sparkling hocks distinguished by their high flavour and refinement, with sparkling moselles vintaged in the best localities and equally excellent in quality.

Sparkling hocks and moselles are made by Messrs. Stock and Sons at Creuznach, afavourite watering-place in the romantic Nahe valley, noted for the picturesque porphyry cliffs which occasionally rise precipitously at the river's edge. Creuznach, where a capital wine is vintaged, on the southern slopes of the Schlossberg, is at no great distance from Bingen. Messrs. Stock and Sons' establishment dates from 1862, and their sparkling wines are mainly made from white grapes, only about one-eighth of white wine from black grapes entering into their composition. The latter is vintaged at Ingelheim, the grapes being pressed under the firm's own superintendence, and only the must resulting from the first squeeze of the press being used. The wine from riesling grapes is usually from the Rhine, and with it is mingled a certain quantity of wine vintaged on the Hessian plain. The vintage generally occurs at the end of October, and the firm remove the new wine to their cellars at Creuznach early in the ensuing spring, and bottle it in the May or June following. They make both dry and sweet varieties of sparkling wines, and their principal markets are England, Germany, the East and West Indies, the United States, and Australia.

BINGEN.

The establishment of G. C. Kessler and Co. at Esslingen—formerly one of the most important of the free imperial cities, and picturesquely situated on the Neckar—was founded as far back as 1826, and claims to be the oldest sparkling wine factory in Germany. The wine employed comes from vineyards in the vicinity of Heilbronn, and others in the Rheingau and the Grand Duchy of Baden, and is more or less a blend of the clevener, traminer, rulander, riesling, and elbling varieties of grape. The vintage takes place in October, and the bottling of the wine is effected during the following summer. Messrs. Kessler and Co. treat their wines after the system pursued at the Clicquot champagne establishment, in which the founder of the Esslingen house held an important position for a period of nearly twenty years. The wines are prepared sweet or dry according to the market they are destined for. The principal business of the firm is with Germany, but they also export to England, the United States, the East Indies, and Australia. Their wines have met with favourable recognition at various exhibitions, notably that of Paris in 1867, when a silver medal was awarded them; and at Vienna in 1873, where they received a medal for progress.

THE NECKAR AT HEIDELBERG.

Wurzburg, one of the most antiquated and picturesque of German cities, is noted for its sparkling Franconian wines vintaged partly in the vineyards that overspread the tall chalk hills which close in around the quaint old university town. The most famous of these vineyards are the Leist and the Stein, the first-named sloping downward towards the Main from the foot of the picturesque Marienberg fort, which, perched on the summit of a commanding height, dominates the city and forms so conspicuous an object in all the views of it. The extensive buildings of the fort not only shield the vines from the winds, but reflect the sun's rays upon them, thereby materially conducing to the perfect ripening of the grapes at a much earlier period than is customary. The Stein vineyard is situated on the opposite side of the Main, and when viewed from the picturesque bridge, studded with incongruous colossal statues—such as Joseph and the Virgin Mary in close proximity to Charlemagne and Pépin—seems to rise up as an immense rampart behind the city. Here the river acts as a reflector, throwing back the sun's rays on the lower portions of the slope, where the finest wine is naturally vintaged. An altogether inferior growth is produced on the hill to the north, known as the Middle Stein, and also in the Harfe vineyard, situated in the rear of the latter. The prevalent vines in the Würzburg district are the riesling, the traminer, the elbling, and the rulander, or pineau gris.

The first sparkling wine establishment at Würzburg was founded in 1842 by Herr Oppmann, the Royal cellar-master, who died in 1866. The position held by this individual was one of considerable importance, for the King of Bavaria is the largest wine-grower in his own dominions, and stores the produce of his vineyards in the famous cellars extending beneath one of the wings of the deserted Residenz, erected at an epoch when Würzburg was subject to episcopal rule. These cellars, vaulted in stone, are on a vast scale, and possibly unequalled in the world. You descend a broad flight of steps, flanked by ornamental iron balustrades, and encounter half-way down a miniature tun, guarded by the Bavarian lions posted in a niche in the wall. Following your guide with lighted candles, you pass between rows upon rows of capacious casks filled with the wine last vintaged, and various wines of recent years; large metal chandeliers—fantastically adorned with innumerable coloured bottles and glasses, and designed to light up the cellars on festive occasions—here and there descending from the arched roof. Eventually you arrive at a gallery where huge casks are poised on massive wooden frames in double tiers one above the other. These cellars are said to be capable of holding upwards of 500 casks, but at the time of our visit there were scarcely half that number, and only a mere fraction of these were filled with wine. The cellars no longer contain any of that archaic wine vintaged in 1546, for which they were formerly celebrated. Indeed, all the historic vintages, once their boast, were removed some years ago to Munich and deposited in the Royal cellars there. Of the ancient ornamental tuns holding their ten thousand gallons each, which the Würzburg cellars formerly contained, only a single one remains, constructed in the year 1784. This tun, carved on the front with the Bavarian arms, is about the dimensions of a fair-sized apartment, and being no longer filled with wine, aDiogenes of the period might take up his abode in it with perfect comfort. Herr Michael Oppmann, who has succeeded to the establishment founded by his father, prepares several varieties of white sparkling Franconian wine, with two kinds of red, and also sparkling hocks and moselles. The first-named wines are vintaged in the best vineyards of Lower Franconia, in the valley of the Main, and the Baden Oberland, the finer qualities being principally produced from the black clevener grape, usually vintaged the first or second week in October. The white grape vintage occurs some fortnight or more later, and the wine is bottled either late in the spring or during the coming summer. Its after-manipulation differs in no respect from that pursued with reference to champagne. Herr Oppmann, whose wines have met with favourable recognition at various foreign and home Exhibitions, prepares both sweet and dry varieties. Their chief market is Germany, although they are exported in fair quantities to Belgium, England, and Northern Europe.

AT AHRWEILER

Another sparkling wine establishment was founded at Würzburg by Herr F.A. Siligmuller in 1843. The wine from white grapes employed by him is vintaged partly in his own vineyards on the Stein and the Harfe, and partly in other Main vineyards, at Randersacker, Escheradorf, &c., the wine used by him from red grapes coming from the Baden Oberland around the so-called Kaisers-stuhl—an isolated vine-clad dolerite mountain bordering the Rhine, and on the verge almost of the Black Forest—and from the neighbourhood of Offenburg, one of the ancient imperial free towns, which has lately raised a statue to Sir Francis Drake, "the introducer," as the inscription says, "of the potato into Europe." The vintage here, which commences fully a fortnight earlier than around Würzburg, usually takes place about the beginning of October, and the wine is bottled in the height of the following summer. Herr Siligmuller's wines, of which there are four qualities, were awarded a medal for progress at the Vienna Exhibition of 1873.

A SPANISH VINTAGE SCENE.

CHAPTER XVIII.

THE SPARKLING WINES OF AUSTRO-HUNGARY, SWITZERLAND, ITALY, SPAIN, RUSSIA, &C.

Sparkling Voslauer—The Sparkling Wine Manufactories of Graz—Establishment of Kleinoscheg Brothers—Vintaging and Treatment of Styrian Champagnes—Sparkling Red, Rose, and White Wines of Hungary—The Establishment of Hubert and Habermann at Pressburg—Sparkling Wines of Croatia, Galicia, Bohemia, Moravia, Dalmatia, the Tyrol, Transylvania, and the Banat—Neuchâtel Champagne—Sparkling Wine Factories at Vevay and Sion—The Vevay Vineyards—Establishment of De Riedmatten and De Quay—Sparkling Muscatel, Malmsey, Brachetto, Castagnolo, and Lacryma Christi of Italy—Sparkling Wines of Spain, Greece, Algeria, and Russia—The Krimski and Donski Champagnes—The Latter Chiefly Consumed at the Great Russian Fairs.

Sparkling wines are made in various parts of Austria and Hungary, and of late years their produce has been largely on the increase. At Voslau, in the vicinity of the picturesque and fashionable summer watering-place of Baden, about twenty miles south of Vienna, Herr R.Schlumberger, one of my colleagues on the wine jury at the Vienna and Paris Exhibitions of 1873 and '8, makes a white sparkling

Voslauer—introduced into England some years since—from the blue portuguese, the burgundy (the pineau noir), the rulander (the pineau gris), and the riesling varieties of grape. It is, however, at Graz, the capital of Styria, picturesquely situated on the river Mur, and surrounded by lofty mountains, where sparkling wines are made upon the largest scale and with the most success. By far the principal manufactory is that of Kleinoscheg Brothers, founded in the year 1850, at an epoch when the larger Styrian wine-growers were directing their attention to the general improvement of their vineyards. The firm gained their knowledge of sparkling wines by practical experience acquired in the Champagne itself, and to-day they unquestionably produce some of the best sparkling wines that are made out of France. They possess extensive vineyards of their own, and are also large purchasers of wines from the best districts, including Pettau, Radkersburg, the Picherergebirge, and Luttenberg, the latter yielding the finest wine which Styria produces, vintaged from the mosler or furmint—that is, the Tokay variety of grape.

White wine from the clevener grape, understood to be identical with the pineau noir of Burgundy and the Champagne, and vintaged early in October, forms the basis of the sparkling wines manufactured by Kleinoscheg Brothers. The produce of several other grapes, however, enters in a limited degree into the blend, including the riesling, the rulander or pineau gris, and the portuguese, the gathering of which is usually delayed several weeks later, and is sometimes even deferred until the end of November. The first and second pressings of the black grapes yield a white must as in the Champagne, while the third and fourth give a pink wine of which the firm make a speciality.

The wines, which are treated precisely after the system pursued in the Champagne, are bottled during the months of July and August, and are made either sweet or dry according to the country they are destined for. Considerable shipments of the dry pale Styrian champagne take place to England, where the firm also send a delicate sparkling muscatel and a sparkling red burgundy, which will favourably compare with the best sparkling wines of the Côte d'Or. They have also a large market for their wines in Austria, Germany, Italy, and Switzerland, and export to British North America, the East Indies, China, Japan, and Australia. From the year 1855 up to the present time the firm of Kleinoscheg Brothers have been awarded no less than sixteen medals for their sparkling wines at various important home and foreign exhibitions.

At Marburg on the river Drave, in the vicinity of the Bacher Mountains, which stretch far into Carinthia, and have their lower slopes covered with vines, Herr F.Auchmann has established a successful sparkling wine manufactory. The raw wine comes from the vineyards around Marburg and from Pettau, some ten or twelve miles lower down the Drave. The vintage commonly lasts from the middle of October until the middle of November. Black grapes of the clevener and portuguese varieties are pressed as in the Champagne, so as to yield a white must, with which a certain portion of white wine from the mosler or furmint grape is subsequently mingled. The bottling takes place as early as April or May. The wines are principally consumed in Austria, but are also exported to Russia, Italy, Egypt, the Danubian Principalities, Australia, &c.

Sparkling wines seem to be made in various parts of Hungary, judging from the samples sent to the Vienna and Paris Exhibitions from Pesth, Pressburg, Oedenburg, Pécs, Velencze, and Kolozsvár. Rose-colour wines are evidently much in favour with the respective manufacturers, several of whom make sparkling red wines as well, but with none of the success of their Styrian neighbours. The best Hungarian sparkling wines we have met with are those of Hubert and Habermann, made at Pressburg, the former capital of Hungary, where its kings, after being crowned, used to ride up the Königsberg brandishing the sword of St. Stephen towards the four points of the compass in token of their determination to defend the kingdom against all enemies. The white sparkling wines are made exclusively from white grapes grown in the neighbouring vineyards of Bösing, Geñnau, and St. Georgen, but the firm make red sparkling wines as well from the produce of the Ratzersdorf and Wainor vineyards. The vintage takes place some time in October, and the wines are bottled both in the spring and autumn, but never until they are fully twelve months old. With these variations the system pursued with regard to the wines is the same as is followed in the Champagne. There are several other sparkling wine manufacturers at Pressburg, and the principal market for these wines is Austro-Hungary, but shipments of them are made to England, the United States, India, Roumania, and Servia. The production of sparkling wine in Hungary is now estimated to amount to one million bottles annually.

In Croatia Prince Lippe-Schaumburg has established a sparkling wine manufactory at Slatina, where he produces a so-called Riesling-Champagner, and it would appear from the collection of Austro-Hungarian sparkling wines exhibited at Vienna by Herr Bogdan Hoff of Cracow, that these wines are also made at Melnik, in Bohemia, at Bisenz in Moravia, at Sebenicodi Maraschino in Dalmatia, at Botzen in the Tyrol, at Tasnad in Transylvania, and at Weiss-Kirchen in the Banat. All these wines had been submitted to examination at the Imperial œno-chemical laboratory at Klosterneuberg, and one was not surprised to find that the majority were pronounced to be of too robust a character for transformation into sparkling wines.

Switzerland long since turned its attention to the manufacture of sparkling wines, not, however, to meet the requirements of its own population, but those of the many tourists with well-lined purses who annually explore its valleys, lakes, and mountains. Neuchâtel champagne has met with a certain amount of success, and at the present time there are a couple of establishments devoted to its production, the best known being that of Bouvier frères. There are, moreover, sparkling wine manufactories at Vevay in the Vaud Canton, and at Sion in the Valais. In the Canton of Neuchâtel the best Swiss red wines are produced—notably Cortaillod and Faverge of a ruby hue and Burgundy-like flavour—and the sparkling wine manufacturers of the district wisely blend a considerable proportion of wine from black grapes with that from white when making their *cuvées*. Vaud, on the other hand, being noted for white wines bearing some resemblance to certain Rhine growths, it is of these that sparkling wines are exclusively made at Vevay.

The Vevay vineyards occupy the heights which skirt the Lake of Geneva on its northern side. The innumerable terraces, steep and difficult of access to the toiling vine-dresser, on which the vines are planted, are the result of centuries of patient labour. Here the vine seems to flourish at an altitude of more than 1,800 feet above the sea level. To compensate for the deficiency of sunshine the leaves are largely stripped from the vines so as to expose the fruit, and thereby assist its ripening.

The sparkling wine factory at Sion, bordering the river Rhône, in the Canton of the Valais, was established in 1872 by MM.de Riedmatten and De Quay, who derive their raw wine from vineyards in the immediate neighbourhood, almost all of which have a southern exposure, and occupy gentle slopes. The soil chiefly consists of a decomposed limestone schist, locally termed "brisé." In these vineyards, and more especially the district known as the Clavaux, some of the best and most alcoholic wines in Switzerland are produced.

The firm originally experimented with the choicer and more powerful growths, and, as may be imagined, soon discovered they were not well adapted for conversion into sparkling wines. To-day they limit themselves to wines produced from what is known as the "fendant" variety of grape, said by some to be identical with the German riesling, and by others to be of the same type as the French chasselas. The vintage in the Valais is the earliest in Switzerland, taking place in favourable years at the close of September, but ordinarily in the course of October. Some fine white candy syrup is added to the wine at the epoch of bottling, in order to provoke the requisite effervescence, which it does so effectually that the tirage is obliged to take place some time between November and May, as at any other period the temperature would be too high and the bottles would burst. MM.Riedmatten and De Quay have two varieties of sparkling wine—their Carte Blanche, which goes under the name of Mont Blanc, and is rather sweet, and their Carte Verte known as Glacier de Rhône, adrier variety and finding a readier sale.

Of late years, since many improvements have been effected in Italy both in the cultivation of the vineyards and the vintaging of the wine, numerous attempts have been made, although on the whole with but indifferent success, to produce a good sparkling wine. The principal seat of the manufacture is Asti, where the Societa Unione Enofila make considerable quantities of a common strong sweet sparkling wine, as well as a sparkling muscatel. Alessandria, Ancona, Bologna, Castagnolo, Genoa, Modena, Naples, Palermo, and Treviso also profess to make sparkling wines, but only in insignificant quantities. Alessandria produces sparkling malmsey and red sparkling brachetto; and on the Marquis Della Stufa's estate of Castagnolo a sparkling wine is manufactured from the currajola variety of grape, one of the best in the Tuscan vineyards. The vines at Castagnolo are cultivated in accordance with the French system, and at the vintage all unripe and unsound grapes are thrown aside. There is an evident flavour of the muscat grape in the Castagnolo sparkling wine, which has the merit of lightness and of being well made. The alcoholic strength is equivalent to rather more than 20° of proof spirit, and the highest quality wine is remarkable for its excessive dryness in comparison with all other samples of Italian sparkling wines that we have met with. Naples appears to confine itself to producing sparkling white lacryma christi, for which, as a curiosity, there exists a certain demand.

Spain of late years has shown itself equally ambitious with Italy to achieve distinction in the production of sparkling wines, and at the Paris Exhibition of 1878 there were samples from the majority of the wine centres skirting the Mediterranean coast, including Gerona, Barcelona, Tarragona, and Valencia. Other samples come from Logroño, in the north of Spain; and years ago sparkling wine used to be made at Villaviciosa, on the Bay of Biscay. To Paris there were also sent samples of sparkling orange wine, an agreeable beverage, and unquestionably preferable to the majority of Spanish sparkling wines composed of the juice of the grape.

Greek sparkling wines, said to be of very fair quality, are made at Athens, Corinth, and Tripoliza, and are exported in moderate quantities to Russia. Algeria, too, is turning its attention to the production of sparkling wines, but solely for home consumption, and at the Paris Exhibition there was a sparkling wine from Uruguay, but of execrable quality.

The sparkling wines of the Crimea and the Don, known in Russia respectively as Krimski and Donski champagnes, are described as being superior to much of the wine which passes in England under the name of champagne. In Russia it is the fashion to speak contemptuously of them, just as rhubarb and gooseberry champagne is spoken of in England, still these Crimean and Don products are genuine wines, and, though somewhat sweet, may be drunk with satisfaction and in moderate quantities with impunity. One of the best Donski brands is that of Abrahamof, and as much as six roubles per bottle is demanded for the finer qualities at Novoi Tscherkash. About a million bottles of the Donski champagne are exported annually, but the wine finds its principal market at the great Russian fairs, where almost every important bargain is "wetted" with sparkling Donski.

VINTAGE SCENE IN THE UNITED STATES.

CHAPTER XIX.

THE SPARKLING WINES OF THE UNITED STATES.

Earliest Efforts at Wine-Making in America—Failures to Acclimatise European Vines—Wines Made by the Swiss Settlers and the Mission Fathers—The Yield of the Mission Vineyards—The Monster Vine of the Montecito Valley—The Catawba Vine and its General Cultivation—Mr. Longworth one of the Founders of American Viticulture—Fresh Attempts to make Sparkling Wine at Cincinnati—Existing Sparkling Wine Manufactures there—Longfellow's Song in Praise of Catawba—The Kelley Island Wine Company—Vintaging and Treatment of their Sparkling Wines—Decrease of Consumption—The Vineyards of Hammondsport—Varieties of Grapes used for Sparkling Wines—The Vintage—After-Treatment of the Wines—The Pleasant Valley and Urbana Wine Companies and their Various Brands—Californian Sparkling Wines—The Buena Vista Vinicultural Society of San Francisco—Its Early Failures and Eventual Success in Manufacturing Sparkling Wines—The Vintage in California—Chinese Vintagers—How the Wine is Made—American Spurious Sparkling Wines.

From the earliest period of the colonisation of America the vine appears to have attracted the attention of the settlers, and it is said that as early as 1564 wine was made from the native grape in Florida. The first attempts to establish a regular vineyard date, however, from 1620, and would seem to have been made in Virginia with European vines, the prospects having become sufficiently encouraging in 1630 for the colonists to send for French vine-dressers to tend their plants. The latter were subsequently accused of ruining the vines by their bad treatment, but most likely this was an error, it having since been made evident that European vines cannot be successfully cultivated east of the Rocky Mountains, where the phylloxera vastatrix prevails. It was in vain that William Penn made repeated attempts to acclimatise European vines in Pennsylvania, that the Swiss emigrants — vine-growers from the Lake of Geneva — made similar trials, they having expended ten thousand dollars to no purpose. In vain, in Jessamine county, Kentucky, Pierre Legaud laboured in the environs of Philadelphia, and Lakanal, the member of the French Convention, experimented in Tennessee, Ohio, and Alabama; all their efforts to introduce the Old World vines proved futile. The attempts that were made by Swiss settlers at Vevay, in Indiana, with the indigenous plants were more successful, and after a time they managed to produce some palatable wine from the Schuylkill muscatel.

Towards the latter part of the 18th century the Mission Fathers had succeeded in planting vineyards in California. It is known that in 1771 the vine was cultivated there, and the San Gabriel Mission in the county of Los Angeles, some 300 miles S.E. of San Francisco, is said to have possessed the first vineyard. A prevalent belief is, that the vines were from roots or cuttings obtained from either Spain or Mexico, but it is also conjectured that they were some of the wild varieties known to be scattered over the country, while a third theory suggests that as attempts to make wine from the wild grapes would most likely have proved a failure, the Fathers planted the seeds of raisins which had come from Spain. The culture must have progressed rapidly, if, as stated, there were planted at San Gabriel in a single spring no fewer than 40,000 vines. These mission vines were mainly of two sorts, the one yielding a white grape with a musky flavour, and the other a dark blue fruit. The latter was the favourite, doubtless from its produce bearing some resemblance to the red wines of Old Castile.

From San Gabriel the planting of the vine extended from mission to mission until each owned its patch of vineland. At the time of the arrival of the Americans in 1846 the smallest of these was five acres in extent, and others as many as thirty acres, and it is calculated the average yield was from 700 to 1,000 gallons of wine per acre. This was owing first to the exceeding richness of the soil, and secondly to its being well irrigated. If the celebrated mission vine grown on one of the sunny slopes overlooking the lovely Montecito valley near Santa Barbara on the blue Pacific had many fellows in the Fathers' vineyards, the above estimate can hardly be an exaggerated one. The stem of this vine, which is four feet four inches in circumference at the ground, rises eight feet before branching out. The branches, under which the country people are fond of dancing, and which are supported by fifty-two trellises, extend over more than 5,000 square feet. This monster vine produces annually from five to six tons of grapes, and one year it yielded no fewer than 7,000 bunches, each from one to four pounds in weight. It is irrigated by water from the hot springs, situated a few miles distant, and is believed to be from half to three-quarters of a century old.

Viticulture and vinification languished in the United States until attention was called in 1826 to the catawba vine by Major Adlum, of Georgetown, near Washington, who thought that by so doing he was conferring a greater benefit on his country than if he had liquidated its national debt. This vine, which is derived from the wild *Vitis labrusca*, was first planted on an extensive scale by Nicholas Longworth, justly looked upon as one of the founders of American viticulture, and gradually supplanted all others, remaining for many years the principal plant cultivated along the banks of the Ohio—the so-called "Rhine of America"—until, ceaselessly attacked by rot, mildew, and leaf-blight, it was found necessary in many places to supplant it by more robust varieties.

Mr. Longworth, about the year 1837, among his numerous experiments at Cincinnati, included that of making sparkling wines from the catawba, isabella, and other varieties of grapes, and to-day there are several manufactories of sparkling catawba and other wines in the capital of Ohio—the self-named "Queen city," which its detractors have jocularly dubbed Porcopolis on account of the immense trade done there in smoked and salted pork. The chief sparkling wine establishments at Cincinnati are those of Messrs. Werk and Sons, whose sparkling catawba obtained a medal for progress at the Vienna Exhibition in 1873, and who have, moreover, largely experimented with ives' and virginia seedlings, delaware and other grapes, in making effervescent wines, though only with doubtful success. Another Cincinnati firm is that of Messrs. George Bogen and Co., whose sparkling wines also met with recognition at Vienna.

The reader will remember Longfellow's well-known song extolling catawba wine, which, with more than a poet's licence, he ranks above the best of the Old World vintages:—

> "There grows no vine
> By the haunted Rhine,
> By Danube or Guadalquivir,
> Nor on island nor cape,
> That bears such a grape
> As grows by the Beautiful River.

> "Very good in its way
> Is the Verzenay,
> Or the Sillery, soft and creamy,
> But Catawba wine
> Has a taste more divine,
> More dulcet, delicious, and dreamy."

On Kelley's Island, Erie county, also in the State of Ohio, awine company, established in 1866, and trading principally in still wines, makes sparkling wines upon a considerable scale exclusively from the catawba variety of grape, which is cultivated in its highest perfection both on the islands of Lake Erie and along a narrow slip of territory not two miles long bordering the southern shore of the lake, and also in the vicinity of Lake Keuka, near Hammondsport, N.Y. The Kelley Island Wine Company, as it is styled, presses the grapes between the middle of October and the end of November, and bottles from about the 20th May until the commencement of July in the year following. Its brands are Island Queen, Nonpareil, and Carte Blanche. Ninety-five per cent. of the wines are dry, and the tendency of the market is in favour of a still drier article. Shipments are principally confined to the United States, the great centre of the trade being St. Louis, on the Mississippi, which has its own sparkling wine establishments, and to-day disputes with Chicago the title of Queen of the West. The company keep some 100,000 bottles of sparkling wines in stock, and possess facilities for bottling five times that quantity whenever the demand might warrant such a step being taken. Of recent years, however, economy has been the rule in American society, and the market for native sparkling wines at any rate is to-day a reduced one.

At Hammondsport, south of Lake Keuka—in other words, Crooked Lake—and in the State of New York, the establishments of the Pleasant Valley and Urbana wine companies, devoting their attention to both still and sparkling wines, are installed. The region, which enthusiastic writers now term the Champagne of America, was colonised in 1793, and vines of the catawba and isabella varieties were first planted for the purpose of making wine in 1854. At the present time there are about 8,000 acres under cultivation with all the better species of vines. The produce from black and white grapes is mingled for the sparkling wines of the district. Of the former but two kinds are considered suitable, the concord and the isabella, both being varieties of the indigenous labrusca, or so-called foxy-flavoured grape. The concord is a hardy and productive plant, producing large and compact bunches of large round sweet grapes, yielding a wine of the obnoxious foxy flavour. The isabella is an equally hardy and productive variety, and its bunches are of good size, although not compact. Its berries, too, are large, oval, and juicy, and marked by a strong musky aroma.

Of the white, or rather pale-coloured grapes—for their hue is usually a reddish one—used for sparkling wines, the principal is the catawba, also of the labrusca variety. The branches are large and tolerably compact; the berries, too, are above the medium size, and have a rich vinous and pronounced musky flavour. Other so-called white species of grapes are the diana and the iona, both, of them seedlings of the catawba; the delaware, the bunches of which are rather small but compact, the berries round, extremely juicy and fresh-tasting, but sweet and aromatic, the wine produced from which is noted for its fragrant bouquet; and, lastly, the walter, avariety obtained by crossing the delaware with the diana. The bunches and berries of the walter are of medium size; the flavour, like that of the delaware, is sweet and aromatic; and the grape is, moreover, remarkable for its agreeable bouquet.

The vintage usually commences about the end of September or the commencement of October, and the grapes, after being carefully sorted, are run through a small mill, which breaks the skins, and admits of the juice running the more readily out when the fruit is placed beneath the press. The latter is worked with a metal screw, and the must is conducted through pipes or hose to casks holding from two to four thousand gallons each, in which it ferments. During the following May the wine is carefully blended, and the operation of bottling commences and lasts for about two or three months. The newly-bottled wine is at first stored in a warm place in order to start the fermentation again, and when the bottles commence to burst it is removed to the subterranean vaults, where it remains stacked in a horizontal fashion until the time arrives to force the sediment down upon the corks. This is accomplished precisely as in the Champagne, the subsequent disgorging and liqueuring being also effected according to the orthodox French system. Altogether a couple of years elapse between the epoch of bottling and shipment, and during this interval each bottle is handled upwards of two hundred times.

The Pleasant Valley Wine Company, established in 1860 for the commerce of still wines, in which it continues to do an extensive business, commenced five years later to make sparkling wines. It grows its own grapes and consumes annually about 1,500 tons of fruit, bottling from 200,000 to 300,000 bottles of sparkling wine in the course of the year. Its brands are the Great Western, of which there is a dry and an extra dry variety, the Carte Blanche, and the Pleasant Valley. Even the extra dry variety of the first-named wine tastes sweet in comparison with a moderately dry champagne, in addition to which its flavour, though agreeable, is certainly too pronounced for a sparkling wine of high quality. The wines, which secured a medal for progress at the Vienna Exhibition of 1873, are sold in every city in the United States, and the company also does a small but increasing trade with England and South America.

The Urbana Wine Company, also established at Hammondsport at the same epoch as its rival, deals, like the latter, in still wines as well. It has three brands— the Gold Seal, of which there is an extra dry variety, the Imperial, and the Royal Rose. At Vienna a diploma of merit was awarded to these wines, for which a considerable market is found throughout the United States and in the West Indies and South America. The Urbana Wine Company produces excellent sparkling wines of singular lightness and of delicate though distinctive flavour. In our judgment the drier varieties are greatly to be preferred. The prices of all the American sparkling wines are certainly high, being almost equivalent to the price of first-class champagnes taken at Reims and Epernay.

In California the manufacture of sparkling wines is carried on with considerable success, and at the Vienna Exhibition the Buena Vista Vinicultural Society of San Francisco was awarded a medal for progress for the excellent samples it sent there. The society was originally organised by Colonel Haraszthy, the pioneer in recent times of Californian viticulture. It commenced manufacturing sparkling wines with the assistance of experienced workmen from Epernay and Ay; but the endeavours, extending over some three or four years, were attended with but indifferent success, very few *cuvées* proving of fair quality, whilst with the majority the wine had to be emptied from the bottles and distilled into brandy. The son of Colonel Haraszthy subsequently succeeded, in conjunction with Mr. Isidor Landsberger, of San Francisco, in discovering the cause of these failures, and for ten years past the wine has been constantly improving in quality owing to the increased use of foreign grapes, which yield a *vin brut* with a delicate bouquet and flavour approaching in character to the finer champagnes. The wine is perfectly pure, no flavouring extracts or spirit being employed in the composition of the liqueur, which, is composed merely of sugar-candy dissolved in fine old wine. AFrench connoisseur pronounces sparkling Sonoma to be the best of American sparkling wines, "clean and fresh, tasting, with the flavour of a middle-class Ay growth, as well as remarkably light and delicate, and possessed of considerable effervescence." The Sonoma valley vineyards produce the lightest wines of all the Californian growths, some of the white varieties indicating merely 15° of proof spirit, and the red ones no more than 17½°.

The vintage takes place towards the end of October, and the grapes are gathered by Chinamen, who will each pick his 12 to 14 cwt. of grapes a day for the wage of a dollar. Light wooden boxes are used for holding the grapes, which are stripped from their stalks on their arrival at the press-house, and then partially crushed by a couple of revolving rollers. An inclined platform beneath receives them, and after the expressed juice has been run off into cask they are removed to the press, and the must subsequently extracted is added to that forced out by the rollers. When white wine is being made from black grapes the pressure is less continuous, and the must is of course separated at once from the skins. The fermentation, which is violent for some ten or twelve hours, ceases in about a fortnight, providing a temperature of from 70° to 75° Fahr. is maintained in the vaults. The wine is racked at the new year, and again before the blending and bottling of it in the spring.

The Californian sparkling wines not only find a market in the eastern States, but are sent across the Pacific to the Sandwich Islands, Japan, China, and even to wine-producing Australia, which has not yet succeeded in producing sparkling wines of its own.

The manufacture of spurious sparkling wines is carried on to some extent in the United States. The raw wine is cleared by fining it with albumen or gelatine and with alum; the latter substance imparting to it great brilliancy. After being dosed with a flavoured syrup the wine is charged like soda-water with carbonic acid gas by placing the bottles under a fountain, and as this gas is derived from marble dust and sulphuric acid, it is liable to be impregnated with both lead and copper, which have the effect of disorganising alike the wine and the consumers of it—nausea, headache, and other ills resulting from drinking sparkling wines made under such conditions.

CHAPTER XX.

CONCLUDING FACTS AND HINTS.

Dry and Sweet Champagnes—Their Sparkling Properties—Form of
Champagne Glasses—Style of Sparkling Wines Consumed in Different Countries—The Colour and Alcoholic Strength of Champagne—Champagne Approved of by the Faculty—Its Use in
Nervous Derangements—The Icing of Champagne—Scarcity of
Grand Vintages in the Champagne—The Quality of the Wine has
little influence on the Price—Prices realised by the Ay and Verzenay Crûs in Grand Years—Suggestions for Laying down Champagnes of Grand Vintages—The Improvement they Develop after a few Years—The Wine of 1874—The proper kind of Cellar to
lay down Champagne in—Advantages of Burrow's Patent Slider
Wine Bins—Increase in the Consumption of Champagne—Tabu-
lar Statement of Stocks, Exports, and Home Consumption from
1844-5 to 1877-8—When to Serve Champagne at a Dinner Party—
Charles Dickens's dictum that its proper place is at a Ball—Advantageous Effect of Champagne at an ordinary British Dinner
Party—Sparkling Wine Cups.

When selecting a sparkling wine one fact should be borne in mind—that just
as, according to Sam Weller, it is the seasoning which makes the pie mutton, beef,

or veal, so it is the liqueur which renders the wine dry or sweet, light or strong. A really palatable dry champagne, emitting the fragrant bouquet which distinguishes all wines of fine quality, free from added spirit, is obliged to be made of the very best *vin brut*, to which necessarily an exceedingly small percentage of liqueur will be added. On the other hand, asweet champagne can be produced from the most ordinary raw wine—the Yankees even claim to have evolved it from petroleum—as the amount of liqueur it receives completely masks its original character and flavour. This excess of syrup, it should be remarked, contributes materially to the wine's explosive force and temporary effervescence, but shortly after the bottle has been uncorked the wine becomes disagreeably flat. Afine dry wine, indebted as it is for its sparkling properties to the natural sweetness of the grape, does not exhibit the same sudden turbulent effervescence. It continues to sparkle, however, for a long time after being poured into the glass owing to the carbonic acid having been absorbed by the wine itself instead of being accumulated in the vacant space between the liquid and the cork, as is the case with wines that have been highly liqueured. Even when its carbonic acid gas is exhausted a good champagne will preserve its fine flavour, which the effervescence will have assisted to conceal. Champagne, it should be noted, sparkles best in tall tapering glasses; still these have their disadvantages, promoting as they do an excess of froth when the wine is poured into them, and almost preventing any bouquet which the wine possesses from being recognised.

Manufacturers of champagne and other sparkling wines prepare them dry or sweet, light or strong, according to the markets for which they are designed. The sweet wines go to Russia and Germany, the sweet-toothed Muscovite regarding M.Louis Roederer's syrupy product as the *beau-idéal* of champagne, and the Germans demanding wines with 20 or more per cent. of liqueur, or nearly quadruple the quantity that is contained in the average champagnes shipped to England. France consumes light and moderately sweet wines; the United States gives a preference to the intermediate qualities; China, India, and other hot countries stipulate for light dry wines; while the very strong ones go to Australia, the Cape, and other places where gold and diamonds and such-like trifles are from time to time "prospected." Not merely the driest but the very best wines of the best manufacturers, and commanding of course the highest prices, are invariably reserved for the English market. Foreigners cannot understand the marked preference shown in England for exceedingly dry sparkling wines. They do not consider that as a rule they are drunk during dinner with the *plats*, and not at dessert, with all kinds of sweets, fruits, and ices, as is almost invariably the case abroad.

Good champagne is usually of a pale straw colour, but with nothing of a yellow tinge about it. When its tint is pinkish this is owing to a portion of the colouring matter having been extracted from the skins of the grapes—acontingency which every pains are taken to avoid, although, since the success achieved by the wine of 1874, slightly pink wines are likely to be the fashion. The positive pink or rose-coloured champagnes, such as were in fashion some thirty years ago, are simply tinted with a small quantity of deep red wine. The alcoholic strength of the drier wines ranges from 18° of proof spirit upwards, or slightly above the ordinary

Bordeaux, and under all the better-class Rhine wines. Champagnes when loaded with a highly alcoholized liqueur will, however, at times mark 30 degrees of proof spirit. The lighter and drier the sparkling wine the more wholesome it is, the saccharine element in conjunction with alcohol being not only difficult of digestion, but generally detrimental to health.

The faculty are agreed that fine dry champagnes are among the safest wines that can be partaken of. Any intoxicating effects are rapid but exceedingly transient, and arise from the alcohol suspended in the carbonic acid being applied rapidly and extensively to the surface of the stomach. "Champagne," said Curran, "simply gives a runaway rap at a man's head." Dr. Druitt, equally distinguished by his studies upon wine and his standing as a physician, pronounces good champagne to be "a true stimulant to body and mind alike, rapid, volatile, transitory, and harmless. Amongst the maladies which are benefited by it," remarks he, "is the true neuralgia, intermitting fits of excruciating pain running along certain nerves, without inflammation of the affected part, often a consequence of malaria, or of some other low and exhausting causes. To enumerate the cases in which champagne is of service would be to give a whole nosology. Who does not know the misery, the helplessness of that abominable ailment, influenza, whether a severe cold or the genuine epidemic? Let the faculty dispute about the best remedy if they please; but a sensible man with a bottle of champagne will beat them all. Moreover, whenever there is pain, with exhaustion and lowness, then Dr. Champagne should be had up. There is something excitant in the wine; doubly so in the sparkling wine, which the moment it touches the lips sends an electric telegram of comfort to every remote nerve. Nothing comforts and rests the stomach better, or is a greater antidote to nausea."

Champagne of fine quality should never be mixed with ice or iced water; neither should it be iced to the extent champagnes ordinarily are, for, in the first place, the natural lightness of the wine is such as not to admit of its being diluted without utterly spoiling it, and in the next, excessive cold destroys alike the fragrant bouquet of the wine and its delicate vinous flavour. Really good champagne should not be iced below a temperature of 50° Fahr., whereas exceedingly sweet wines will bear icing down almost to freezing point, and be rendered more palatable by the process. The above remarks apply to all kinds of sparkling wine.

In the Champagne what may be termed a really grand vintage commonly occurs only once, and never more than twice, in ten years. During the same period, however, there will generally be one or two other tolerably good vintages. In grand years the crop, besides being of superior quality, is usually abundant, and as a consequence the price of the raw wine is scarcely higher than usual. Apparently from this circumstance the sparkling wine of grand vintages does not command an enhanced value, as is the case with other fine wines. It is only when speculators recklessly outbid each other for the grapes or the *vin brut*, or when stocks are low and the *vin brut* is really scarce, that the price of champagne appears to rise.

That superior quality does not involve enhanced price is proved by the amounts paid for the Ay and Verzenay crûs in years of grand vintages. During the present century these appear to have been 1802, '06, '11, '18, '22, '25, '34, '42, '46,

'57, '65, '68, and '74—that is, thirteen grand vintages in nearly eighty years. Other good vintages, although not equal to the foregoing, occurred in the years 1815, '32, '39, '52, '54, '58, '62, '64, and '70. Confining ourselves to the grand years, we find that the Ay wine of 1834, owing to the crop being plentiful as well as good, only realised from 110 to 140 francs the pièce of 44 gallons, although for two years previously this had fetched from 150 to 200 francs. In 1842 the price ranged from 120 to 150 francs, whereas the vastly inferior wine of the year before had commanded from 210 to 275 francs. In 1846, the crop being a small one, the price of the wine rose, and in 1857 the pièce fetched as much as from 480 to 500 francs, still this was merely a trifle higher than it had realised the two preceding years. In 1865 the price was 380 to 400 francs, and in 1868 about the same, whereas the indifferent vintages of 1871, '72, and '73 realised from 500 to 1,000 francs the pièce. It was very similar with the wine of Verzenay. In 1834 the price of the pièce ranged from 280 to 325 francs, or about the average of the three preceding years. In 1846, the crop being scarce, the price rose considerably, while in 1857, when the crop was plentiful, it fell to 500 francs, or from 5 to 20 per cent. below that of the two previous years, when the yield was both inferior and less abundant. In 1865 the price rose 33 per cent. above that of the year before; still, although Verzenay wine of 1865 and 1868 fetched from 420 to 450 francs the pièce, and that of 1874 as much as 900 francs, the greatly inferior vintages of 1872-73 commanded 900 and 1,030 francs the pièce.

Consumers of champagne, if wise, would profit by the circumstance that quality has not the effect of causing a rise in prices, and if they were bent upon drinking their favourite wine in perfection, as one meets with it at the dinner-tables of the principal manufacturers, who only put old wine of grand vintages before their guests, they would lay down champagnes of good years in the same way as the choicer vintages of port, burgundy, and bordeaux are laid down. Champagne of 1874 was a wine of this description, with all its finer vinous qualities well developed, and consequently needing age to attain not merely the roundness but the refinement of flavour pertaining to a high-class sparkling wine. Instead of being drunk a few months after it was shipped in the spring and summer of 1877, as was the fate of much of the wine in question, it needed being kept for three years at the very least to become even moderately round and perfect. In the Champagne one had many opportunities of tasting the grander vintages that had arrived at ten, twelve, or fifteen years of age, and had thereby attained supreme excellence. It is true their effervescence had moderated materially, but their bouquet and flavour were perfect, and their softness and delicacy something marvellous.

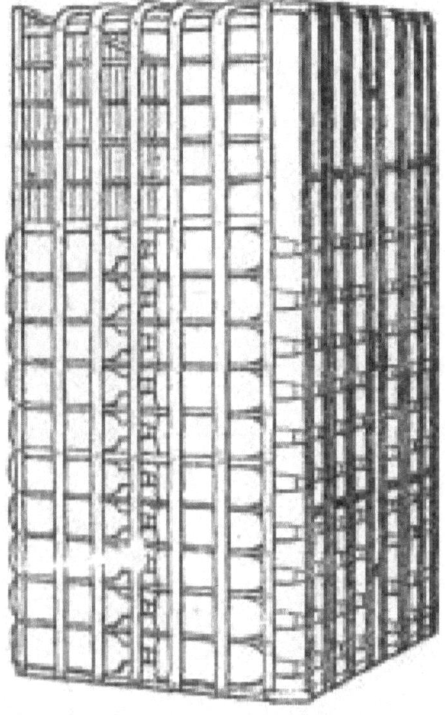

A great wine like that of 1874 will go on improving for ten years, providing it is only laid down under proper conditions. These are, first, an exceedingly cool but perfectly dry cellar, the temperature of which should be as low as from 50° to 55° Fahr., or even lower if this is practicable. The cellar, too, should be neither over dark nor light, scrupulously clean, and sufficiently well ventilated for the air to be continuously pure. It is requisite that the bottles should rest on their sides to prevent the corks shrinking, and thus allowing both the carbonic acid and the wine itself to escape. For laying down champagne or any kind of sparkling wine an iron wine-bin is by far the best. Imuch prefer the patent "slider" bins made by Messrs. W.andJ. Burrow, of Malvern, they being better adapted to the purpose than any other I am acquainted with. In these the bottles rest on horizontal parallel bars of wrought-iron, securely riveted into strong wrought-iron uprights, both at the back and in front. The bins can be obtained of any size—that is, to hold as few as two or as many as forty dozen—and they can be had furnished with lattice doors, secured by a lock. One great advantage is that with them there is no waste of space, for individual compartments can be at once refilled with fresh bottles after the other bottles have been removed. These "slider" bins are especially adapted for laying down champagne, as they admit of the air circulating freely around the bottles, thus conducing to the preservation of the metal foil round their necks, and keeping the temperature of the wine both cool and equable.

WINE-CELLAR FITTED WITH BURROW'S PATENT SLIDER BINS.

When binning the wine the bottles are held by their necks and slid into their places with such ease and safety that a child might be entrusted with the work. The bottles can be withdrawn from the bin with equal or even greater facility. Breakage is avoided from each bottle having an independent bearing, which prevents the upper bottles from either falling or weighing down upon those below, and thereby crashing together. The larger engraving shows a wine-cellar fitted up entirely with. Burrow's patent "slider" wine-bins, while the smaller represents a bin adapted to laying down twenty dozens of champagne, and the dimensions of which are merely 5feet 8inches by 3feet.

From the subjoined table it will be seen that the consumption of champagne has almost trebled since the year 1844-5, aperiod of little more than thirty years. Another curious fact to note is the immense increase in the exports of the wine during the three years following the Franco-German war, when naturally both the exports and home consumption of champagne fell off very considerably. No reliable information is available as to the actual quantity of champagne consumed yearly in England, but this may be taken in round numbers at about four millions of bottles. The consumption of the wine in the United States varies from rather more than a million and a half to nearly two million bottles annually.

STATISTICAL TABLE, 1844-1878

OFFICIAL RETURN BY THE CHAMBER OF COMMERCE AT REIMS OF THE TRADE IN
CHAMPAGNE WINES FROM APRIL, 1844, TO APRIL, 1878.

Years, from April to April.	Manufacturers' Stocks.	Number of Bottles Exported.	Number of Bottles sold in France.	Total number of Bottles Sold.
1844-45	23,285,218	4,380,214	2,255,438	6,635,652
1845-46	22,847,971	4,505,308	2,510,605	7,015,913
1846-47	18,815,367	4,711,915	2,355,366	7,067,281
1847-48	23,122,994	4,859,625	2,092,571	6,952,196
1848-49	21,290,185	5,686,484	1,473,966	7,160,450
1849-50	20,499,192	5,001,044	1,705,735	6,706,779
1850-51	20,444,915	5,866,971	2,122,569	7,989,540
1851-52	21,905,479	5,957,552	2,162,880	8,120,432
1852-53	19,376,967	6,355,574	2,385,217	8,740,790
1853-54	17,757,769	7,878,320	2,528,719	10,407,039
1854-55	20,922,959	6,895,773	2,452,743	9,348,516
1855-56	15,957,141	7,137,001	2,562,039	9,699,040
1856-57	15,228,294	8,490,198	2,468,818	10,959,016
1857-58	21,628,778	7,368,310	2,421,454	9,789,764
1858-59	28,328,251	7,666,633	2,805,416	10,472,049
1859-60	35,648,124	8,265,395	3,039,621	11,305,016
1860-61	30,235,260	8,488,223	2,697,508	11,185,731
1861-62	30,254,291	6,904,915	2,592,875	9,497,790
1862-63	28,013,189	7,937,836	2,767,371	10,705,207
1863-64	28,466,975	9,851,138	2,934,996	12,786,134
1864-65	33,298,672	9,101,441	2,801,626	11,903,067
1865-66	34,175,429	10,413,455	2,782,777	13,196,132
1866-67	37,608,716	10,283,886	3,218,343	13,502,229
1867-68	37,969,219	10,876,585	2,924,268	13,800,853
1868-69	32,490,881	12,810,194	3,104,496	15,914,690
1869-70	39,272,562	13,858,839	3,628,461	17,487,300
1870-71	39,984,003	7,544,323	1,633,941	9,178,264
1871-72	40,099,243	17,001,124	3,367,537	20,368,661
1872-73	45,329,490	18,917,779	3,464,059	22,381,838
1873-74	46,573,974	18,106,310	2,491,759	20,598,069
1874-75	52,733,674	15,318,345	3,517,182	18,835,527
1875-76	64,658,767	16,705,719	2,439,762	19,145,481

| 1876-77 | 71,398,726 | 15,882,964 | 3,127,991 | 19,010,955 |
| 1877-78 | 70,183,863 | 15,711,651 | 2,450,983 | 18,162,634 |

Distinguished gourmets are scarcely agreed as to the proper moment when champagne should be introduced at the dinner-table. Dyspeptic Mr. Walker, of "The Original," laid it down that champagne ought to be introduced very early at the banquet, without any regard whatever to the viands it may chance to accompany. "Give champagne," he says, "at the beginning of dinner, as its exhilarating qualities serve to start the guests, after which they will seldom flag. No other wine produces an equal effect in increasing the success of a party—it invariably turns the balance to the favourable side. When champagne goes rightly nothing can well go wrong." These precepts are sound enough, still all dinner-parties are not necessarily glacial, and the guests are not invariably mutes. Before champagne can be properly introduced at a formal dinner the conventional glass of sherry or madeira should supplement the soup, awhite French or a Rhine wine accompany the fish, and a single glass of bordeaux prepare the way with the first *entrée* for the sparkling wine, which, for the first round or two, should be served, briskly and liberally. Awine introduced thus early at the repast should of course be dry, or, at any rate, moderatelyso.

We certainly do not approve of Mr. Charles Dickens's dictum that champagne's proper place is not at the dinner-table, but solely at a ball. "Acavalier," he said, "may appropriately offer at propitious intervals a glass now and then to his danceress. There it takes its fitting rank and position amongst feathers, gauzes, lace, embroidery, ribbons, white satin, shoes, and eau-de-Cologne, for champagne is simply one of the elegant extras of life." This is all very well, still the advantageous effect of sparkling wine at an ordinary British dinner-party, composed as it frequently is of people pitchforked together in accordance with the exigencies of the hostess's visiting-list, cannot be gainsayed. After the preliminary glowering at each other, *more Britannico*, in the drawing-room, everybody regards it as a relief to be summoned to the repast, which, however, commences as chillily as the soup and as stolidly as the salmon. The soul of the hostess is heavy with the anxiety of prospective dishes, the brow of the host is clouded with the reflection that our rulers are bent upon dragging us into war. Placed between a young lady just out and a dowager of grimly Gorgonesque aspect, you hesitate how to open a conversation. Your first attempts, like those of the Russian batteries on the Danube, are singularly ineffectual, only eliciting a dropping fire of monosyllables. You envy the placidly languid young gentleman opposite, limp as his fast-fading camellia, and seated next to Belle Breloques, who is certain, in racing parlance, to make the running for him. But even that damsel seems preoccupied with her fan, and, despite her *aplomb*, hesitates to break the icy silence. The two City friends of the host are lost in mute speculation as to the future price of indigo or Ionian Bank shares, while their wives seem to be mentally summarising the exact cost of each other's toilettes. Their daughters, or somebody else's daughters, are desperately jerking out monosyllabic responses to feeble remarks concerning the weather, lawn tennis, operatic *débutantes*, the gravel in the Row, the ill-health of the Princess, and kindred topics from a couple of F.O. men. Little Snapshot, the wit, on the other side of the Gorgon, has tried to lead up to a story, but has found himself, as it were, frozen in the bud. When lo! the butler softly sibillates in your ear the magic word "champagne," and as it flows, creaming and frothing, into your glass, achange comes over the spirit of your vision.

The hostess brightens, the host coruscates. The young lady on your right suddenly develops into a charming girl, with becoming appreciation of your pet topics and an astounding aptness for repartee. The Gorgon thaws, and implores Mr. Snapshot, whose jests are popping as briskly as the corks, not to be so dreadfully funny, or he will positively kill her. Belle Breloques can always talk, and now her tongue rattles faster than ever, till the languid one arouses himself like a giant refreshed, and gives her as good as he gets. The City men expatiate in cabalistic language on the merits of some mysterious speculation, the prospective returns from which increase with each fresh bottle. One of their wives is discussing the E.C.U. and the S.S.C. with a hitherto silent curate, and the other is jabbering botany to a red-faced warrior. The juniors are in full swing, and ripples of silvery laughter rise in accompaniment to the beaded bubbles all round the table. And all this is due to champagne, that great unloosener not merely of tongues but of purse-strings, as is well known to the secretaries of those charitable institutions which set the wine flowing earliest at their anniversary dinners.

RECIPES FOR WINE CUPS

A few recipes for sparkling wine cups gathered from various sources will conclude our work. Not having personally tested these we leave the responsibility of them to their respective authors—Soyer, Tovey, Terrington ("Cooling Cups and Dainty Drinks"), &c.—premising that it is the merest folly to use a high-class champagne or a fine sparkling hock for a beverage of this description. Sparkling saumur, or the newly-introduced sparkling sauternes, and the cheaper hocks and moselles, will do equally well at a greatly reduced cost. In all cases, too, the kind of liqueur, the amount of sugar, and the flavouring with borage, verbena, pine-apple, or cucumber, may be varied to suit individual tastes. For soda or seltzer water we have invariably substituted Apollinaris, which is far better adapted for effervescent drinks of this description by reason of its purity and softness, its freedom from any distinct flavour, and above all its powerful natural effervescence.

Soyer's elaborate recipe for champagne cup for a large party is as follows:—

Prepare three ounces of oleo-saccharine by rubbing some lumps of sugar against the outside of a lemon or Seville orange and scraping away the sugar as it absorbs the essential oil contained in the rind of the fruit. Put the oleo-saccharine with the juice of four lemons in a vessel, add a quart bottle of Apollinaris water (Soyer says soda-water, but Apollinaris is certainly preferable), and stir well together until the sugar is dissolved. Then pour in one quart of syrup of orgeat and whip the mixture up well with an egg whisk in order to whiten it. Next add a pint of cognac brandy, aquarter of a pint of Jamaica rum and half a pint of maraschino; strain the whole into a bowl, adding plenty of pounded ice if the weather is warm, and pour in three bottles of champagne, stirring the mixture well with the ladle while doing so in order to render the cup creamy and mellow.

A less potent and pretentious beverage, and better suited for a summer drink, is the subjoined:—

Dissolve two tablespoonfuls of powdered sugar in a quart of Apollinaris water. Add a wineglass of curaçoa, a sprig of green borage or a couple of slices of cucumber with the juice and fine shavings of the outside peel of a lemon, and a pound of bruised ice. After the whole has been well stirred pour in the champagne and serve.

Other recipes are as follows:—

Prepare an ounce of oleo-saccharine, add to it a large wineglass of maraschino, aliqueur glass of cognac, and the juice of half a lemon. Mix well together, and add several slices of pine-apple, and a large lump or two of ice. On to this pour first a large bottle of Apollinaris water, and next a bottle of sparkling wine.

Mix with the contents of a bottle of chablis or sauternes a liqueur glass of chartreuse and a tablespoonful or two of powdered loaf sugar. When the latter is dissolved throw in a pound and a half of pounded ice and a sprig of borage. Pour over these a quart of Apollinaris water and a bottle of sparkling saumur. For the chablis or sauternes half a bottle of light claret may be substituted.

To a gill of good pale sherry add a liqueur glass of maraschino and a few lumps of sugar which have been well rubbed over the rind of a Seville orange, the juice of which is also to be added to the mixture. After the sugar is dissolved throw in a sprig of borage or a slice or two of cucumber and some pounded ice. Then add a quart bottle of Apollinaris water and a bottle of champagne or some other sparkling wine.

The following cup for a party of twenty is said to be of Russian inspiration:—

Pour on to some sprigs of borage or a few slices of cucumber a pint of sherry and half a pint of brandy, then rub off the fine outside peel of a lemon with a few lumps of sugar, and add these with the strained juice of the lemon and of three oranges. Pour into the mixture half a pint of curaçoa, awineglass of noyau, acouple of bottles of German seltzer-water, three bottles of soda-water, and three bottles of champagne. Sweeten and ice to taste.

Here is a recipe for a cup made with chablis and sparkling red burgundy:—

With a bottle of chablis mix a liqueur-glass of chartreuse and then dissolve in it some powdered sugar. Add two pounds of ice in largish lumps, aslice or two of cucumber, and a sprig of lemon-scented verbena, or substitute for these a few slices of pine-apple. Pour in a quart bottle of Apollinaris water, mix well together, and add a bottle of sparkling burgundy just before serving.

The following refer to sparkling hock and moselle cups:—

To a bottle of sparkling hock add a quarter of a pint of lemon water ice and a liqueur glass of pine-apple syrup. After mixing them add a slice of cucumber, alump or two of ice, and a bottle of Apollinaris water.

Add to the strained juice of a couple of lemons an ounce and a half or more of powdered loaf sugar and a wineglass of maraschino. Mix well, and pour in a couple of bottles of iced sparkling hock and a large bottle of iced Apollinaris water.

Dissolve a couple of ounces of sugar in a gill of dry sherry, add the thin peel of half an orange, afew slices of pine-apple, peaches, or apricots, with some pounded ice, and then pour in a bottle of sparkling moselle and a bottle of Apollinaris water.

With half a pint of lemon water ice mix a bottle of iced sparkling moselle, add a few drops of elder-flower water and a bottle of iced Apollinaris water. Instead of the lemon ice half the quantity of pine-apple ice may be used with the juice of half a lemon, and the elder-flower water may be dispensed with.

THE PRINCIPAL SPARKLING WINE BRANDS.

. *In this list whenever a manufacturer has various qualities the higher qualities are always placed first.*

CHAMPAGNES.

Firms and Wholesale Agents.	Brands.	Qualities.	On side of Corks.
AYALA & CO., Ay Ayala, 7, Little Tower Street, London Rinck & Unger, 50, Park Place, New York		Carte Blanche	Extra.
		Carte Noire	Première.
		Second	
BINET FILS & CO., Reims Rutherford & Browne, Old Trinity House, 5, Water Lane, London.		Extra	Binet fils & Cie.
		First Second	" "
BOLLINGER, J., Ay. L. Mentzendorf, 6, Idol Lane, London. E. and J. Burke, 40, Beaver Street, New York.		Very Dry Extra	Very Dry Extra quality.
		Dry Extra	Dry Extra quality.
BRUCH-FOUCHER & CO., Mareuil L. Ehrmann, 34, Gt. Tower Street, London.		Carte D'Or First Second	

CLICQUOT-PONSARDIN, Veuve, Reims (WERLE & CO.) Fenwick, Parrot, & Co., 124, Fenchurch Street, London. Schmidt Bros., New York.		Dry	England.
		Rich	"
DE CAZANOVE, C., Avize J. R. Hunter, 46, Fenchurch Street, London		Extra First Second Third Fourth	Extra qualité.
		Fifth	
DEUTZ & GELDER-MANN, Ay J. R. Parkington & Co., 21, Crutched Friars, London.		Gold Lack (Extra Dry and Dry)	Gold Lack.
		Cabinet (Extra Dry and Dry)	Cabinet.
DUCHATEL-OHAUS, Reims Woellworth & Co., 70, Mark Lane, London		Carte Blanche (Dry and Rich) Verzenay (Dry and Rich) Sillery (Dry and Rich)	
DUMINY & CO., Ay Mogford, Courtenay, & Co., 16, Mark Lane, London Anthony Oechs, New Street, New York		Extra	Maison fondée en 1814.
		First	

FARRE, CHARLES, Reims Hornblower & Co., 50, Mark Lane, London Gilmore & Gibson, Balti- more Mel & Sons, San Francisco		Cabinet (Grand Vin)	Cabinet Grand Vin.
		Carte Blanche	Carte Blanche.
		Carte Noire	Carte Noire.
		Sillery Sec	Sillery Sec.
		Sillery	Sillery.
		Ay Mousseux	Ay.
FISSE, THIRION, & Co., Reims Stallard and Smith, 25, Philpot Lane, London See author's Errata.		Cachet d'Or (Extra Dry and Medium Dry)	Cachet d'Or.
		Carte Blanche (Dry, Medium Dry, and Rich)	Carte Blanche.

See author's correction.		Carte Noire (Dry and Medium Dry).	Carte Noire.
GIBERT, GUSTAVE, Reims Cock, Russell, & Co., 63, Great Tower Street, London Hays & Co., 40, Day Street, New York		Vin du Roi	
		Extra	
		First	
		Second	
All these wines are prepared Extra Dry, Dry, or Rich.		Third	

Firm		Brand	
GIESLER & CO., Avize F. Giesler & Co., 32, Fenchurch Street, London. Purdy & Nicholas, 43, Beaver Street, New York		Extra Superior	
		India	India.
		First	
		Second	
		Third	
HEIDSIECK & CO., Reims. Theodor Satow & Co., 141, Fenchurch Street, London Schmidt & Peters, 20, Beaver Street, New York		Dry Monopole. Monopole (Rich) Dry Vin Royal Grand Vin Royal (Rich)	
IRROY, ERNEST, Reims. Cuddeford & Smith, 66, Mark Lane, London O. de Saye, 18, South William Street, New York W. E. Hepp, 101, Gravier Street, New Orleans		Carte d'Or, Dry	Carte d'Or, Sec.
		Carte d'Or	Carte d'Or.
KRUG & Co., Reims Inglis and Cunningham, 60, Mark Lane, London A. Rocherau & Co., New York Hillman Bros. & Co., San Francisco		Carte Blanche	Carte Blanche, England.
		Private Cuvée	Private Cuvée, England.
		First	England.
		Second	

MOËT & CHANDON, EPERNAY Simon & Dale, Old Trinity House, 5, Water Lane, London, Agents for Great Britain and the Colonies Renauld, François, & Co., 23, Beaver Street, New York J. Hope & Co., Montreal		Brut	Imperial, England.
		Creaming	Creaming, England.
		Extra Superior	Extra Superior, England.
		Extra Dry Sillery	
		White Dry Sillery	White Dry, England.
		First Quality	England.
		Second Quality	
MONTEBELLO, DUC DE, MAREUIL-SUR-AY John Hopkins & Co., 26, Crutched Friars, London Cazade, Crooks, & Reynaud, 25, South William St., N.Y.		Cuvée Extra	Cuvée Extra.
		Carte Blanche	Reserve.
		Carte Bleue	Cte. Bleue.
		Carte Noire	Cte. Noire.
MUMM, G. H., & CO., REIMS W. J. and T. Welch, 10, Corn Exchange Chambers, Seething Lane, London F. de Bary & Co., 41 and 43, Warren Street, New York		Carte Blanche	Cuvée Extra.
		Extra Dry	Extra Dry.
		Extra	Extra.
		First	First.
		For America only.	
		Cordon Rouge	Cordon Rouge.
		Extra Dry	Extra Dry.
		Dry Verzenay	Dry Verzenay.
MUMM, JULES, & CO., REIMS Jules Mumm & Co., 3 & 4, Mark Lane, London		Extra Dry Dry	

PÉRINET & FILS, Reims John Barnett & Son, 36, Mark Lane, London Wood, Pollard, & Co., Boston, U.S. Hooper and Donaldson, San Francisco		Cuvée Réservée (Extra Dry)	Cuvée Reservée.
		White Dry Sillery	White Dry Sillery.
PERRIER-JOUËT & CO., Epernay A. Boursot & Co., 9, Hart Street, Crutched Friars, London		Cuvée de Réserve	Extra
		Pale Dry Creaming First	
		Second	
		Third	
PIPER, H., & CO., Reims (KUNKELMANN & CO.) W. Foster Newton & Son, 3, Maiden Lane, E.C., London John Osborn, Son, & Co., New York and Montreal		Très-Sec (Extra Dry) Sec (Very Dry) Carte Blanche (Rich)	Kunkelmann & Co.
PFUNGST FRÈRES & CIE., Ay, Epernay J. L. Pfungst & Co., 23, Crutched Friars, London		Carte d'Or (Dry, Extra Dry, and Brut)	Carte d'Or.
		Sillery Crêmant (Extra Dry and Brut)	Sillery Crêmant.
		Carte Noire (Dry, Extra Dry, and Brut)	Carte Noire.
		Cordon Blanc (Full, Dry, and Extra Dry)	Cordon Blanc.

Brand / Agents	Trade Mark		
POL ROGER & CO., EPERNAY Reuss, Lauteren, & Co., 39, Crutched Friars, London		Vin Réservé.	
POMMERY, VEUVE, REIMS (POMMERY & GRENO) A. Hubinet, 24, Mark Lane, London Charles Graef, 65, Broad Street, New York		Extra Sec (Vin Brut)	Veuve Pommery.
		Sec	
ROEDERER, LOUIS, REIMS Grainger & Son, 108, Fenchurch Street, London		Carte Blanche	Reims, Carte Blanche, Gt.-Britain.
ROEDERER, THÉOPHILE, & CO., MAISON FONDÉE EN 1861, REIMS Théophile Roederer & Co., 150, Fenchurch Street, London		Crystal Champagne, Special Cuvée	Special Cuvée.
		Extra Reserve Cuvée	Reserve Cuvée.
		Extra Superior Carte Blanche Dorée	Carte Blanche Dorée
		Extra Quality Carte Blanche	Carte Blanche.
		First Quality Carte Noire	Carte Noire.
		Verzenay	Verzenay.
ROUSSILLON, J., & CO., EPERNAY J. Roussillon & Co., 15, New Broad Street, London D. St. Amant & Son, 13, South William Street, New York		First Cuvée Second Cuvée Dry Verzenay	
		Sillery Sec	1874 Extra Sec.

RUINART, PÈRE ET FILS, REIMS Ruinart, Père et Fils, 22, St. Swithin's Lane, London		Carte Anglaise Dry Pale Crêmant Extra Dry Sparkling Carte Blanche First	
DE SAINT-MARCEAUX & CO., REIMS Groves &, Co., 5, Mark Lane, London Hermann Batjer & Bro., New York		Vin Brut	
		Carte d'Or (Extra Dry)	Very dry.
		Bouzy Nonpareil (Dry)	Vin Sec.
		Carte Blanche (Medium)	
		Second (Medium)	
See author's corrections.		Third (*id.*) *For America only.* Dry Royal	

SAUMUR AND SAUTERNES.

Firms and Wholesale Agents.	*Brands.*	*Qualities.*	*On side of Corks.*
ACKERMAN-LAU-RANCE, ST. FLORENT, SAUMUR J. N. Bishop, 41, Crutched Friars, London Timothy Stevens, 29, Beaver Street, New York Chapin and Gore, 70, Monroe Street, Chicago		Carte d'Or	Carte d'Or.
		Carte Rose	Carte Rose.
		Carte Bleue	Carte Bleue.
		Carte Noire	Carte Noire.

DUVAU, LOUIS, Aîné, Château de Varrains, Saumur Jolivet and Canney, 3, Idol Lane, London	DUVAU	Carte d'Or, Extra Superior Carte d'Argent, Extra Carte Blanche, Superior Carte Rose, Ordinary	
LORRAIN, JULES, Château De la Côte, Varrains, near Saumur J. Lorrain, 73, Great Tower Street, London	JULES LORRAIN	Carte d'Or Carte Blanche Carte Rose Carte Bleue	
ROUSTEAUX, A., St. Florent, Saumur Cock, Russell, & Co., 63, Great Tower Street, London I. H. Smith's Sons, Peck Slip, New York Law, Young, & Co., Montreal	A. ROUSTEAUX	Extra	
	A. ROUSTEAUX	First	
	A. ROUSTEAUX	Second	
	A. ROUSTEAUX	Third Sparkling Vouvray, Superior Sparkling Vouvray	
NORMANDIN, E., & CO., Châteauneuf-sur-Charente P. A. Maignen, 22, Great Tower Street, London	E. NORMANDIN & Cº	Sparkling Sauternes (Extra Dry) Sparkling Sauternes (Dry)	

BURGUNDIES.

Firms and Wholesale Agents.	Brands.	Qualities.
ANDRÉ & VOILLOT, BEAUNE Cock, Russell, & Co., 63, Great Tower Street, London P. W. Engs and Sons, 131, Front Street, New York		Romanée (White) Nuits (do.) Volnay (do.) Saint-Péray Pink and Red Wines
LATOUR, LOUIS, BEAUNE Reuss, Lauteren, & Co., 39, Crutched Friars, London		Romanée (White) Nuits (do.) Volnay (do.) Saint-Péray (do.) Chambertin (Red) Nuits (do.) Volnay (do.)
LIGER-BELAIR, COMTE, NUITS AND VÔSNE Fenwick, Parrot, & Co., 124, Fenchurch Street, London		Carte d'Or (White) Carte Noire (do.) Carte Verte (do.) Carte Noire (Red) Carte Blanche (do.)

HOCKS AND MOSELLES.

Firms and Wholesale Agents.	Brands.	Qualities.
DEINHARD & CO., COBLENZ Deinhard & Co., 6, Idol Lane, London H. G. Schmidt & Co., 38, Beaver Street, New York		First
		Second
		Third

EWALD & CO., RUDESHEIM-ON-RHINE Simon and Dale, Old Trinity House, 5, Water Lane, London		Sparkling Hock Nonpareil (Extra Dry and Dry) Sparkling Moselle Muscatel Nonp. (Dry) Sparkling Moselle (Nonp.) Scharzberg (Dry)
HOCHHEIM ASSOCI-ATION, HOCHHEIM-ON-MAINE F. Class & Co., 31, Crutched Friars, London		Sparkling and Creaming Johan-nisberg Hochheim First (White or Red) Do. Second (do.) Do. Third (do.) Do. Fourth (do.) Hocks and Moselles Nonpareil First Second Third
		Fourth
KESSLER, G. C., & CO., ESSLINGEN George Saurmann, 7, Cross Lane, St. Mary-at-Hill, London		Kaiser Wein Sparkling Hock Do. Neckar
LAUTEREN, C. SOHN, MAYENCE Reuss, Lauteren, & Co., 39, Crutched Friars, London		Sparkling Johannisberg Hock No. 1 Do. No. 2 Do. No. 3 Moselle, Dry, No. 1 Do. No. 2 Do. No. 3 Moselle, Muscatel, No. 1 Do. No. 2 Do. No. 3

MÜLLER, MATHEUS, ELTVILLE M. Muller, 15, Philpot Lane, London		Flower of Sparkling Johannisberg Sparkling Johannisberg Pearl of the Moselle Extra Superior Moselle Nonpareil Sparkling Moselle Nonpareil Sparkling Hock Fine Sparkling do. Fine Sparkling Moselle Sparkling Assmannshäuser, Superior (Red) Sparkling Assmannshäuser (do.)
		Sparkling Hock (Ordinary) Sparkling Moselle (do.)
OPPMANN, MICHAEL, WÜRZBURG		Franconia Wine: Nonpareil Stein Wine Blue Label White Label Sparkling Moselle, First Do. do., Second Do. Hock, First Do. do., Second
SILIGMÜLLER, F. A., WÜRZBURG		Cabinet *(On side of cork:)* Cabinet.
		Carte d'Or Carte Blanche Carte Noire
STÖCK, JOS, & SÖHNE, CREUZNACH John Barnett & Son, 36, Mark Lane, London		Johnnnisberg, supr. Scharzberg, do. Johannisberg, ordin. Scharzberg, do. Hock, superior Moselle, do. Hock, ordin. Moselle, do. Red Hock, First Do., Second Do., Third Do., Fourth

STYRIAN, HUNGARIAN, AND SWISS WINES.

Firms and Wholesale Agents.	Brands.	Qualities.
KLEINOSCHEG BROTHERS, Graz, Styria Davis and Littlewood, 4 and 5, Botolph Lane, London		Dry Pale Styrian Muscat Champagne. Dry Pale Styrian Champagne Sparkling Burgundy (Red)
HUBERT & HABERMANN, Pressburg, Hungary C. O. Pattenhausen, 40, Great Tower Street, London		Sparkling White Sparkling Red (Carlovitz)
DE RIEDMATTEN, DE QUAY, & CIE., Sion, Valais, Switzerland		Carte Verte, Glacier du Rhône Carte Blanche, Mont-Blanc

AMERICAN WINES.

Firms and Wholesale Agents.	Brands.	Qualities.
KELLEY'S ISLAND WINE CO., Kelley's Island, Ohio		Island Queen Nonpareil Carte Blanche
PLEASANT VALLEY WINE CO., Hammondsport, N.Y.		Great Western (Dry and Extra Dry) Carte Blanche Pleasant Valley Paris Exposition
URBANA WINE CO., Hammondsport, N.Y.		Gold Seal (Extra Dry) Gold Seal Imperial Royal Rose

AUTHOR'S ERRATA

The subjoined corrections are necessary in the following brands (See pages 212 and 213):—

<table>
<tr>
<td rowspan="2">FISSE, THIRION, & Co., Reims
Stallard and Smith, 25, Philpot Lane, London</td>
<td rowspan="3"></td>
<td>Cachet d'Or (Extra Dry and Medium Dry)</td>
<td>Cachet d'Or.</td>
</tr>
<tr>
<td>Carte Blanche (Dry, Medium Dry, and Rich)</td>
<td>Carte Blanche.</td>
</tr>
<tr>
<td>N.B.—The brand on the corks is an anchor instead of an eagle.</td>
<td>Carte Noire (Dry and Medium Dry).</td>
<td>Carte Noire.</td>
</tr>
<tr>
<td colspan="4">GIBERT, GUSTAVE, Reims.
Cock, Russell, and Co.'s address is 23, Rood Lane, London.</td>
</tr>
<tr>
<td colspan="4">GIESLER & CO., Avize.
The corks of the firm's Extra Superior quality wine are branded "Extra Superior" on the side.</td>
</tr>
<tr>
<td colspan="4">IRROY, ERNEST, Reims.
The New York agent is F. O. de Luze, 18, South William Street, New York.
W.E. Hepp is no longer M. Irroy's agent for New Orleans.</td>
</tr>
</table>

The following are the correct brands of MM. de Saint-Marceaux & Co.:—

DE SAINT-MARCEAUX & CO., Reims Groves &, Co., 5, Mark Lane, London Hermann Batjer & Bro., New York		Vin Brut	
		Carte d'Or (Extra Dry)	Very dry.
		Bouzy Nonpareil (Dry)	Vin Sec.
		Carte Blanche (Medium) *For America only.* Dry Royal	
		Second (Medium)	
		Third (*id.*)	

Lector House believes that a society develops through a two-fold approach of continuous learning and adaptation, which is derived from the study of classic literary works spread across the historic timeline of literature records. Therefore, we aim at reviving, repairing and redeveloping all those inaccessible or damaged but historically as well as culturally important literature across subjects so that the future generations may have an opportunity to study and learn from past works to embark upon a journey of creating a better future.

This book is a result of an effort made by Lector House towards making a contribution to the preservation and repair of original ancient works which might hold historical significance to the approach of continuous learning across subjects.

HAPPY READING & LEARNING!

LECTOR HOUSE LLP
E-MAIL: lectorpublishing@gmail.com

9 789389 560725